Zion & Bryce Canyon

EXPLORER'S GUIDES

Zion & Bryce Canyon

A GREAT DESTINATION

Christine Balaz

The Countryman Press ✳ Woodstock, Vermont

FIRST EDITION

Interior photographs by the author unless otherwise specified
Maps by Erin Greb Cartography, © The Countryman Press
Book design by Joanna Bodenweber
Composition by Eugenie S. Delaney

Explorer's Guide Zion & Bryce Canyon: A Great Destination
978-1-58157-143-1

Published by The Countryman Press, P.O. Box 748, Woodstock, VT 05091
Distributed by W. W. Norton & Company, Inc., 500 Fifth Avenue, New York, NY 10110
Printed in the United States of America

10 9 8 7 6 5 4 3 2 1

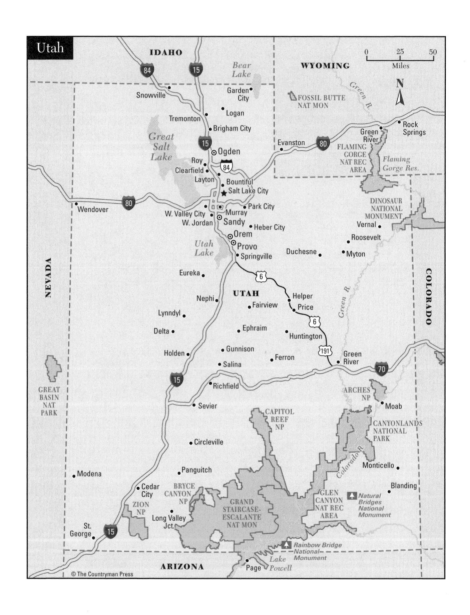

Contents

Introduction

IMAGINE A TRIP TO UTAH. What do you expect to see? Salt Lake City? Moab? Park City? The Mormon Temple? Or perhaps you picture Utah's wilderness. For scenery, Utah is one of the most well-endowed states in the United States. And not surprisingly, many people travel to Utah expressly to experience its spectacular and varied wilds, the most unique and best preserved of which is showcased within the boundaries of its numerous national parks.

Utah has 5 national parks in all—6 if you count Monument Valley Tribal Park. Or 7, if you count the 1.9-million-acre Grand Staircase–Escalante National Monument (GSENM). In addition to Zion, Bryce Canyon, Arches, Canyonlands, and Capitol Reef national parks, Utah also contains 45 state parks and 8 national monuments scattered across its 84,899 square miles of diverse terrain. Many of these are situated on national park-grade territory, with incredible views and clean, well-maintained facilities.

Utah's national parks share a common theme of exposed sandstone and the wild shapes that nature carves into it with her tectonic powers of uplift and subduction and erosive powers of wind and water. The Colorado Plateau, which dominates the state's southern half, has been so radically deformed by these powers that it has transformed into a giant sandstone sculpture garden, with each of Utah's parks enclosing a distinct variation on theme and medium.

Zion National Park, with its sheer, 2,500-foot sandstone walls, showcases the amazingly solid and smooth features of Zion Canyon's Navajo sandstone, exposed dramatically by the waters of the Virgin River. The Colorado and Green rivers 150 miles to the east slice deeply into the Wingate and Cedar Mesa strata of Canyonlands, giving this park its soaring buttes and dramatic rock needles. The main attraction of Bryce Canyon and Cedar Breaks is the loose, brightly oxidized mud and crumbling layers that readily yield to erosive forces. These areas highlight the exposed rainbows of these

LEFT: Though tall, the broad Boulder Mountain Plateau has no distinct peaks to speak of.

The Parade of Elephants, in the windows section of Arches, as viewed from the south.   David Sjöquist

subterranean strata hiding beneath the Paunsaugunt Plateau. And there isn't a person in the world who doesn't know about the Entrada sandstone windows of Arches National Park. With more than 2,000 of these registered formations greater than 3 feet in diameter, this park contains the densest collection of natural arches and windows in the world.

Beyond the national parks and their emblematic landforms, there are dozens of state parks that offer similarly dramatic vistas and opportunities for outdoor recreation. Less famous than their national peers, these parks have a simpler infrastructure and are less crowded, allowing for a much freer, less structured exploration of nature's beauty. One of Utah's biggest and best nonnational park areas is GSENM. This enormous 1.9-million-acre protected area offers vast stretches of slot canyons, hiking, mountain biking, petroglyphs, ruins, and miles upon miles of roads and trails leading into its wilds, offering unlimited exploration. Boulder Mountain, a massive and broad bulge north of Boulder, Utah, offers a high aspen- and evergreen-forested landscape in the Dixie National Forest. Covered in lakes, streams, and campsites, this nearby plateau presents a completely separate climate and set of opportunities than the nearby GSENM.

Among southern Utah's best (or most famous) state parks is Koda-chrome Basin, quite near to Bryce Canyon National Park and not entirely unlike Monument Valley. Snow Canyon, conveniently just outside St. George and very near Zion National Park, intimates Nevada's Red Rock Canyon, with its bright orange color schemes and gently rounded sandstone domes. Other worthy destinations on the list include Goblin Valley near Arches, Petrified Forest outside Escalante, and Coral Pink Sand Dunes on the Arizona border.

These state parks offer a supplement to the national parks tour, exhibiting yet other, bite-size vistas and historical sites distinct from nearby areas.

Typically smaller and only moderately developed, these cost less to enter than the national parks. Dead Horse Point State Park showcases an extremely small but beautiful peninsula of land teetering over the Colorado River, 2,000 feet below. Additionally, this park contains a new and well-built trail system for mountain bikers of all levels. Snow Canyon State Park, northwest of St. George, offers clean facilities, beautiful hiking trails, camping, and multipitch rock climbing. Anasazi State Park displays the ruins and artifacts left behind by indigenous peoples, illustrating the history of a culture that left behind more than one hundred structures on this site between 1160 and 1235 A.D. And different still, the Frontier Homestead near Cedar City depicts the lives of early Mormon pioneers sent by Brigham Young to colonize southern Utah in 1850. These are just a sampling of Utah's diverse, state-run parks.

Given Utah's desert climate and hot summers, it may come as a surprise to you that its prime park-visiting season falls outside the winter months. In fact, most of its parks are typically best visited in late spring or early fall—with some areas like Cedar Breaks National Monument even being unreachable during the snowy season. Because of its high elevation, Utah's desert is vulnerable to the elements. It can be covered in snow one day and bake under intense sun the next. In terms of cold weather and snow accumulation, the most extreme and commonly visited location detailed in this book is Cedar Breaks National Monument. With an elevation nearly 2 miles above sea level, the monument's roads can remain utterly buried under snow into early June, despite plowing efforts. Sometimes it remains closed even through the middle of this month.

As a rule of thumb, the St. George area of Utah typically is the state's warmest. With its far southern location and relatively low elevation, it enjoys comfortable daytime temperatures, sometimes even in January—depending on the weather, of course. However, nearby Zion National Park stays cooler and more susceptible to inclement weather because of its mountainous topography and the shading of its deep and narrow canyons.

The region of Moab, Canyonlands, and Arches experiences a more moderate weather pattern, with elevations falling between those of the lofty Cedar Breaks and low-altitude St. George. Still considered high desert, this area cools off dramatically when the sun goes down, with its temperatures plunging quickly and registering substantially below freezing on most winter nights.

Whether you plan to visit the state for a quick, drive-by tour of the more famous parks or backpack for weeks into deep wilderness, you will experience geology, wildlife, and history unlike that of any other state during your tour of Utah. You can stay in hotels and dine in fine restaurants, or sleep in a tent and cook over a camp stove. But whatever you do, bring plenty of sunscreen, water, and memory cards for your camera.

The Way This Book Works

UTAH IS A VAST STATE encompassing five national parks, the 1.9-million-acre Grand Staircase–Escalante National Monument, dozens of state parks, fun towns, uncountable other points of interest, and scenic roads connecting them all. This book, which centers around Utah's national parks—and therefore its southern half—contains one chapter for each of the national parks: Zion, Bryce Canyon, Capitol Reef, Arches, and Canyonlands. The Grand Staircase—Escalante National Monument and City of Moab, both famous and worthy destinations, each get their own chapters as well. These seven chapters have been organized in order of a logical driving route from Utah's southwestern corner (Zion), up through its south- central portion (Bryce, Capitol Reef, Grand Staircase–Escalante), and across toward its southeastern pocket (Arches, Canyonlands, and Moab).

Those unsure of their exact time frame and route should first begin planning their trip by reading "Overview of Southern Utah: Its History, Parks, and Monuments." After a history lesson of the Colorado Plateau, this chapter introduces the national parks, summarizing each park's general layout, major attractions, and nearby amenities, and then fleshes out the rich and complex terrain that connects the parks. Utah's numerous state parks and national monuments, located along the same driving route, are briefly described in the following section: "The Best of Utah's Southern National Monuments, State Parks, and Surrounding Areas." After selecting the national parks to include in your itinerary, peruse the nearby state parks and other points of interest. In this way, you can select which parks, monuments, and sites should take precedence on your trip.

The chapter entitled "Planning Your Trip: Where to Go, When to Go, What to Take" discusses other facets of trip planning, such as the state's layout, suggested trips of various lengths, seasons, desert climate and wildlife, and how to best prepare for your trip—including what you should bring and what you should leave at home. It also points out the potential hazards the environment can present to you, as well as those that you may pose to it.

Once you have decided on the parks and monuments you would like to visit, take a look at the book's main chapters. Each begins with an overview of the park or area, discussing its characteristics, size, layout, elevation, and attractions. The "Pick Your Spot" section discusses the nearby towns you can choose among as possible base camps and the best places to sleep within those areas. "Local Flavors" describes those towns' best restaurants and cafés.

Next, each chapter walks you through a sample 48-hour itinerary. Assuming you'll arrive in the afternoon or evening, it details how you will arrive in the area, where to eat, and what do to for the next two days. This will include the area's best entertainment options (if they exist!), restaurants, hikes, sightseeing, and other must-do's—all listed from the time you arrive to the time you depart.

The remainder of each chapter provides suggestions for extending your visit, giving you supplementary (or alternative) options to those listed in the 48-hour itinerary. These are broadly categorized under "Recreation," "Accommodation and Restaurants," and "Camping." Given the nature of this region, the recreation category tends to be the richest, with possibilities for hiking, biking, horseback riding, rock climbing, bird-watching, and more. If the park happens to fall into a more developed corner of the state, you'll find a listing of additional hotels, B&Bs, and eateries here.

And, finally, the "Camping" section at the end of each chapter will help you decide where best to pitch your tent or park your RV. These paragraphs detail the in-park campgrounds, as well as the possibilities for reservations, or lack thereof. It also provides location and contact information for nearby commercial campgrounds. Finally, it discusses free, out-of-park, wild camping for those wanting to escape into the great outdoors and save a few dollars.

So whether you just want to head to one park, or tour the entire state, this book will serve as a planning tool and orientation guide. Its maps, photographs, and background information can help you feel comfortable and well prepared to make your trip match your goals. All business addresses, phone numbers, and Web sites are listed when possible and relevant. Whether you want to check a showtime, or make reservations for camping or dining, you should be covered. And don't forget to phone for reservations while in town; cell phone service is not reliable in southern Utah. Finally, if you just can't find what you're looking for, check the index in the back of the book to get you pointed in the right direction.

Overview of Southern Utah

ITS HISTORY, PARKS, AND MONUMENTS

NATURAL AND HUMAN HISTORY

The Geologic Picture

Anyone visiting the southern portion of Utah must surely wonder how its peculiar, unique, and varied natural features came about. When viewing the thousands of natural rock windows in Arches National Park; the sheer, streaked Navajo sandstone walls of Capitol Reef's Grand Wash Narrows; the ragged, teethlike spires of the Needles; or the dead-vertical, deep red cliffs of Zion Canyon, you can't help but wonder how so many different colors, shapes, and sizes of sandstone could ever coexist in such close proximity.

To understand any of these individual "sculptures," one must also understand the bigger picture. The southeastern half of Utah occupies about one quarter of an area known as the Colorado Plateau. This massive region, centered exactly around the Four Corners of Arizona, Utah, Colorado, and New Mexico, occupies an area of 140,000 square miles—approximately the size of Montana.

Elevation in the area ranges from 3,000 feet at its southern portion, the Colorado River, to 14,000 feet in its northeastern corner, the Colorado Rocky Mountains. That's more than 2 vertical miles of relief. A complex composite of many plateaus divided by several north–south running fault lines, the region contains rocks believed to be as old as 3.8 billion years. As one might guess, the oldest specimen, called Vishnu schist, appears at the lowest elevation of the region—along the Colorado River and at the bottom of the Grand Canyon.

LEFT: Looking northwest from Gooseberry Mesa

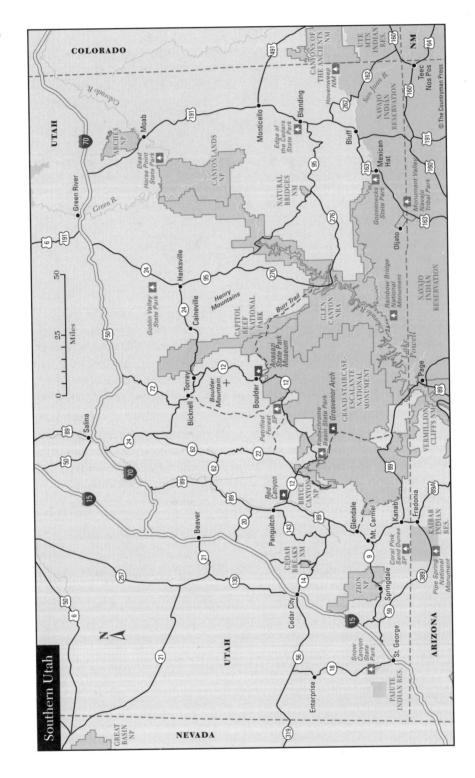

Southern Utah

Despite great amounts of tectonic activity, much of the Colorado Plateau has been a low-lying (even sea-level) expanse for most of its recent history. For long periods of time, it received sedimentary deposits from other higher areas. Into its fault lines seawater seeped, creating massive salt deposits over time. Then about 5 million years ago, a monumental uplift occurred, pushing the Colorado Plateau and the already high Rocky Mountains upward by a vertical mile. This huge regional change occurred as a collection of faults was reactivated, effectively tipping up the northern portion of the plateau.

Much of the deformation visible today was actually caused by streams carving their course over and into this newly lifted land. As the plateau rose, the area's waters found their way downward to the new lowest-elevation destination, eating their way through the path of least resistance. These superimposed rivers ate their way through the land as it rose, resulting in what looks today like streams chewing straight through mountains. Over time, the rising earth and the perpetual need for water to obey gravity has created wild canyons, gorges, and valleys. Wind, too, has done its part.

The biggest determining factor in the shape of the remaining features is the properties of the rock itself. Canyonlands' deep red, completely sheer Wingate sandstone cliffs came to be so as the surface of these iron-rich rocks oxidized into a hard varnish, preserving and coloring the rock faces. Smooth, white Navajo sandstone domes formed as wind buffs this softer rock into round shapes.

At different points in the plateau's history, magma has seeped upward through deep, subterranean faults, pooling and then cooling underground, much like unpopped pimples. Not actually reaching the surface of the earth, these underground bubbles gradually cooled, creating plugs of volcanic rock. Gradually exposed by uplift and subsequent erosion, these appear today as the laccoliths of the Henry and La Sal mountains.

Other, formerly underground phenomena include salt deposits caused by ocean water seeping into faults. As these massive salt beds were lifted and eroded onto the earth's surface, they faced the erosive forces of wind and water. The naturally weaker salt deposits eroded more readily than their host stone, leaving behind the 2,000 rock windows of Arches National Park.

Other peculiar rock sculptures formed as a result of adjacent layers of rock weathering differently. Discrepancies in hardness and water solubility of sandstone strata sometimes manifest in strange ways. When a more durable rock layer happens to find itself sitting atop more easily disintegrating rock, erosion can create mushroom-shaped formations called hoodoos. These exist all over the region, and in a particularly high concentration in Goblin Valley State Park.

Humans in the Region

Though not as visible as geology's impact on the region, humans, too, have left their tracks in the area for thousands of years. This story has many chapters, including early nomads, indigenous farmers, European trappers and explorers, Mormon pioneers, immigrant railway workers, miners, infamous outlaws, and eventually modern inhabitants and tourists.

The first of these groups appeared in southern Utah roughly 12,000 years ago. Generally grouped under the name Desert Archaic Culture, these peoples populated the area lightly and primarily lived as hunter-gatherers. With distinctly dry conditions and wild seasonal climactic swings, Utah has always been a challenging environment for human life. As such, these primitive people spent most of their waking hours procuring food and shelter, with only enough surplus time and energy to craft useful implements such as baskets and tools of stone, bone, and wood.

The general classification of indigenous people changed roughly around 400 A.D., as elements of the Fremont culture began to coalesce. Though this group still primarily hunted and gathered for subsistence, a major distinction arose; with the emergence of the Fremont culture came the area's first agriculture in the form of squash, beans, and maize. As the growing of crops inherently required a somewhat fixed, residential lifestyle, the dwellings of these people evolved into permanent, masonry structures. Culturally, these more stable populations were able to engage in more elaborate crafts such as pottery and ceremonial art.

The next major societal shift came with the arrival of the well-known Anasazi tribe. Originating south of the Colorado River, this group came into greater Utah and maintained a presence until roughly 1300 A.D. Like the Fremont people, they managed a relatively stable and domestic lifestyle. When compared with other North American tribes, the Anasazi erected complex settlements and engaged in rather enriched artistic and religious endeavors. Significant settlements contained stone houses, multihousehold dwellings, granaries, and religious structures. Anasazi crafts included ornate baskets, tools of natural materials, and refined pottery. Today their cultural remains are perhaps the most visible of any group—other than European descendants, of course. The bulk of cliff dwellings, rock art, stone structures, and artifacts found in the area can be attributed to this collective. Eventually, climactic changes and other emerging cultures forced the Anasazi to gradually retreat southward. Some of the most famous and dense evidence of the Anasazis' presence in Utah can be seen at Hovenweep National Monument, in the southern portion of the state, and along the Colorado border.

Around the time the Anasazi retreated, the Numic era began in Utah. This Shoshonean language group existed successfully as a hunter-gatherer culture. Subfactions included the Ute, Southern Paiute, Goshute, and Northern Shoshone tribes. Not needing a stable climate to subsist, these generally nomadic groups traveled in small bands and readily adapted to the variable conditions. These were the peoples first encountered by white explorers, religious men, trappers, and traders during the 1700s and 1800s.

The Dominguez-Escalante Expedition of 1776 is credited as being one of the earliest European ventures to successfully penetrate into modern-day Utah. Escalante, originally of Spain, and Dominguez, of Mexico, were both Franciscan priests. They left Mexico to scout out a plausible route from Santa Fe, New Mexico, to California's Spanish missions. These men and nine others, including a cartographer, traveled through western Colorado and as far north as the Salt Lake Valley before winter turned them around. Notes and maps taken by the expedition would help develop the future Old Spanish Trail, a route from Santa Fe, up through Utah, and down south again toward Los Angeles.

The next—and by far most famous—group of people to enter Utah were the Mormons. Called the Church of Jesus Christ of Latter-day Saints (LDS), this religion was founded on April 6, 1830, by Joseph Smith in western New York. Only one year later, Smith was seeking to found a New Jerusalem in North America and relocated the church to Kirtland, Ohio. Troubles with the locals and financial scandal ousted them and landed the remaining Mormons in Far West, Missouri. Quickly afterward, they were banished by the governor and left behind a story of violence and unrest; shortly thereafter, they set up shop in a swampy area called Nauvoo, Illinois.

This theme of rejection and relocation continued. Joseph Smith and his brother, Hyrum (who would have been Joseph's successor in the church), were murdered by an angry mob in Carthage, Illinois. Thereafter, Brigham Young took over leadership of the Mormons and led them yet farther westward to Nebraska. Seeing a clear pattern of alienation in the greater society, LDS leaders began to consider relocating to a place all their own. They specifically sought a barren and isolated area, one that was completely unsettled by other groups. Trusting that the inherent industriousness and fervent beliefs of his religious followers would aid them in civilizing even the most challenging of landscapes, Young set out westward toward the Great Basin. The group contained 143 men, 3 women, 2 children, more than 70 wagons and 90 horses, as well as dozens of oxen, mules, cows, dogs, chickens, and a year's worth of provisions.

With careful planning, a vanguard scout team, and communication with mountain men like Jim Bridger, the team arrived in the Salt Lake Valley on July 24, 1847. Young, upon viewing the area declared, "This is the place." Today, This Is the Place Heritage Park marks the site of this announcement. This sits at the mouth of Emigration Canyon, a popular road biking spot for locals. That the Mormon pioneers arrived on July 24th explains the modern Utah holiday, Pioneer Day. Sometimes called the Days of '47, this celebration utterly trumps the Fourth of July in the Beehive State. So next time you're in Utah during the latter half of July, you won't have to wonder whether your calendar is off.

During the next decades, Mormons continued to immigrate to the area. Following the now established routes of the forerunning pioneers, the majority of the nation's Mormons trekked westward from Missouri and Illinois. Thousands of Mormons made the westward trek to Utah, covering the 1,000-plus-mile journey on foot, pushing their belongings in their famous handcarts or wheelbarrow-like wagons. More well-off church members made the journey with horses and wagons. Though church endowments were low at the time, the church nevertheless supplemented members' provisions when possible.

Just a bit more than a decade later, Major John Wesley Powell came to Utah as the most successful and meticulous early explorer of the state's wilderness. A very active soldier, cartographer, and geologist for the Union Army during the Civil War, Powell lost his arm to a minié ball—but even so returned to battle again. In fact, Powell's missing arm did very little to slow his brilliant course. Of his lifetime's many accomplishments, his 1860s and '70s explorations of the western interior were among his greatest.

Though he made one short trip in 1867, Powell's most famous mission was his 1869 Powell Geographic Expedition, which ran the Green and Colorado rivers from Wyoming down through the Grand Canyon. Powell and his team did the entire journey in wooden rowboats—well before whitewater boating was even a concept. On this most illustrious campaign, Powell, who was an expert geologist and a highly skilled drawer, traveled 930 miles from Green River, Wyoming, to the mouth of the Virgin River. The entire way, Powell made excruciatingly detailed notes on this entirely uncharted territory. He frequently left the boat to scramble up dangerously craggy canyon walls to gain better vistas of the surrounding areas. Though his drawings were clear and detailed, Powell repeated the same trek just two years later with a photographer. Though it would make this naturalist turn over in his grave to hear it, today's Lake Powell was named after this man.

It was also around this time that railroads made their way into northern Utah. The First Transcontinental Railroad, originally called the Pacific Railroad, was completed at Promontory Point (near Tremonton) on May 10, 1869. Traveling between Omaha and Sacramento, this railroad, which passed through Utah about 70 miles north of Salt Lake City, had immediate impacts on the area. First, once-employed railroad workers suddenly became jobless men. Needing work and money, many of these Americans and immigrants found work at nearby mines, like those in Park City. Sec-

The Court of the Patriarchs in Zion National Park

ond, this state-of-the-art mode of transportation connected Utah to the greater U.S. Both of these exposed the Mormons to new and generally undesired "heathen" immigration.

Life in Utah would become turbulent after this. Mormons, who had trekked to Utah specifically to escape the outside world, had hoped to avoid being surrounded by so-called gentiles in their Zion. Nonetheless, non-Mormons continued to arrive in the area. The divided populations lived adjacent to, but not with, one another. Each group built its own schools and even government buildings, unwilling to cooperate with the other party. Though Utah has largely modernized and integrated in the 140 years since that time, this feeling is sometimes palpable in Latter-day Saints strongholds.

The railways brought not only people to and through Utah but also goods. Freight and passenger trains loaded with valuables became the booty of famous bad guys such as Robert LeRoy Parker and Harry Longabaugh, who made a living robbing the trains during the end of the nineteenth century. Better known as Butch Cassidy and the Sundance Kid, these two infamous men roamed the frontier on horses, hitting loaded trains and then fleeing to the hills with the loot. Knowing the area particularly well, the men could completely evade the law in their hideouts. Though they traveled all over the west, including in Wyoming and Colorado, southern Utah was one of their favorite stomping grounds. Robber's Roost, in southeastern Utah near Escalante, was one of their hangouts, and today is one of the state's more popular technical canyoneering areas. In fact, this is where Aron Ralston took a solo trip, became pinned by falling boulders, and famously amputated his own arm on the spot to survive.

During the twentieth century, the southern portion of Utah underwent significant Mormon and mining development. Once Salt Lake City had been successfully established, Mormons focused a good portion of their energy on colonizing a larger region. Towns swiftly sprang up across Utah. In the interest of founding a sovereign nation, the State of Deseret, Mormons worked fervently to establish many cities to help create the new country they hoped to found. By 1855, they had already established the Elk Mountain Mission in modern-day Moab, and by 1861, they had established townships in the St. George area. But though the southwestern portion of the state was relatively easy to reach by a route that approximately follows the mellow and open path of I-15, the southeastern portion of Utah was quite a different story.

The San Juan portion of Utah was one of the last settled in the region. And anyone who's driven from Salt Lake City to the southeastern corner of Utah can imagine the difficulties faced by wagon trains attempting to travel through this land with no roads or bridges. Mountain ranges, high plains, and the San Rafael Swell occupy the northern portion of the journey. And

The sun begins to rise over Gooseberry Mesa.

Utah's largest rivers, the Green and Colorado, stand in the way of travelers in the southern half of this route. Crossing either of these rivers means not just fording streams but also descending into the deep canyons they have eroded into the earth. With steep walls sometimes more than 2,000 feet tall, the Green and Colorado river canyons would have posed an enormous challenge even to hikers. But with wagons, livestock, and the huge amount of provisions required to establish a town, the task was even greater.

In 1879, a group of 236 Mormons set out to settle this region of the state. Hoping to find a direct route from Escalante to present-day Bluff, they ignored existing, roundabout routes and made a beeline to the Glen Canyon along what is now the Hole-in-the-Rock Road. If you drive this route today, you will see that the first 40 miles are fairly reasonable; however, the last bit would have posed an enormous challenge to those earlier settlers. To cross the Colorado River, the group had to descend the sheer walls of Glen Canyon, cross the river, and then ascend the other equally treacherous side. Group leaders located a weakness in the walls that would hopefully provide a safe path down to water level. But, it wasn't that simple. Roughly six weeks of improvements ensued. During this time, the pioneers blasted, carved, and reinforced the route with logs, pulleys, and more. Eventually this "road" down to the river was completed, and the group made the crossing safely. Even though an equally strenuous uphill journey awaited them on the other side, they crossed slickrock, mesas, and cliffs to successfully establish Bluff in 1880.

The most recent decades in southern Utah have been much less adventuresome. The middle of the twentieth century brought the uranium mining industry to the region. Today, you can still see many of these mine shafts, which can be recognized as door-size tunnels in mountainsides. Townships grew into what they are today, and roads were created to connect them. National parks, recognized for their beauty, became established, and tourism was born. The advent and popularization of extreme sports like mountain biking and rock climbing began attracting people from all over the world. Today, Moab is one of the world's most famous mountain biking destinations, made so by its rather unique and abundant slickrock wilderness. Zion National Park and Indian Creek (near the Needles District of Canyonlands National Park) with their special and pristine sandstone cracks bring rock climbers from all over the world.

Visitors today may easily access the region by way of the Salt Lake International Airport or McCarran International Airport in Las Vegas, Nevada. A large network of scenic byways and tourist-friendly townships covers the region, providing comfort and pleasure. If you decide to visit, make sure to stack the odds in your favor. Get a thorough vehicle checkup before you head out. Pack ample water, sunblock, and food. And then bring some more water. Though this portion of Utah has largely been tamed, you must never forget the unforgiving nature of the desert.

NATIONAL PARKS

Zion National Park

Between the 11,000-foot Colorado Plateau and the depths of the Grand Canyon sits the complex and dramatic Grand Staircase. Zion occupies nearly a vertical mile of this topographical descent, with elevations ranging from 8,700 feet all the way down to 3,600 feet. Contained within this cross section of earth and climes is a wild range of sedimentary geology and natural ecosystems, beautifully sliced into the open by the waters of the Virgin River. Though most visitors to Zion head directly to the Zion Canyon area of the park, Kolob Canyon should not be forgotten. With its separate entrance on the northwestern side of the park, it offers a refreshingly vacant, hikeable portion of the park with much less infrastructure and crowding than the park's main, southern portion.

Zion National Park's most distinguishing feature is the Navajo sandstone, with cliff faces that reach up to 2,500 feet and tower above the narrow, cottonwood-lined Zion Canyon below. These soaring buttresses provide excellent free- and aid-climbing routes for rock climbers technically adept enough to leave the ground. But for all others, Zion offers a number of diverse hiking trails, short and long, paved and dirt. You can hike the famously exciting Angels Landing Trail to an exposed viewpoint thousands of feet above the deck, or stroll just a quarter mile to Weeping Rock. After the spring runoff has cleared, you can explore the upper reaches of Zion Canyon in the Zion Narrows by walking along the bed of the Virgin River.

Utah's most popular park, Zion receives almost 3 million visitors every year. To best handle this traffic, the National Park Service has implemented a mandatory shuttle system for the Zion Canyon portion of the park, in operation during spring, summer, and fall. This shuttle is free for anyone inside the park and provides a safe, hassle-free means to sightsee without the responsibility of driving, or the tedium of parking.

Outside Zion

Nearest the main entrance of Zion is the town of Springdale, a small, tourist-friendly village with restaurants, hotels, developed campgrounds, rental shops, guide services, cafés, and the like. Moving farther west from the park and toward I-15, there are many small towns along the way—as well as other opportunities for hiking and mountain biking like the trails of the famous Gooseberry Mesa and Hurricane Rim. To the far southwest of Zion Canyon stands St. George, just above the Arizona border. St. George is a bustling, small city with a university, several golf courses, restaurants, hotels, auto mechanics, shopping centers, and a hospital.

Kolob Canyon, the park's northern sector, sits immediately adjacent to I-15. The nearest sizable town to this portion of the park is Cedar City, about 20 miles north along that interstate. Cedar City also can be considered a "real" town, comparable to St. George, including a university, though it is not quite the trendy retirement community as its southern counterpart.

Traveling east from Zion National Park, you'll find a series of tiny towns and businesses clustered around highway junctions. Because of their location between Zion and the many parks and monuments to the east, they offer a bit more than typical villages of their size. But don't expect a lot more here than a pricey tank of gas and establishments with limited hours.

Bryce Canyon National Park

With a misnomer for a name, Bryce Canyon is actually not a canyon at all. Rather, it consists of more than a dozen amphitheaters carved into the Paunsaugunt Plateau, revealing over 1,000 vertical feet of exposed geology. A canyon is, by definition, created by a river eating or eroding a ravine or

A supernatural view gained by looking up from the bottom of the Bryce Amphitheater

gorge into the earth. However, Bryce Canyon was created by chemical and physical weathering forces carrying soils and rocks from the top to the bottom. The sedimentary strata exposed by this natural stripping can be seen as a horizontal rainbow of reds, oranges, pinks, and yellows. These bright bands stretch across the wide expanses in parallel layers, showing up on the many, individual formations across the park—from the amphitheater walls to the globular hoodoos and crumbling fins.

Bryce sits rather high up, between 6,620 and 9,115 feet—though not as high as Cedar Breaks National Monument—and can be visited year-round. However, during many of those months, you'll be visiting on cross-country skis. For T-shirt-and-shorts weather, come during the peak of summer—and bring a sweatshirt with you in case the breeze picks up.

To explore Bryce, you should plan to do some hiking—or at the very least, take the shuttle bus into the park for easy viewing from the road. You are permitted to drive your car, but parking is limited. And the bus, which costs nothing, allows for unlimited gawking. Plus if you ride the shuttle, you may explore various sections of the Rim Trail without having to retrace your steps to a parked car.

Several of the hiking trails in Bryce meander down toward the bottom of these amphitheaters and around, between, and sometimes even through the park's colorful rock formations. As these trails are meticulously maintained by the park service, they are usually quite accessible and tame, regardless of their length and steepness.

Outside Bryce Canyon

Bryce Canyon sits in a rather remote portion of Utah, northeast of Zion National Park, and roughly between Cedar Breaks and the Grand Staircase–Escalante national monuments. Those coming to Bryce shouldn't plan to see any shopping centers or amusement parks. That said, the roads leading to and away from Bryce carry millions of national parks visitors every year, and so spawn an industry of their own. Along the way, you'll see numerous small towns, bed & breakfasts, and gas stations.

The nearest town to Bryce Canyon is Tropic, to the east. Amazingly, this town has been around since 1891. But in all that time, it has still only managed to collect a population of roughly 500 people. Though small, this town has gotten hip to the tourist traffic passing through it, and therefore offers a range of amenities to visitors. Tropic is located on UT 12; perhaps the state's most famous scenic byway, this road connects Tropic to Cannonville, Henrieville, and eventually the Grand Staircase–Escalante National Monument. If you have time, consider heading all the way east on this road to experience stunning scenery and reach the more contemporary amenities of Escalante and Boulder.

Of all Utah's national parks, this is perhaps my favorite for its incredibly expansive views and relative emptiness. Though by no means a deserted wild area, this park receives significantly fewer visitors than Zion National Park and has a much less structured, lower-key feel.

Capitol Reef National Park preserves a major portion of the 100-mile-long Water Pocket Fold, North America's largest exposed monocline. This incredible uplift of rock has brought to the surface brilliant colors of diverse sandstones including Wingate, Navajo, and Chinle formations. This fantastic feature was called a reef by early travelers, as it posed a fiercely rugged and seemingly impenetrable barrier to travelers attempting to move in an east–west direction. Only five rivers actually cut a path through the reef from the east to the west; the gravel bed of one constitutes Grand Wash trail—one of the more popular and easier hiking trails in the park.

Those visiting Capitol Reef can view much of its grandeur from the roadside. In fact, a large chunk of the area's beauty can be seen along UT 24 without even turning onto the park's main road, called Scenic Drive, which splits south off the main highway. In addition to the numerous hikes and natural viewpoints of the park, you can explore the remains of Fruita, a 19th-century Mormon settlement whose buildings and orchards have been preserved by the National Park Service. If you only have a few hours to spend in Capitol Reef, I recommend visiting in the late afternoon when the sun bathes its mainly west-facing cliffs in warm, brilliantly saturating light.

Outside Capitol Reef

The nearest town to Capitol Reef is Torrey, rife with gas stations, cafés, B&Bs, national and local motels, and the like. This town, though small, caters to the needs of tourists. Settled in 1880, Torrey has a quaint feel and a tree-lined Main Street. Surrounding Torrey and Capitol Reef, the red rock desert stretches for miles. Mixed private and Bureau of Land Management (BLM) lands outside Capitol Reef have seen little or no development and offer the occasional cost-free camping areas.

Southwest of the park, the massive and broad Boulder Mountain Plateau looms high above the surrounding landscape. This huge feature has a peak elevation of 11,313 feet at Bluebell Knoll, as well as 80 lakes up to 52 acres in size and a generous collection of developed and wild campgrounds. Following UT 12 from the Capitol Reef/Torrey area southward to Boulder, Utah, you climb high onto the shoulders of this massive mountain. Along this route stand several scenic pullouts with signs explaining the features below, including Capitol Reef, the Circle Cliffs, the Henry Mountains, and more. The Wildcat Ranger Station, located right off UT 12, opens its doors (with very limited hours) from Memorial Day weekend into October.

Arches National Park

Part of Utah's eastern national park (and Moab) circuit, Arches is Utah's most emblematic park, featuring more than 2,000 recorded natural arches with openings greater than 3 feet across. These rather unique formations, in addition to a collection of accompanying fins and spires, sit atop rounded sandstone domes and among the remains of petrified sand dunes and fossilized dinosaur footprints. Located at a moderate elevation, between 4,085 feet at the visitors center and 5,653 feet at Elephant Butte, Arches gets pretty chilly during the winter, but nevertheless bakes in the summer. Especially if you want to do some hiking in this park, you should plan to visit during the spring and fall seasons.

As in the other parks, Arches offers the possibility to view much of its terrain via scenic drives. Arches has two main roads—or rather one main road to the Devil's Garden and Fiery Furnace portion of the park with a significant spur leading east toward the Delicate Arch viewpoints and trail heads.

Outside Arches

Once outside Arches, you don't have far to go before you get to Moab. In fact, the turnoff to the park sits just 8 miles north of town via the major highway, US 191. Moab has nearly everything you could want or need before, during, or after an outdoors adventure, including restaurants, cafés, outdoor rental and retail outfits, a big and fairly modern library, hotels, and even beer- and wine-making operations. Not bad! For more information on Moab, check out chapter 7.

If you head north from Arches, you must travel 27 miles on US 191 until you reach I-70. From there, the town of Green River is just 17 miles to the west. This small, interstate town offers several truck-stop-style gas stations, the John Wesley Powell River History Museum, and Ray's Tavern. This grill makes the best burger in the vicinity.

Canyonlands National Park

This park, centered around the junction of the Colorado and Green rivers, consists of three major parts and one smaller "island" of land. The slice north of the Y goes by Island in the Sky; the eastern portion is called the Needles; the western chunk, by far the park's most remote and rugged, goes by the somewhat ominous name of the Maze; and the final piece, which sits off the northwestern corner of the Maze, is called Horseshoe Canyon.

Island in the Sky has been fitted with a nearly literal title, stemming from the fact that its namesake mesa actually is somewhat of a rock island, standing more than 1,000 feet taller than its immediate surroundings and 2,000 feet above the Green and Colorado rivers, below. Island in the Sky

Island in the Sky has a fitting name. Gordon McArthur

offers many hiking and backpacking trails, including the famous White Rim Road, a 100-mile loop that traces around the mesa and is very popular for multiday mountain biking and jeep outings. You can take a short day hike here, backpack, or simply head to the Grand View Point to enjoy a vista of the entire park.

The Needles' name becomes apparent to even the most casually observing visitor, with jagged Wingate sandstone teeth jutting out of the high desert floor. This portion of the park also offers a network of backpacking and hiking opportunities, a scenic drive, and various points of archaeological interest, including a cowboy camp and Puebloan ruins.

The Maze, 2.5 hours from the town of Green River, is reached by driving 24 miles of paved and 46 miles of dirt roads. The Hans Flat Ranger Station stands at the entrance to this wild portion of Canyonlands, beyond which lead several miles of winding, high-clearance-requiring dirt roads. This portion of the park has been left nearly untainted by development, rendering it nearly pristine for a real backcountry experience. Those planning to enter this portion of the park should do so with a proper high-clearance, four-wheel-drive vehicle or the fitness, self-sufficiency, and time to explore the park on foot.

And Horseshoe Canyon, a tiny and isolated chunk of the park, centers around an incredibly dense collection of ancient rock art of the Barrier Canyon style. Its most famous panel is called the Great Gallery and features clear and detailed figures up to 7 feet in height. Visitors to this canyon must be prepared to hike down into it to check out the art.

Outside Canyonlands

Canyonlands National Park's four districts are some of the more remote of Utah's national parks—particularly the Maze and the Horseshoe Canyon sections. The northern portion of the park, Island in the Sky, is accessed via UT 312. This state highway arches up and away from the park to the northeast and connects promptly with US 191 just north of Arches National Park. When visiting Island in the Sky, think about visiting Dead Horse Point State Park (see "The Best of Utah's Southern National Monuments, State Parks, and Surrounding Areas," below), also along this road. To the south of the park is Moab, to the north is I-70.

The southeastern portion of the park, the Needles, is reached via UT 211. This highway splits off US 191, 37 miles south of Moab (or just 14.5 miles north of Monticello, Utah). This road heads west across high desert plains before plunging down into a beautiful valley carved between Wingate sandstone bluffs by Indian Creek. This incredible area is home to some of the world's most famous crack climbing, and people travel from all over the world just to climb on these cliffs. As you drive through the canyon, see if you can't spot a few of them—as well as the rock art on what's called Newspaper Rock, near the top (eastern) end of the canyon.

Outside the Maze and Horseshoe Canyon, you'll find exclusively wild, nearly untamed lands. This section of Canyonlands requires more time and backcountry knowledge to access than most any other national park in the country. The ranger station is roughly 2.5 hours from Green River and I-70, via 24 miles of the paved UT 24 and 46 miles of maintained dirt road. The Maze shares its western border with the Glen Canyon Recreation Area.

THE BEST OF UTAH'S SOUTHERN MONUMENTS, STATE PARKS, AND SURROUNDING AREAS

It would be a mistake to assume Utah's only worthy sights stand within the boundaries of national parks. In fact, you'll notice that almost every highway in Utah's southern half bears the scenic drive symbol on any road map. You'll also notice many state parks and national monuments along these routes. Of course, all of these denote worthy destinations, whether they hold scenic or historic value. Below stand descriptions of the best destinations, listed in order along the route from Zion National Park (chapter 1) in the southwest, through Bryce Canyon (chapter 2), Capitol Reef National Park (chapter 3), along UT 12 and the northern portion of Grand Staircase–Escalante National Monument (chapter 4), along UT 24, and eventually down into Arches National Park (chapter 5), Canyonlands (chapter 6), Moab (chapter 7), and beyond via US 191 and toward Arizona. All of the state parks listed below charge day-use fees (usually $6, but sometimes more); Interagency Annual Passes are not accepted.

Snow Canyon State Park

In the southwest corner of Utah, Snow Canyon State Park (435-628-2255; www.stateparks.utah.gov) protects a brilliantly colored, red rock canyon just outside St. George. Despite being located near one of Utah's most rapidly growing towns, this park offers unadulterated desert vistas that closely resemble the famous Red Rock Canyon near Las Vegas, Nevada. This quiet and well-maintained state park provides clean facilities, hiking and biking trails, camping, and even rock climbing. With elevations between 3,150 and 5,023 feet, this area enjoys a mild climate in the depths of winter. A state park since 1958, it is situated in the East and West Snow canyons, which cut deeply into the Red Mountains and converge in the center of the park. These two canyons carve beautiful sheer cliffs and rounded domes into the soft and colorful local sandstones and are topped by black lava flows. Of the 11 trails in the park, most are fairly short and access various historic and natural points of interest; a few stretch for longer distances (up to 7 miles) and can be used for jogging or biking trips through stands of sagebrush and juniper trees. Contained in the park are pioneer markings dating back to 1883, petrified sand dunes, scenic overlooks, ancient pinyon trees, sandy washes, natural potholes, and a 200-foot-wide rock arch. Many of the trails are handicapped accessible. The park also contains several rock climbs, including multipitch traditional routes and single sport pitches.

Coral Pink Sand Dunes State Park

Farther east along Utah's southern border is Coral Pink Sand Dunes State Park (435-648-2800; www.stateparks.utah.gov) between Zion National Park and Kanab. Of all Utah's magnificent and spectacular desert formations, this is one of the most unique and contains the Colorado Plateau's only major sand dune area. Resembling a snippet of the great Middle Eastern and African deserts, this are contains over 3,700 acres of rosy pink Navajo sandstone dunes replete with a gorgeous backdrop of red cliffs and the deep blues of the Moquith and Moccasin mountains. These dunes, formed by winds blasting down the notch between these two ranges, have an estimated age of 10,000 to 15,000 years. A protected area, Coral Pink Sand Dunes State Park provides habitat to the majority of the planet's remaining Welsh's milkweed, which appears on the federal list of threatened species. A popular place for ATVs and dirt bikes, these lands can also be enjoyed by hikers, campers, horseback riders, and others interested in desert wildlife and photography. ATVs are restricted to certain trails and designated areas. Information on the park and visitor tips can be obtained at the visitors center. For those on longer trips, the campgrounds here offer showers and bathrooms.

Heading northeast toward Bryce Canyon National Park, you'll get a preview of what's to come at Red Canyon (Dixie National Forest, 435-865-3700), just east of the junction of US 89 and UT 12. Here, UT 12 passes through multiple red rock tunnels as it meanders through the brightly colored, muddy-looking rock formations. Regardless of whether you take the time to stop and explore, this canyon offers surprisingly orange and red rocks appearing beneath the carpet of evergreen forests. A visitors center, open from Memorial Day to Labor Day, details a bit of the area's historical, geological, and natural information. Multiple different trails have been created for hikers, bikers, ATVers, and horseback riders. Stop to stretch your legs, have a picnic en route from one park to another, or set up camp for the evening. Situated at an elevation of almost 7,000 feet, this canyon provides a cool respite from lower elevation recreation areas during the hotter seasons of the year.

Kodachrome Basin State Park

Farther along UT 12 and nearer to the town of Escalante, watch for the turnoff to Kodachrome Basin State Park (435-679-8562; www.stateparks .utah.gov). Nine miles of (very low speed limit) pavement lead south toward this state park, a quiet garden of rock spires. Almost 70 of these rock "pipes" reach from the juniper- and sage-covered desert floor up toward the sky, and range from two all the way up to 52 meters in height. Exposed in the rock pillars of the park are 180 million years of geologic history, with the oldest and lowest stratum of sandstone being the Winsor Member of the Carmel Formation and the newest being Tropic Shale at "just" 95 million years of age. More recently, during a 1949 National Geographic expedition to the area, photographers used Kodachrome color film, notorious for capturing this range of colors well. Because of this, the valley was dubbed Kodachrome. Fourteen years later, this area received designation as a state park, but because of copyright issues with the Kodak company, its first official name was Chimney Rock State Park. However just a few years later, the state gave the park its current name with Kodak's permission. One of the park's most popular activities is camping; though generally low key, the park's campgrounds (containing 27 sites) are full of RVs, campers, and tents. The other popular attraction in this relatively petite park is hiking along the park's many trails. If you stop by and stay the night, you should consider stargazing, as Kodachrome Basin suffers little light pollution and therefore affords great views of the celestial bodies above.

Kodachrome Basin State Park is hard to miss.

Drive a bit farther along the same access road to visit Grosvenor Arch, about 11 miles southeast of Kodachrome Basin State Park. This double arch actually consists of two side-by-side arches sharing the same middle pillar. The formation stands about 152 feet tall and spans a width of about 90 feet. It sits in the northwestern portion of the Grand Staircase–Escalante Monument (see chapter 4) and was one of the first famous singular attractions within its bounds. Named after Gilbert Hovey Grosvenor, the president of the National Geographic Society from 1920 to 1954, this arch starts red at the top, fading in intensity through shades of orange to white sandstone at its feet. With a paved, sidewalklike trail leading nearly to its base, this

A classic sandstone pipe in Kodachrome Basin.

A wide valley showcases Kodachrome Basin's fins and pipes.

site is fully accessible to those in wheelchairs. A campground, picnic sites, and toilets are located at the site.

Escalante Petrified Forest State Park

Once you've returned north to UT 12, and driven eastward and nearly to the town of Escalante, you'll notice a turnout to the north leading to the Escalante Petrified Forest State Park (435-826-4466; www.stateparks .utah.gov). On the way up to the park's entrance, you'll pass the dam that contains the waters of the Wide Hollow Reservoir. Here, you'll pay a small fee to enter the park (additional charges for camping, if desired). If you wish to hike the 1.25-mile trail leading up to the namesake petrified wood chunks, bear right and park at the signed area. This well-maintained trail leads uphill to the top of a plateau via switchbacks. As you climb, you'll gain views of the reservoir and camping below, as well as the town of Escalante to the southeast. Once at the top, the trail makes a loop, around which many pieces of petrified wood are situated immediately nearby. Some of

The junction between the Sleeping Rainbow Trail and the Main Trail in the petrified forest of Escalante State Park.

these are quite large. In fact, many are complete cross sections of massive logs, with the bark still preserved around the entire piece. If you wish to add extra mileage to the hike, follow signs for the Sleeping Rainbow Trail, which tacks on another 30 minutes of steep walking. The trail's name comes from the Navajo description for the colorful Capitol Reef and Colorado Plateau landscape to the east.

Anasazi State Park Museum

Traveling yet farther along on UT 12 between the towns of Escalante and Boulder, you'll trace almost exactly along the northern edge of the 1.9-million acre Grand Staircase–Escalante National Monument and its many natural attractions (as detailed in chapter 4). Anasazi State Park Museum (460 North UT 12, Boulder; 435-335-7308; www.stateparks.utah.gov) sits just off the highway near Boulder, on an archaeological dig called the Coombs Site. Inhabited approximately 1160–1235 A.D., this is among the area's largest Ancestral Puebloan villages, home to as many as 200 people at one time. Today, many of the buildings remain in varying degrees of completeness. Though some of the structures have been cordoned off, visitors may tour other, more intact buildings. The Anasazi, believed to be the predecessors of today's Puebloan Indians, resided in the Four Corners Region roughly 200–1300 A.D. This people obtained food using a blend of hunting and agriculture, thus leading a more "residential" lifestyle. They built permanent villages and left behind many remains in the form of artifacts, dwellings, and ruins of other storage structures like granaries. The Coombs Site is certainly not the only instance of this culture in the area; a stop by the museum will help you understand the many structural ruins, pictographs (paintings), and petroglyphs (etchings) scattered along your journey through southern Utah. If heading into the southeastern portion of Canyonlands National Park (see chapter 6), make sure to stop by Newspaper Rock on your way into the Needles, or by the Great Gallery in the Horseshoe Canyon Unit; these are among the densest collections of rock art around.

Some pieces of the petrified wood are quite large in Escalante State Park.

Dixie National Forest/Boulder Mountain

Continuing along UT 12 as it bends to the north, you'll leave the town of Boulder and quickly climb onto the large plateau known generally as Boulder Mountain, in the Dixie National Forest (435-865-3700; www.fs.fed.us/dxnf). Part of the Aquarius Plateau, this broad and lofty mound tops out at 11,317 feet above sea level. UT 12 carves a meandering path high on its flanks, passing many dirt side roads, developed campgrounds, and lake access spurs along the way. In all, the area

UT 12 traces along the top of the Grand Staircase–Escalante National Monument and up over Boulder Mountain.

has roughly 80 lakes up to 52 acres in size. You can't help but notice the scenic vistas along the way; to enjoy these, stop at any of the several pull-outs overlooking the complicated Grand Staircase region to the south and east. Signs explain and illustrate the sights below, including Capitol Reef National Park and the 100-mile-long Waterpocket Fold, the Henry Mountains, and Circle Cliffs. Though the highway remains open all year (except in the cases of extreme weather), recreation becomes severely limited due to snowpack in the winter and spring months.

From Boulder Mountain, you can't help but see the massive Henry Mountains to the southeast. This range, like the La Sal Mountains near Moab, formed as a result of volcanic activity. Roughly 23 to 31 million years ago, magma forced its way up into the earth's crust, but never erupted onto its surface. These domes cooled into laccoliths of diorite. Gradually, the crust above these domes eroded away, exposing the five major rocky peaks of this range. One of Utah's most rugged and remote regions, these mountains are accessed only by unmarked dirt roads. Though they are often passable even by low-clearance cars, they can degrade to the point at which only four-wheel-drive vehicles can maneuver them. In 1941, a herd of 18 American bison was transplanted to this range from Yellowstone National Park. Since that time, this group has grown to contain more than 200 individuals and is the only free-roaming herd in the lower 48 states for which the government issues hunting permits. However, bison are not the only animals roaming these slopes; take precautions as mountain lions and rattlesnakes live there as well—in addition to numerous other nonthreatening species. In these mountains, you can camp, hike, and even rock climb, but there are no developed trails or campgrounds. Watch out for midsummer precipitation; this range receives a significant amount of its annual moisture during the summer months. Looking from a distance, you'll easily understand why, as the soaring, lonely peaks rise high in the sky, catching and draining a cloud system all its own. The Henry Mountains rise steeply from 3,700 feet at the valley floor to more than 1.5 vertical miles to 11,600 feet at the top of Mt. Ellen. If you visit this range without a trailer (which you can't feasibly tow up its dirt roads anyway), consider looping back west and toward Boulder via the Burr Trail. Detailed in chapter 3, this dramatic road cuts an extremely twisted path just south of the Henry Mountains.

Goblin Valley State Park

Traveling east, Capitol Reef National Park is the next major stop. Once through this park, though, the sights and points of interest grow farther and farther apart as you travel UT 24 eastward. The exception to this is Goblin Valley State Park (435-275-4584; www.stateparks.utah.gov/parks/goblin-valley), 32 road miles northeast of Hanksville. Perhaps Utah's most peculiar and famous park, this area has been designated a state park since 1974. Previously called Mushroom Valley, this park includes nearly 3,700 acres of peculiar top-heavy hoodoos. These orange Entrada sandstone formations—which quite resemble mushrooms—form when soft sandstone underneath harder capstone erodes more quickly, leaving larger boulders on top of

High on Boulder Mountain, views of the surrounding landscape can be seen through aspen trees.

Skirting around the southeastern tip of the Henry Mountains on the Burr Trail.

thinner pillars. Humans have long been fascinated by these features, as evidenced by ancient rock art panels and the more recent reports of early 20th-century cowboys. This park, with an elevation of approximately 5,000 feet, remains open throughout the year and has a visitors center, open daily. People are free to hike among these rock creatures and explore the barren slickrock valley floor. Though not allowed to ride in the park, mountain bikers and ATV users commonly re-create along the network of dirt roads outside the boundaries.

Dead Horse Point State Park

Once you've completed the UT 24 traverse and have begun the southern trek toward Moab, keep your eyes out for the Canyonlands and Dead Horse Point State Park (435-259-2614; www.stateparks.utah.gov) turnout, 9 miles north of town. Twenty-three miles down UT 313, this park features a vista of the snaking Colorado River meandering approximately 2,000 feet below the lookout. One of the most popular and accessible areas in the state for photography, Dead Horse Point is a high peninsula of land, bounded by sheer cliffs falling off below its rim. This seeming rock island is connected to the mainland by a thread of land just 30 feet wide. In the late 19th century, cowboys corralled a group of wild horses onto this "island" and strung a fence across, blocking them from the mainland. For reasons unknown, they deserted the horses there. Trapped without water, the horses died of dehydration. The park offers three developed and pet-friendly trails, including a new mountain biking area, the Intrepid Trail System, which gives a taste of the area's famous slickrock bike riding as well as single track and sandy washes. These nested trails are as short as 1 mile or as long as 9 and offer both easy and challenging riding. This park is more developed than others, offering events (check online) and even a café. It's also a bit pricier than most of Utah's other parks, charging $10 for its day-use entry fee.

Edge of the Cedars State Park

Heading south from Canyonlands National Park (chapter 6) and Moab (chapter 7), you'll pass through the small, high desert towns of Monticello and Blanding. While in Blanding, look for Edge of the Cedars State Park (600 West 400 North; 435-678-2238; www.stateparks.utah.gov), on the western side of town. This park features an ancient Puebloan village and modern museum explaining its cultural and historical background. The pueblo itself was occupied 825–1125 A.D., by a faction of the pre-Columbian Native Americans. Part of a small village containing six dwellings and ceremonial structures, the excavated area today grants an enlightening view into the lives of these bygone people. A log ladder leads down into a reconstructed *kiva* or ceremonial room, which has been stabilized and preserved to allow visitors inside. The accompanying on-site museum illustrates the human history of the area, beginning with the ancient Anasazi Indians and working through the more modern Navajo and Ute tribes. It also includes pioneer history and holds a large number of artifacts. One of its biggest claims to fame is its extremely large Anasazi pottery collection, among the biggest in the entire southwestern United States.

Hovenweep National Monument

Southeast from Edge of the Cedars by about 50 miles (and 1.5 hours), on the border with Colorado, is the Hovenweep National Monument (970-562-4282; www.nps.gov/hove). This monument features one of the most major archaeological sites in the entire southwestern region of the U.S. With a human history reaching more than 10,000 years into the past, Hovenweep has been visited and impacted by numerous cultures. The first permanent structures here date back to around 900 A.D., when people were first able to inhabit the area on a year-round basis—made possible by implementing agricultural practices. For a few centuries, this community flourished, growing to a size of roughly 2,500 by 1200 A.D. Needless to say, a population of that size with such a substantial length of stay was sure to pass on a wealth of artifacts. To help visitors experience these extensive ruins, the monument maintains a trail system that accesses its many cultural sites. The most popular path, the Square Tower Group Trail, stretches 2 miles and begins at the visitors center. The first segment of this trail is paved, allowing access to those in wheelchairs. After this, the dirt path offers many viewpoints along the way. Other, less-maintained trails reach into outlying sites, including Goodman Point, Cutthroat Castle, and more. Those with ample energy may hope to visit a lot of these sites, as their access trails typically are a mile or less each way. Unlike most national parks, backpacking is *not* permitted here; however, Hovenweep does offer a 30-site campground, primarily intended for tents.

Goosenecks State Park

Directly on the route connecting Arches, Moab, Blanding, Hovenweep, and Edge of the Cedars to the world-famous Monument Valley is the Goosenecks State Park (435-678-2238; www.stateparks.utah.gov). Located at the far eastern tip of the Glen Canyon National Recreation Area, this park affords views of the San Juan River from the top of a 1,000-foot canyon, as it approaches Lake Powell, the country's second biggest man-made reservoir. This river has flowed though the area for millions of years. Long after it has established its path, a massive tectonic uplift began. However, even as the bedrock slowly rose, the San Juan maintained its erosive path, cutting into the climbing plateau much more quickly than tectonics could lift the earth. Today, this particularly loopy meander reveals approximately 300 million years' worth of sedimentary layers on the canyon walls. At this point, the San Juan travels a distance of 6 river miles in only about a quarter the straight-line distance. This small (10-acre) park is almost entirely undeveloped and serves as a designated viewpoint of this remarkable geological phenomenon. However it does offer a shaded pavilion for picnicking, pit toilets, and primitive campsites. The entire park (including its campsites) costs nothing to enter.

Monument Valley Navajo Tribal Park

On the final stretch south toward Arizona on US 163, you'll catch one last fantastic site, the Monument Valley Navajo Tribal Park (435-727-5870; www.navajonationparks.org). Perhaps the most iconic and photographed desert vista in the U.S., this valley features numerous fins of shale, sandstone, and siltstone. All sitting atop talus pedestals, these rise as much as 1,000 feet above the surroundings—a barren, sandy valley floor composed of red Cutler siltstone. Though the turnoff to the park is just north of the border, the valley itself is situated in Arizona. The entirety of Monument Valley sits within the northern portion of the 26,000-square-mile Navajo Nation. The park features a 17-mile, well-maintained dirt road that loops through the spires, mesas, and buttes. A scenic brochure, which can be picked up at the park's visitors center, briefly outlines 11 of the named features. A 3.2-mile, self-guided hiking path called the Wildcat Trail traces a loop around the West Mitten Butte. Because of the area's cultural significance to the tribe, the majority of its backcountry areas may be entered on a guided tour only. Visit the monument's Web site for a listing of guide services. This park is administered by the Navajo Nation; National Park Service Interagency Annual Passes are not accepted.

Glen Canyon National Recreation Area

Occupying a vast and rather difficult-to-access, arrow-shaped portion of southern Utah is the Glen Canyon National Recreation Area (928-608-6200; www.nps.gov/glca). This enormous land tract surrounds the waters of Lake Powell, a reservoir capturing the waters of the Colorado and San Juan rivers. Pinned behind the Glen Canyon Dam near Page, Arizona, this man-made lake stretches as far north as the now-defunct Hite Marina on UT 95. The recreation area centers around this reservoir and shares its northeastern border with the Maze portion of Canyonlands National Monument. Its southeastern filament follows the San Juan River, petering out just west of Mexican Hat, Utah, with an overlook at Goosenecks State Park. Created largely for water storage and electrical production, this reservoir today is one of Utah's most popular areas for motorized water recreation: jet skis, houseboats, speedboats, and the like. Though the recreation area is huge, the dramatically steep walls of the now-flooded Glen Canyon keep access points to a select few. The most popular put-in points are near Page, Arizona. This town is accessed via US 89, which traces through the southern portion of the Grand Staircase–Escalante National Monument on its approach. Others come to the area by approaching through Hanksville, driving UT 95. Still others arrive at the Bullfrog Marina, driving UT 276 along the eastern slopes of the Henry Mountains. Because of evaporation and persistent drought, the waters of the reservoir have sunk more than 100 feet, creating a visible, white "bathtub ring." The receding shoreline of the lake has most impacted many of its marinas, particularly those with very gradual shorelines. The Hite Marina, once at the northern tip of the lake, now sits high above and back from the lake. Though the ownership tried to adapt to the dropping shoreline by extending the boat ramp, the marina is no longer operational. Today, it looks more like a landing strip than a marina.

The Hite Marina at the northern tip of Lake Powell looks more like a landing strip than a boat ramp.

Planning Your Trip

WHERE TO GO, WHEN TO GO, WHAT TO TAKE

POINT B TO POINT Z: UTAH'S LAYOUT

The first thing to consider when planning any trip to or within Utah is the weather. With such a huge amount of topographical relief, the southern portion of this state is as diverse in its weather patterns as it is in its vistas. To be sure, the tallest attractions like Cedar Breaks National Monument—with an elevation above 10,000 feet—close when snowpack becomes too deep. In high snow years, this can mean that Cedar Breaks (and therefore all of its through roads) remains closed well into mid-June. Utah has a handful of highways that traditionally close during the winter. For information on these roads and their status, check with the Utah Department of Transportation (www.udot.utah.gov).

That said, if all roads are open, your route depends entirely on the amount of time you have at your disposal. If you study any map, you'll see that all highways connecting the parks are littered with other sideshow attractions: state parks of all varieties, viewpoints, national forests, national monuments, friendly towns, restaurants, campgrounds, and the like, all welcoming visitors to spend unlimited time in the area.

Anyone driving around and in the parks should allow ample time. Given a distance of 60 miles between destinations, you should expect to spend much more than an hour driving. Once you leave the interstate and enter the topography of the Grand Staircase, the roads pass through meandering curves, climb up and drop down steep passes, have low speed limits, and offer numerous scenic vistas. The resulting slow traffic is a natural result of road conditions and an often high volume of cars. Additionally, you

LEFT: Photographs do not give the Hog's Back portion of UT 12 justice.

can expect to encounter roadside villages, wildlife, and any number of other traffic-retarding agents. But if you simply plan ahead and expect this, you can relax and enjoy these sites.

Utah's far western attractions include Zion National Park, in the southwestern corner, and Cedar Breaks National Monument, to its north. UT 9, also called the Zion–Mt. Carmel Highway, runs east–west through Zion and straight into US 89. A number of state highways (subject to snow closure from autumn into early summer) lead from Cedar Breaks to US 89. This major north–south highway boasts pleasant scenery and many gas stations as it leads toward the famous UT 12.

Looking out from the North View of Cedar Breaks National Monument

UT 12 runs in a huge crescent, trending roughly east and then northeast from its junction with US 89. Punctuated with a handful of genuinely charming tourist-friendly towns, this is one of Utah's most famous roadways. It connects a lifetime's worth of parks, monuments, recreation areas, and ecosystems. Along this route stands Kodachrome Basin State Park, Bryce Canyon National Park, Escalante Petrified Forest State Park, the Grand Staircase–Escalante National Monument (GSENM), Anasazi State Park, portions of the Dixie National Forest, Boulder Mountain, the Ashley National Forest, and the towns of Escalante and Boulder. The wild Burr Trail also departs from this road, connecting the town of Boulder to the southeastern edge of the Henry Mountains, cutting through the southern portion of Capitol Reef National Park along its way.

North of all this, UT 24 carves a squat U-shaped path that begins and ends at I-70, but stays to the south of it. At the center and southernmost point of this curve (and just east of its intersection with UT 12), this highway slices right through the heart of Capitol Reef National Park. This highway traverses quite a different set of ecosystems than UT 12. Though less spectacular than other designated scenic drives, it nevertheless offers a wide variety of beautiful sights along the way.

A somewhat substantial stretch of land stands between the western sights (Cedar Breaks, Zion, Bryce Canyon, Grand Staircase–Escalante, and

Capitol Reef) and the eastern destinations (Arches, Canyonlands, Goblin Valley, Dead Horse Point, Natural Bridges, and Edge of the Cedars). I-70 and UT 24 represent the only "real" highways spanning this middle zone. And though quite a void exists between these two major park areas, it can be passed in a matter of hours. Don't forget to check out Goblin Valley State Park (north of Hanksville) if traversing this "gap" via UT 24.

US 191 serves as the major artery connecting I-70 to Arches National Park, Dead Horse Point State Park, Canyonlands National Park, Moab, Hovenweep National Monument, the iconic Monument Valley Navajo Tribal Park, and the numerous small towns and roadside attractions in between. Though mainly a two-lane, undivided highway, it nevertheless functions as a major throughway with typically fast speed limits allowing for quick passage. For those coming from different landscapes, this offers views of handsomely barren high desert and plains. But despite its beauty, it certainly is not as breathtaking and unique as its western counterpart, UT 12.

CAMPING AND HIKING

Best Hikes and Viewpoints

The most spectacular and stunning hike in Utah's busiest national park, Angels Landing, climbs 1,488 feet for over 2.7 miles in the heart of Zion Canyon. The trail ascends to the top of a thin peninsula of rock 1,500 feet above the Virgin River. This hike is classified as strenuous and features extreme exposure at the top, so it is not for everyone. However, the entirety

Monument Valley is a desolate piece of land. David Sjöquist

of the journey offers a variety of diverse and unique trail segments that make even an incomplete trek worth it. Though very steep, the first 80 percent of the trail is paved. From the canyon bottom, it winds up the mountainside via dozens of zigzagging switchbacks. It quickly ascends steep slopes before entering the shady Hidden Canyon. Another burst of heavily fortified switchbacks called Walter's Wiggles climbs steeply to a lookout point. At this point, the final 0.5-mile ascent to the summit is visible. From here, the way becomes much more exposed and challenging. If you decide to make a summit bid, be absolutely sure that no thunderstorms are approaching. The rest of the journey has been reinforced with carved steps and hand chains, but all hikers should be mindful of their footing every step along the way. Lethal vertical drops on either side flank the narrow ridge. A flat plateau awaits at the final destination, perfect for picture taking or even a quick picnic. This hike should not be taken with small children or those afraid of heights, and it should never be attempted in the event of a storm.

On the other end of the exposure spectrum, the Capitol Reef Narrows Hike offers a completely low-key, nearly flat trek along the bottom of the Grand Wash. Descending imperceptibly over the course of 2.5 miles, this sandy, usually dry riverbed passes the Cassidy Arch (and trail) along its way. Along the journey, the sandstone walls of the gulch grow taller and the width of the passage decreases until the trail enters what's called the Narrows. Here, cliffs on either side rise hundreds of feet above the wash, hardly more than 15 feet apart. For obvious reasons, this hike should be avoided if there is any threat of flash flooding; check with the park rangers before attempting this journey.

In the same national park, Sunset Point offers one of the most spectacular views of the complex Waterpocket Fold. Requiring only 50 feet of walking, this truly should be visited at sunset, when the sinking sun casts a saturating glow over the west-facing cliffs of Capitol Reef. Here the deep reds of Wingate and Chenille sandstones complement the paler Navajo sandstone varieties. A late afternoon visit here provides memorable views of the many spires, domes, monoliths, cliffs, arches, and canyons created by the fantas-

Angels Landing itself from the trail

The Walter's Wiggles on Angels Landing Trail

tic geological uplift and subsequent erosion of this 65-million-year-old monocline.

In Bryce Canyon National Park, the Queen's Garden/Navajo Loop Trail offers a moderate-level, roughly 3-mile journey down into Bryce's muddy fins and spires. Descending about 300 vertical feet from Sunrise Point, a pleasant trail leads through a rainbow of sand and mud to reach the spires of the Queen's Garden. Touring through a menagerie of bizarre and unlikely seeming rock features, this trail passes through several man-made archways. After a while, the Navajo Loop Trail bends back uphill through a narrow canyon, taking dozens of visually striking switchbacks between glowing cliffs to return to the top of the amphitheater rim. This surreal environment offers a fun hike to active kids and adult photographers alike.

The single-most popular hike in the GSENM, Calf Creek Falls Trail, requires 3 miles of relatively easy hiking along the namesake Calf Creek to reach this 125-foot-tall falls. This trail begins at the Calf Creek Campground and Recreation Area, just east of Escalante. It rolls along the desert hillsides above the river, leading imperceptibly upward to reach its goal. On the approach to the falls, the trail jogs up and down the canyon hillside, staying fairly near its bottom. About halfway, look east of the river to see an 800- to 1,000-year-old granary, located high on the cliffs and just below the canyon's rim. The trail terminates in a stone amphitheater. Here the waterfall cascades through a V-shaped notch at the top of a Navajo sandstone cliff, streaming downward in a thin ribbon. The water lands in a broad, shallow pool that many people wade in. These chilly waters offer brisk refreshment after the hike in and before the return trek out. Bring plenty of drinking water, as this hike is quite exposed to the sun and is warmer than most expect.

Near the northern entrance to Canyonlands National Park stands Dead Horse Point State Park. Situated on a thin, almost islandlike peninsula of land, this relatively developed state park offers sweeping views of the area's complex and deep river canyons. Below the park, millions of geologic years have been exposed by the Colorado River eroding 2,000 feet into the desert's surface. The landscape on all sides is composed of tall red mesas, crumbling orange talus piles, parallel bands of purple sandstone, green trees along the river, and the brown waters of the Colorado River.

Sunlight filters down into the narrow and deep slot canyons of the Navajo Loop Trail.

Island in the Sky Grand View Point, in nearby Canyonlands National Park, offers another panoramic view of the desert plateaus and mesas and the handiwork of the rivers eroding into them. Flat plateaus end in blunt, curving edges. Spires shoot skyward from the floor, and vast areas of barren desert basin lie all around this point. This viewpoint provides a yawning vista full of sandstone and starkly beautiful desert nothingness.

A trip to Utah would hardly be

complete without a viewing of the emblematic Delicate Arch in Arches National Park. Appearing on Utah's license plate and pictured throughout the state, this unlikely natural arch stands nearly alone atop—and near the steepening edge of—a smoothly sloping, sandstone dome. A few different options exist for viewing this arch. Trails that range in length from 50 yards to 1.5 miles provide near and far views of the 52-foot-tall feature. Those hiking to the arch itself can actually wander underneath and around it; however, it is illegal to climb on it.

The hike to Calf Creek Falls is perhaps the most popular in the entire monument.

Camping Inside and Outside the Parks

Each of Utah's national parks has at least one campground. These on-site facilities offer numerous advantages, such as a minimal commute to the park, drinking water, and pit toilets. But they also have some negative aspects, including crowding and a compromised experience of nature. However busy they may get during peak season, they are typically quite clean and well maintained. Those interested in tent or RV sleeping inside the park should check ahead of time to see whether reservations are possible. Most parks offer online and telephone booking services for an additional fee.

Alternative private and state camping options usually exist within reasonable driving distance of the parks. Many of the small- and midsize towns outside the parks have numerous, private campgrounds that not only offer picnic tables and fire rings but also provide full bathrooms, showers, electricity, and sometimes even pools and other recreational facilities. State parks usually operate their own campgrounds with similar facilities and prices to their national park peers—but often with less crowding and more availability. National Forest campgrounds exist in areas such as Boulder Mountain, north of the GSENM. These offer a bit of community and minimally developed sites and usually cost less than the in-park campgrounds.

And finally, many totally undeveloped and free campsites exist in Utah, some of which can be found near a few of the parks. Most often on BLM land, these are almost entirely unregulated. To anticipate where and how to find these different types of options on the fly, a gazetteer can prove quite useful. These relatively detailed maps indicate the location of public and private land, as well as point out most of the developed campgrounds in an area.

In the Zion area, there is a handful of free camping opportunities just outside the park. The most well known and easily accessible is called Mosquito Cove. West of Springdale, and just off UT 9 (between mile markers 23 and 24), this popular, riverside area has long been used by locals and park visitors alike. There is no charge to camp here, and there are no developed sites or facilities. That said, people have clearly been careless about burial of human waste and disposal of garbage. Those visiting the area should try to not worsen the situation. During wet springs, the cove sometimes closes due to high river levels. In this case, an alternate and quite scenic option is Gooseberry Mesa. This nationally famous slickrock mountain biking area also offers free, undeveloped camping on public lands. When camping in this area, be sure to only occupy sites that already bear visible signs of use. To reach this area, head to Rockville (west of the park) and turn south on Bridge Road. This road picks its way up to the top of the obvious plateau south of Rockville, winding to its top via switchbacks. It is advisable to approach this area during daylight hours, as the road forks numerous times along the way, sometimes leading in the wrong direction or onto private land.

Heading northeast toward Bryce Canyon National Park, you drive through a healthy patch of BLM lands centered around the junction of US 89 and UT 12. Though ownership in this area is a bit patchy, all lands to the west of US 89 and north of Hatch in this region are public. A number of dirt roads depart from the main highway and head west.

Once in the GSENM proper, camping is pretty much unlimited. However all people camping inside the monument are required by the BLM to have a permit. These can be obtained at any of the numerous visitor centers (see chapter 4). Though many developed campgrounds can be found in places like Red Canyon, Kodachrome Basin State Park, Calf Creek Recreation Area, and in the town of Escalante, infinite backcountry sites exist. As the monument rangers will tell you, all camping should be done at preexisting sites.

North of the GSENM, the Dixie National Forest area, known generally as Boulder Mountain, boasts several developed, pay campgrounds as well as uncountable backcountry camping options. Finding a site there is as simple as following any of the numerous dirt roads branching off UT 12 between Boulder and Grover. The bulk of the land in this area is either owned by Dixie National Forest or the BLM, so is generally open for public use. A gazetteer comes in handy for locating acceptable sites. If you don't have one, but would like to camp here anyway, consider stopping at the

Entering Capitol Reef National Park from the west on UT 24

Wildcat Ranger Station, located on the west side of the highway approximately halfway between Boulder and Torrey. Be aware that this station offers limited office hours, closing promptly at 4:30 during the summer and completely during winter (end of September through May).

The nearby vicinity of Capitol Reef National Park has a scenic camping area on BLM land just a few miles outside the park and immediately off UT 24. Easily visible in the red desert landscape, this multisite area sits on the northern side of the highway and consists of multiple undeveloped but well-worn sites separated from each other by rolling knolls, small boulders, and occasional juniper shrubs. At this site, you're only about five minute away from the first pit toilet in Capitol Reef National Park (but still outside the pay zone).

The Arches, Island in the Sky, and Moab region of Utah is comprised almost entirely of public lands along the US 191 corridor, 5 or more miles south of I-70. To the east and west, dirt roads extend into the high desert plateaus, reaching far enough from the highway to afford seclusion from the noise pollution of the busy throughway. Nearer to UT 313, camp to the west side of US 191, as the eastern side of the road is privately owned.

Anyone approaching the Needles District, in the southern portion of the Canyonlands National Park, will drive directly through Indian Creek Canyon on UT 211. This area endures heavy use from rock climbers, and therefore has many campsites somewhat far off the highway. Several miles west of Newspaper Rock, keep an eye out for a pit toilet and kiosk to the left. Taking this turnoff for Beef Basin Road leads to a number of campsites. The road fords a stream and quickly forks. Taking the left fork will lead to miles of dirt road that reach a cottonwood stand full of campsites; taking the right branch will bring you over a shorter (but more rugged) stretch of road to several marked (but undeveloped) campsites beneath the Bridger Jack Mesa.

For more detailed information on the camping near each state park, see the camping portion of the "Extend Your Stay" section at the end of each chapter.

SUGGESTED TRIPS: SHORT AND LONG

Two to Three Days: Cedar Breaks, Zion, and Bryce Canyon

If you only have a weekend to spend in the southwestern corner of Utah, consider taking a Zion-centric trip. If coming from the north, head to Cedar Breaks National Monument to catch the sunset. The approach drive from Parowan up to Brian Head Resort and then Cedar Breaks National Monument is a scenic and very steep (grades up to 13 percent!) canyon road that passes through beautiful forests and by cliff bands on its ascent. Consider camping in the park here, or getting a hotel room in Cedar City, just to the south and on I-15.

Spend your first day visiting the main area of Zion National Park, Zion Canyon. On the way into the park, have breakfast or a midmorning coffee in the town of Springdale. Mountain bikers may decide to spend the morning checking out Gooseberry Mesa, a slickrock and single-track trail just south of and above the small town of Rockville (see the biking portion of "Extend Your Stay," chapter 1). Others may head directly into the park.

On the way into the canyon, park your car in Springdale. Go to any of the (very visible) bus stops along UT 9/Main Street, and hop on a shuttle heading into the park. (Alternatively, if you plan to head east toward Bryce Canyon, drive into the park and leave your car at the visitors center parking lot.) Load a day pack with a tube of sunblock, a lunch, and a few liters of water per person. Stop inside the impressive, ecofriendly visitors center to learn a bit about the park and select a hike or two. If you have the legs for only one fairly strenuous journey, strongly consider heading to the top of Angels Landing, perhaps Utah's most spectacular and exposed vista approachable without technical rock climbing. Just be sure the weather forecast holds no lightning or high winds.

Get back in the car and head

Brian Head Resort

The Rim Trail traces along the edge of Bryce Amphitheater for miles.

east on UT 9, also know as the Zion–Mt. Carmel Highway. Plan to spend a little more time driving this road than the point-to-point mileage would suggest. This scenic route climbs steeply out the eastern side of Zion National Park, navigating several switchbacks on its journey before heading through the 1.1-mile Mt. Carmel Tunnel. Once past the tunnel, you emerge on a high-altitude layer of sandstone domes completely unlike anything in Zion Canyon, below. These colorful and stratified mounds rise above the meandering highway. Eventually the domes flatten out to a vegetated plateau at Mt. Carmel Junction.

Taking UT 89 to the north, you'll reach UT 12 in about an hour. Follow signs to end up in Bryce Canyon National Park. Though the bus system in the park is not actually mandatory, I strongly suggest parking your vehicle outside the entrance station and hopping aboard a shuttle. Bryce Canyon features a nearly flat, nonloop Rim Trail that has many access points and overlooks the colorful strata below. Taking the bus allows you to walk segments of this trail and explore other side trails without obligatorily returning to the same parking lot. If you wish to explore the depths of the canyon, head downhill about 300 vertical feet on the nearly 3-mile Navajo Loop Trail. This heads down into the Queen's Garden and through crazy, built-up switchbacks. Stop for a snack in the General Store before heading north from Bryce on US 89 and back to I-15 on UT 20.

Two to Three Days: Arches, Moab, Canyonlands, and Dead Horse Point

Those with just a few days to investigate the southeastern portion of Utah should consider making a home base in the town of Moab and checking out the very nearby and famous Arches National Park. Just 8 miles north of town via US 191, this is a driver-friendly park, whose most famous vistas can easily be taken in from the roadside pullouts. However, its singular most emblematic feature, Delicate Arch, requires a slight bit of walking to see and can be viewed from a number of trails. Two of these are short—with one being less than a quarter mile in length. Another departs from the Wolfe Ranch area and covers 1.5 miles of walking across open slickrock domes to reach the base of the Arch.

After leaving the main section of the park, head south toward Moab.

Stop by the Courthouse Wash parking area (0.5 miles north of the Colorado River) and hike about 0.5 miles across the Courthouse Wash Bridge and uphill to gain views of a major rock art panel of the Barrier Canyon style. Cruise the remaining miles into Moab to eat dinner and get some sleep.

To visit Canyonlands National Park, you can either head south to visit the Needles District or head north to check out Island in the Sky. If you opt for the southern route, you'll pass by Newspaper Rock on your descent into Indian Creek along UT 211. This 200-square-foot, densely engraved slab of rock is overhung by a natural, protective roof that has preserved these Basketmaker, Fremont, and Puebloan images for roughly 2,000 years. Located right off the road, this panel costs nothing to view. Farther down the road, this narrow river drainage opens up as you drive through Indian Creek Canyon, perhaps the world's greatest crack-climbing destination. If you look to the north, you'll perhaps even see climbers ascending some of the deep red Wingate sandstone buttresses.

Once you've entered Canyonlands National Park, take your time to stop in the visitors center and check out the park's scenic drives. Look to the northeast and enjoy views of Island in the Sky mesa to the north and the La Sal Mountains near Moab, which rise dramatically above the red desert foreground.

To hit the Island in the Sky District of Canyonlands, head north from Moab on US 191 and then west on UT 313. If time allows, be sure to stop by the well-developed Dead Horse Point State Park (see "The Best of Utah's Southern National Monuments, State Parks, and Surrounding Areas," earlier in this chapter), accessed via a spur road departing to the south from this same state highway. Then motor on a few more miles to the southwest to access the park. If you're short on time, drive to Grand View Point and check out soaring views of the entire park, below. If you have more time, consider any of the short or long hikes within the park.

Five to Seven Days: The Complete Parks Tour

This itinerary could be compacted into less than a week by those spending only short amounts of time in each of the national parks and a few of the nearby state parks. Or it could easily be extended to a month by those wanting to explore the off-road attractions and the many worthy destinations in the area. Those wishing to do a truly complete tour of all Utah's national parks and monuments should probably hold off until at least mid-June to allow for adequate melting of snow. Arbitrarily, this suggested route follows roughly a west-to-east direction of travel and is roughly in the neighborhood of Zion National Park, and terminates around Arches and south toward Monument Valley.

UT 143 as it climbs south from Parowan to Brian Head and Cedar Breaks National Monument.

For a scenic and relatively efficient order to visit these destinations, first head toward the town of Parowan. If you have time, check out the Parowan Gap Petroglyphs, about 10 miles west of the city. Then head southeast on UT 143 toward Brian Head and Cedar Breaks National Monument. This route is *not* recommended for vehicles towing trailers, as the road climbs at a continuously steep pitch, reaching grades of 13 percent along the way. If you wish to hit Zion National Park, retrace your path and head south along I-15. Enter Zion through the town of Springdale. If you want to get dinner, stay in a hotel, or camp, this town provides good opportunities to do so.

After visiting Zion, head east through the Mt. Carmel Tunnel and toward US 89. Travel north until you reach UT 12, one of Utah's most stunning roadways. Motoring along, you almost immediately enter into the deep reds and oranges of Red Canyon, and the road heads through a few small, rock tunnels. Shortly afterward, you'll come to the turnoff to Bryce Canyon National Park. A relatively high-elevation area, Bryce provides good temperatures for hiking during warm days.

After Bryce Canyon, UT 12 quickly enters the Grand Staircase–Escalante National Monument (GSENM). This 1.9-million-acre beast offers lifetimes' worth of backcountry-style adventures ranging from casual day hikes to technical slot canyon routes. Highlights in the area include Kodachrome Basin State Park, Escalante Petrified Forest State Park, the Devil's Garden scenic area, and the Calf Creek Falls Trail and Campground. The two towns in the north central portion of this beauty, Escalante and Boulder, both offer a number of resources to tourists. Escalante provides more diverse and affordable lodging, as well as cafés, restaurants, and even outfitting services. Boulder is a much smaller town, but is the home of the Hell's Backbone Grill and adjoining Boulder Mountain Lodge. The Grill offers the area's best and freshest cuisine, including fresh vegetables and other goodies grown right on the property.

Because of the steepness of UT 143, this highway is not recommended for vehicles pulling trailers.

From here, an optional southern route (which bypasses Goblin Valley State Park, Arches, Canyonlands, Dead Horse Point, and Moab) departs to the east. This partly paved, partly dirt road heads into the remote southern

Red Canyon offers mountain biking trails and a taste of Bryce's colors. Kami Hardcastle

region of Capitol Reef National Monument and along a historic route
called the Burr Trail. The most famous and distinctive portion of this route,
the Muley Twist, is a crazy, switch-backing section of dirt road so named as
its narrow zigzags were thought to be severe enough to twist a mule. After
this road drops down from the Waterpocket Fold, it traces along the southern skirts of the Henry Mountains and runs into UT 276 near the Bullfrog
Marina on Lake Powell (south of Hanksville). Though this route is navigable by almost any passenger vehicle, it takes you deep into Utah's backcountry and is recommended only to those self-sufficient in the wilderness. Take
your car to the mechanic before embarking on this journey.

If you wish to stay on the northern, less wild route, remain on UT 12
as it passes through Boulder and bends to the north. Notice the massive,
broad mountain to the north; this route ascends high onto the shoulders of
this Dixie National Forest plateau commonly called Boulder Mountain.
Called the Land of 1,000 Lakes, this area contains roughly 80 lakes, the
largest of which is 52 acres in size. Those wishing to camp will enjoy the
many developed and primitive spots along the way. With most of the road at
or around 8,000 feet in elevation, this area affords great summer sleeping
and re-creating temperatures. Along the way, be sure to stop at any or several of the scenic turnouts and read the signs detailing the complex geology
below. Capitol Reef's Waterpocket Fold, the Circle Cliffs, Henry Mountains, and much more can be spotted from many points along the way.

UT 12 drops as quickly as it climbs, dumping you in the vicinity of
Torrey and Grover, on the western outskirts of Capitol Reef National
Park. If possible, try to hit this park in the late afternoon or early evening
and position yourself in a vantage point—such as Sunset Point—to enjoy
the ever-deepening hues of red and
orange. As most of this feature's
diverse and stunning cliffs face
west, the setting sun brilliantly saturates their reds, oranges, and yellows. It actually costs nothing to
drive UT 24 through this park; it is
along this road that some of the historic buildings and orchards of
Fruita can be seen. If time allows,
definitely consider a trip south from
UT 24 and into the belly of Capitol
Reef for an easy hike to the Narrows portion of Grand Gulch. As
a national park, Capitol Reef has
much more of an unstructured feel

The road winds up as it approaches the
Muley Twist.

than its other Utah peers, with a self-service pay station, extremely friendly rangers, and little infrastructure. Those who appreciate the wilder aspects of the desert will enjoy the less developed nature of this place.

Moving eastward, UT 24 passes out of Capitol Reef and bends slightly to the north. As you drive, look to the south and notice the Henry Mountains, looming beyond Hanksville. After passing through this town, take the opportunity to visit Goblin Valley State Park. Here, thousands of hoodoos have gathered to render an otherworldly environment. Motor along the same highway to reach I-70. Taking this eastward, you pass through Green River and its John Wesley Powell River History Museum. This midsize museum presents the interesting and awe-inspiring story of the one-armed explorer responsible for charting the western interior in the late 1800s.

Head south toward Moab on US 191, bearing right on UT 313. This road heads southwest toward the Island in the Sky portion of Canyonlands National Park, passing by Dead Horse Point State Park on the way. Both afford bird's-eye views of the complex canyons and exposed sedimentary geology below. Once back on US 191, the road quickly enters Moab. This outdoorsy tourist town caters to all kinds of visitors, offering everything from cafés and restaurants to guide services, bike rentals, boating expeditions, and more. This town also offers the region's best opportunity to rest and refuel.

South of Moab, US 191 climbs and meanders along the high desert plateaus. Keep your eyes peeled for a turnout to the east, UT 211, leading to Canyonlands National Park's Needles District. The drive into the park stretches for about 40 miles beyond the turnout. Along the way, the road maintains its high plains position for a while before dropping into the head of Indian Creek Canyon. On its initial descent, it passes by Newspaper Rock, an amazingly concentrated rock art panel just off the road. Indian Creek, a spectacular basin rimmed by sheer, Wingate sandstone buttresses, is a world-renowned rock climbing area offering hundreds of "splitter" crack climbs. The highway follows the canyon as it deepens and broadens before again reascending into the Needles District. Check out the visitors center near the entrance and visit some of the ancient Puebloan ruins of the park or explore the complex network of hiking trails.

As you return UT 191, the tour nears its completion, passing through Monticello and Blanding. Follow signs for US 163 West to hit Mexican Hat and eventually Monument Valley Tribal Park. Though this Navajo Nation park actually exists in Arizona, the turnoff for it comes just north of the border. Have your camera ready, as this final destination is likely the most iconic view of the American Southwest.

The summit of UT 143 is often buried in snow, even in early June.

For suggested two-day, park-specific trips, turn to the chapter of your desire. Each main chapter in this book begins with a detailed, 48-hour itinerary that suggests an ordered trip from the time you arrive on the first afternoon to the time you depart two days later. This running list uncovers each area's "best-of" dining, entertainment, and recreation options. As some of these selections might not exactly tickle your fancy, each 48-hour itinerary also provides some alternatives listed under the heading "If you like this . . . ," as well as a much more substantial list of extra or substitute options listed in the "Extend Your Stay" section of each chapter. Here you can find any of the area's additional worthy dining, lodging, recreation, and camping opportunities.

WHEN TO GO: SEASONS, WEATHER, AND ELEVATION

Before embarking on any journey in Utah, be aware of the elevation of your destination. Though almost all of the national parks remain open year-round, Cedar Breaks National Monument and UT 143 close during the winter and spring. Others remain only partially open, and all are subject to temporary closures if severe weather demands it.

Furthermore, spring runoff can severely limit access to areas like Zion National Park and GSENM, whose narrow canyons can be devastatingly wiped out by high waters. Late winter and early spring freeze-thaw cycles can also loosen and trundle huge rocks in any of these areas, closing roads and, more often, trails.

Despite sometimes lofty heights, southern Utah bakes in the sun and endures spicy hot summer temperatures. If you plan to visit during July and August, you should consider being the most active in the higher parks like Bryce Canyon and Cedar Breaks and staying inside buildings and cars in lower elevation parks like Zion, Arches, and Canyonlands. It is still completely possible to hike around and explore these areas during the summer,

Flash Flooding

Utah's sandstone deserts have little top soil and even less vegetation. The region's characteristic slickrock domes and intermittent narrow canyons have little capacity to absorb precipitation. Rather than soaking into the soil, most of the rain falling onto these areas drains immediately downward. This runoff gathers into area streams, collecting into larger rivers, and surges through the area's canyons. Many of these canyons happen to be popular destinations among hikers and canyoneers. Anyone planning to enter any type of canyon or wash—even a popular one like the Zion Narrows or Capitol Reef's Grand Wash—should check all regional weather forecasts. Even if the weather directly above a canyon is perfectly dry, a nearby thunderstorm can dump rain onto the mountains or the upper slopes of a drainage system, thereby flooding with remote precipitation. Without perceivable warnings, water levels can rise several meters. In narrow canyons with sheer sandstone walls, this means certain danger and likely death for anyone trapped inside its walls. Each year offers plenty of safe days to explore Utah's beautiful sandstone gorges, gulches, canyons, and ravines. To ensure a safe experience, you must be aware of the area's greater topography and river systems and check all relevant forecasts before making any decisions to go.

but you should prepare yourself by wearing plenty of sunscreen and clothing that provides protection from the sun (sun hat and lightweight long-sleeved shirt), as well as carrying generous amounts of water. Consider hiking and exploring during the cooler, early morning hours. Stack the odds in your favor by looking out for potential storm hazards like lightning and flash flooding.

Additionally, thunderstorms can be quite limiting to afternoon activities. Especially in locations with major topographical relief and/or outcrops or exposure like Zion, Bryce Canyon, Cedar Breaks, Canyonlands, and Arches, storm systems can build during a sunny day and strike suddenly. Hiking trails like Zion's Angels Landing are extremely exposed to rain, wind, and lightning for long stretches and become hazardous to pass when wet. During big storms snow can fall, even during summer months, making paths yet more slippery and impassable than a rain shower would. So it's a good idea to check the weather before heading out on any major hike, particularly if it is a ridge-type trail or if it features any type of hilltop exposure.

The ultimate time to visit the area for reduced snowpack and ideal daytime high temperatures (and nighttime lows) is during the autumn months of September and October. Statistically, these weeks offer the most pleasant temperatures, the least amount of precipitation, reasonably long daylight hours, and tolerable nighttime cooling. However, increased crowding during these months is the price you pay for these more temperate conditions. For some visitors, this is acceptable; for others, this can be too much, particularly in the busiest areas like Zion Canyon.

If you are crowd-phobic, consider visiting during the off-seasons. You can visit during the peak of summer and avoid the worst heat by hiking in the early morning or sunset hours—when the light is best for photography anyway! Or you can bring your cross-country skis and tour Bryce Canyon National Park in the winter months and enjoy the spectacular contrast of white snow atop the soil's red rainbows. Or take a midnight boat tour down the Colorado River and into Moab under the light of a full moon. Regardless of your priorities, these areas can be enjoyed during any season and any time of day. It just requires a bit of planning and proper clothing.

Desert Wilderness: Preservation and Safety

Aside from the regions' obvious similarities—sandstone and desert ecosystems—each of Utah's national parks, monuments, state parks, and other attractions offers a unique set of rewards and potential challenges. When planning a visit, you must consider this area to be generally inhospitable to life and come prepared with ample water, food, sun protection, and a well-maintained vehicle. Though this situation is ever changing, cell phone service in the area is not reliable, and visitors should travel with some degree of self-sufficiency. That said, when touring the region's main attractions, you will almost never be faraway from other visitors like yourself.

Even if you come prepared to handle the elements, please think twice before bringing small children and pets. Little bodies with sensitive skin are affected much more severely by the bright desert sun, burning and parching more quickly than adults. Pets, too, suffer greatly in the heat. Unable to sweat, dogs cannot cool themselves efficiently enough to withstand the uninterrupted sunlight of these sandstone deserts.

If you are visiting the parks during peak season (late spring through early autumn), you'll notice that many implement a shuttle bus system. Some parks like Zion have enacted mandatory bus transportation in certain areas; others like Bryce Canyon offer the option. Though bus riding requires a few minutes of planning and bag packing, many people choose to ride buses. Leaving your car parked allows for unlimited and undistracted sightseeing and usually features an informational audio recording pointing out the highlights of the park visible from the bus. Additionally, many of the parks feature long trails with different access points; using the shuttle bus system allows you to begin and end all hikes as desired and without the need to return to a certain parking lot. All bus systems contain plenty of vehicles, and you'll never have to wait more than 10 or 15 minutes at any particular bus stop. The best part of the buses? They cost nothing to ride.

Finally, you should come with ample time and patience. Even though the distances through and among these parks appear short on a map, the roads of the Colorado Plateau and the Grand Staircase are characteristically hilly, winding, and often crowded. If you drive with haste, these twisty roads will only be an annoyance. Even empty, these highways' curves, climbs, and corners present a hindrance to quick driving times. But considering that millions of

Leave Pets at Home

The National Park Service severely restricts pet access in the name of preserving these special natural places. Though pets technically may enter the parks, they almost always must remain on pavement, and may not be left unattended in vehicles. So if you plan to explore the parks' off-road offerings at all, leaving the pets at home would be the wisest choice by a long shot.

Prickly pear cactus can produce pink or yellow blossoms.

Checklist: The Essentials

Water: When packing water, don't skimp. To be on the safe side, bring at least a gallon a day per person. If you plan to camp and cook, add more to that figure. And don't forget to bring extra in the event your vehicle breaks down and you become stranded. A few extra gallons can make the difference between an annoying wait and a desperate escape. If you plan to be active, consider bringing some electrolyte drinks to help your body stay hydrated.

Sunblock: Leave the SPF 8 at home. When you're in the desert, you should consider bringing sunblock with an SPF of 30 or higher, especially if your trip will involve sweating and prolonged hikes.

Food: Bring a variety of high-energy snacks with sufficient protein and fat content. Energy bars, cheese and crackers, and bread and peanut butter can take you a long way. Don't count on a cooler actually keeping anything cold in a solar-collecting car.

Spare tire, jack, and wrench: If possible, bring a full-size spare tire. At the very least, be sure your doughnut has enough pressure, and double-check for the necessary tire-changing tools.

Maps: A general road atlas will guide you along most highways without a problem. But those planning to explore beyond the major roadways should bring a Utah gazetteer and possibly an even more detailed maps of the specific region they will be probing.

Sleeping bag and blankets: Even those not planning to camp should bring some backup insulation. Firsthand experience says that those with car problems can be stranded for 12 hours or more—even if the car breaks down on a main highway and the authorities have been alerted. This delay can grow exponentially if the malfunction happens in the backcountry. A set of warm blankets can transform a night out from a miserably cold experience into an unexpected—but tolerable—camping trip.

Camera: Many of the towns along the way offer coffee shops with electrical outlets for recharging. But it still doesn't hurt to pack an extra battery and memory card.

National Parks Interagency Annual Pass: These all-inclusive yearlong passes cost $80 and are accepted at all national parks. Unfortunately, neither the state parks nor the Monument Valley Navajo Tribal Park accept the pass. Depending on your trip, you might consider purchasing a less expensive area-specific pass.

other visitors in all sorts of vehicles share these roads, you can count on being stuck behind RVs, tractor trailers, jalopies, rubberneckers, and more. But if you accept this fact and allow plenty of time, these roads can provide some of the most beautiful and fun scenic drives of your life.

Preserving the Wild

Looking around the region, it's clear to see that this corner of the world does not readily support life. The only indigenous species have radically adapted to survive in these inhospitable conditions. Fluctuating rapidly from burning hot to bitter cold, wet to parched, and windy to still, the region presents a great challenge to any living specimen within its confines.

Fragile, Living Earth

Cryptobiotic soil, though hard to spot by the untrained eye, contributes vastly to stabilizing the soil. A slow-growing and extremely delicate blend of algae and bacteria, this nearly invisible, symbiotic carpet lives on the soil's surface and literally holds the desert in place. Please respect this soil, too often destroyed by footprints and decimated by off-road vehicle traffic. Whenever possible, stick to existing trails and roads. These ecosystems take decades to develop and can be destabilized by the slightest human error.

That said, humans must respect the fragility of the area. The root structure of the precious few plants that survive functions to stabilize the soil and keep the desert from becoming a barren dust bowl. Take care to not trample or destroy the more obvious flora. Do not gather firewood; the decomposition of this debris helps the soil maintain a healthy constitution. Many shops (including grocery stores) sell bundles of firewood for just a few dollars.

Take care not to disturb the animals. A crafty bunch, the species of the area typically seclude themselves from humans and take shelter during the heat of the day. But of course, higher elevations present completely different environments. While snakes, lizards, and rodents thrive in the low deserts, larger animals like mountain lions, deer, and bears prowl the high mountain forests. Regardless of location, the best policy with food is to keep it sealed, stored, and safely away from your campsite. Tempt the animals as little as possible, whether it means protecting your food from disappearing or yourself from animal attack.

Use provided restroom facilities whenever possible. Most high-use areas offer permanent, pit-style toilets. If you find yourself "caught short" away from one of these, do your best to perform your business well away from any trails and waterways and bury your excrement sufficiently (at least

Watch out for these little guys in southern Utah.

six inches deep). Bring a lighter and burn any paper that you've used. It doesn't hurt to pack a small spade in the trunk of your car for precisely this purpose. Many outdoors shops also sell Wag Bags, sealable human waste disposal systems that help people pack out solid waste in a sanitary fashion. Especially along popular bodies of water like the Green River, these bags are mandatory for boaters.

Keep in mind that the desert offers many hazards to human health. Several varieties of rattlesnake reside in these areas, but usually offer a warning to those approaching. However, as humans kill more and more rattlesnakes, they have evolved away from rattling—causing many snakes to *not* warn approaching humans and pets. Other, more benign (but still painful) things to avoid are scorpions and the many species of low-growing cactus living in Utah. Many other plant species have adopted a spiny form and can easily poke into your skin.

Finally, be aware of the weather. The desert climate swings wildly from one extreme to the next. The combination of heat, sun, wind, and lack of shade conspire to parch and burn you. But on the other hand, the nighttime cooling or storm-induced cold, wind, and lack of sun can chill you into hypothermia. Prepare yourself with water, more water, sunblock, insulating layers, sun hat, extra food, a well-maintained car, a fully inflated spare tire, and perhaps even an extra quart of oil.

All of these warnings can make the desert seem quite ominous. But those arriving self-sufficient and prepared to tread lightly can enjoy the area without harming themselves or the ecosystems.

1

Zion National Park

PARK OVERVIEW

Covering 229 square miles and 5,060 vertical feet, Zion National Park show-cases the stunning Zion and Kolob canyons and their sometimes 2,000-foot-tall, absolutely sheer sandstone walls. Slicing into the colorful geology of the Colorado Plateau, the unassuming Virgin River has carved out a rainbow of sandstones. From the pearly white Temple Cap Formation atop the canyon rims, down through shades of orange and yellow Navajo sandstone, to the deep red Moenave and Chinle formations at the canyon floor, Zion Canyon forms a gash reaching nearly half a vertical mile into the earth's surface.

The bottom of this deep and narrow gorge enjoys a carpet of soft sand, gentle grass, and shady cottonwood trees. Visitors to the canyon enjoy pleas-ant surroundings while simultaneously being utterly dwarfed by the looming walls overhead. Deer, lizards, and nearly 300 bird species are commonly sighted among the low-lying brush and shrubbery. In a corner of the world that is otherwise hot, dry, and vulnerable to intense sun, Zion offers wildlife a inviting reprieve and a cold drink of water.

Throughout history, people have recognized this nook of southwestern Utah to be incredibly special. For as many as 12,000 years, people have occupied the area, drawn to it because of its wildlife, life-giving water, and unique beauty. Established in 1919, Zion is Utah's oldest national park. And with 2.7 million visitors annually, it is by far and away the state's most popu-lar. Situated near the far southwestern corner of Utah, it is easily reached by I-15 and sits within close proximity of St. George.

LEFT: Fall comes to Kolob Canyon in early November.

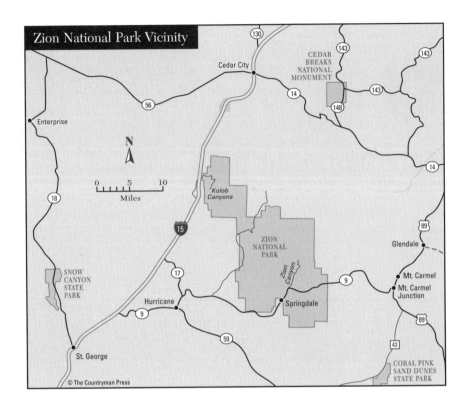

Zion National Park Vicinity

While in Zion, you can test your legs—and vertigo tolerance—on the strenuous and exposed Angels Landing Trail as it climbs up to and on top of a rock peninsula 1,400 feet above the valley floor. Or simply sightsee along the roadside while riding the park's free shuttle buses. Take a walk along the Virgin River on the Pa'rus Trail or sit in on a ranger-given talk. Ride a bus into the heart of Zion Canyon and explore the upper reaches of the Zion Narrows on foot. When you're finished, you can drive back out to the west through Springdale and past Gooseberry Mesa, or take the Zion–Mt. Carmel Highway eastward as it ascends to the top of the Colorado Plateau via numerous switchbacks and through the 1.1-mile-long Zion—Mt. Carmel Tunnel.

View down Angels Landing Trail

The Zion–Mt. Carmel Highway climbs high above Zion Canyon on the eastern side of the park.

ZION AND KOLOB CANYONS

Unofficially divided into two sections, the "main" and busiest portion of the park is its southern member, Zion Canyon. This is where you will find the bulk of attractions like the Zion Human History Museum, Zion Canyon Visitor Center, Zion Lodge, and shuttle buses. Here, too, is where you will find the park's most famous and developed hiking trails. In fact, a majority of people coming to Zion National Park visit only this southern portion.

The Zion Human History Museum

Because Zion Canyon receives the brunt of the visitors, and because it is located in such an inherently space-restricted area, anyone touring the Zion Canyon proper during peak season must either ride a shuttle bus or a bicycle (see sidebar below). Fear not; the buses come at frequent intervals to several designated stops, cost nothing to ride, and travel in both

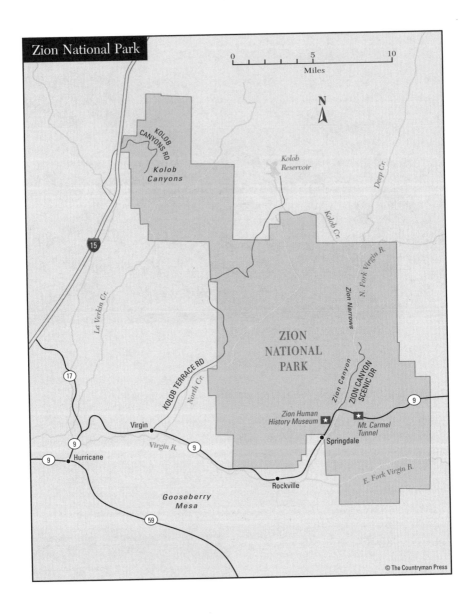

Zion National Park

0   5   10
Miles

N

Kolob Canyons Rd

Kolob Canyons

Kolob Reservoir

Deep Cr.

Kolob Cr.

N. Fork Virgin R.

15

La Verkin Cr.

Zion Narrows

ZION NATIONAL PARK

17

KOLOB TERRACE RD

North Cr.

Zion Canyon

ZION CANYON SCENIC DR

9

Virgin

Zion Human History Museum

Mt. Carmel Tunnel

9

Virgin R.

9

Springdale

9

Hurricane

Rockville

E. Fork Virgin R.

Gooseberry Mesa

59

© The Countryman Press

directions. To get to the southern portion of the park, take UT 9 (also called the Zion–Mt. Carmel Highway), either from I-15 at exit 16 if coming from the south, or exit 27 if arriving from the north.

The Kolob Canyons portion of the park, though contiguous to the Zion Canyon section, has a completely different access road. Because this section of Zion National Park is much less developed than its southern counterpart, hardly any traffic comes here at all. Aside from views afforded by the Kolob Canyons Road and the viewpoint at the terminus of the road, all exploration

Zion's Shuttle Bus System

Zion National Park receives an estimated 2.7 million visitors each year. And with most of them aiming straight for the heart of the park, Zion Canyon, it is easy to imagine this causing some serious traffic problems. Despite the largeness of the park, the actual canyon floor is quite cramped and tiny, with only enough free space for the Virgin River and a 23 total miles of roadway.

The bus system dates back to 1994 when Zion reported receiving 2.5 million visitors—nearly all of which arrived in personal vehicles. In order to handle the incredible bottlenecking problem, the park supervisors enacted a mandatory bus system that has been in place ever since. Now if you arrive at the park between April 1 and October 30 and wish to visit the Zion Canyon Scenic Drive (a spur road branching northward from UT 9), you will have to ride a shuttle bus—unless you plan to cycle or walk.

However restrictive this might seem, this mandatory bus system actually accomplishes quite bit in the way of clearing up congestion in the park. And with a generous number of stops along the route, the buses are easy to catch. Starting as far west as the town of Springdale, these clearly signed pickup and drop-off points allow you to park wherever you choose, whether at your hotel, near the visitors center, or at the junction of the Zion Canyon Scenic Drive and UT 9. Buses travel in both directions and come as frequently as once every seven minutes.

The shuttle buses in Zion have huge windows for easy viewing.

When planning your day, be sure to check the earliest and latest pickup times. The first bus usually heads into the park before sunrise; the last bus out of the canyon departs approximately just after dark. But with many stops along the way and exact times changing per season, it's a good idea to look at the park brochure to be completely certain you won't have to walk out of the park at night.

True, riding the buses requires visitors to plan ahead and pack the day's food, water, sunscreen, and clothing. But it also means passengers are able to enjoy the scenery without trying to steer a vehicle. Plus, each bus features an audio accompaniment that points out major landmarks and explains tidbits of the park's history. Keep in mind that no pets are allowed on the buses, and the buses do not operate during the winter months (November 1 through March 31).

must be done out of the vehicle and on foot. Precisely because of this, Kolob Canyons have, in some respects, much more of a wilderness aura. Most visitors to the park's northern half spend their time hiking and backpacking. To get there, take the Kolob Canyons Road, located right off I-15 at exit 40.

Pick Your Spot
Where to stay and what you'll find nearby . . .

SPRINGDALE

Likely the best choice for visitors with more money than time to spare, Springdale offers a fairly substantial number of lodging and dining choices for a small town. But being situated rather far from any major cities and sitting right next to Utah's most famous national park, these amenities come with a slight convenience tax.

Those who desire immediate proximity to the park and an intimate setting should look into the Zion Canyon Bed & Breakfast (101 Kokopelli Circle; 435-772-9466; www.zioncanyonbandb.com). A four-guest-room establishment located within 1.5 miles of the park's entrance, this B&B provides an upscale, comfortable slumber amid Desert Southwest décor. Those staying here are within comfortable walking distance of Springdale's center and therefore its restaurants and shops.

For a more anonymous sleeping experience, check into the Zion Park Motel (865 Zion Park Boulevard; 435-772-3251). Also situated quite near the park, this locally owned motel offers standard amenities, as well as a backyard with picnic tables, a swing set, and a small swimming pool. Just because the day in the park is over, doesn't mean you have to confine yourself to a bedroom for the night. Lodging options range from double-queen single rooms up through family-size suites.

The Zion Park Motel in Springdale

Operated locally since 1972, the Bumbleberry Inn (897 Zion Park Boulevard; 435-772-3224; www.bumbleberry.com) provides motel-style lodging in the center of town yet is set back from the main road enough to also offer a quiet night of sleep. Named after the homemade bumbleberry pies baked here, the property also contains Wildcat Willies Grill & Saloon and a small theater. All guests are privy to an outdoor pool, Wi-Fi, air conditioning, and an exercise room. The Zion National Park shuttle bus makes a stop right at the inn.

ST. GEORGE

Though about an hour from Zion National Park, many people choose to base themselves in St. George because of its expanded dining and cultural opportunities, as well as its less costly lodging. Most of the hotels in the area bear the names of familiar national brands. Because of this, most of the beds in St. George cost quite a bit less than the boutique accommodations characteristic of Zion's immediate vicinity.

The Ramada Inn (1440 East St. George Boulevard; 435-628-2828; www.ramadainn.net) represents one such option, offering relatively higher-end lodging for a reasonable price. Located just east of I-15 at exit 8, this provides access to St. George's in-town amenities as well as a quick escape to Zion. Immediately near the hotel

stands a collection of casual restaurants. Just a block away is Winger's Grill & Bar, the later function of which is rather uncommon in this generally conservative part of Utah. To get to Winger's from the hotel, travel south on River Road.

If you feel like pampering yourself, consider booking ahead with The Inn at Entrada (2588 West Sinagua Trail; 435-634-7100). One of the singularly most luxurious and exclusive resorts in the area, it offers golf, spa services, and other special packages. Rooms vary from one-bedroom suites, up through *casitas* of various sizes, and culminate in five-bedroom masterpiece suites. Located at the inn is the Kokopelli Restaurant and Lounge (435-634-7100), which offers outdoor patio dining with views over St. George, below. If you plan to dine here, reservations are strongly recommended. A dress code is enforced, so inquire when booking your dinner.

CEDAR CITY

Cedar City will be an unlikely place to bed down if your primary target is the Zion Canyon portion of Zion National Park. However, if you plan to visit the Kolob Canyons section, Cedar City makes for a great home base. Just 30 minutes to the north of the Kolob Canyons Visitor Center, this large town has plenty of nontouristy, lower-cost choices for hotels, restaurants, and coffee; if you're looking for any of these, simply follow Main Street as it traverses through the center of town.

Right on Main Street you'll find the Best Western Town & Country Inn (189 North Main Street; 435-586-9900; www.best western.com), among the higher-end lodging in the area. This hotel has all the basic accoutrements expected by modern travelers, such as a fitness center, free Wi-Fi, and pool. Plus, it's ecofriendly, meaning that it operates in compliance with one of the ecofriendly labeling committees of North America.

If you prefer a locally owned establishment, check out the Garden Cottage Bed & Breakfast (16 North 200 West; 435-586-4919; www.thegardencottagebnb.com). Don't be frightened away by its overtly floral themes. The rooms here have been handsomely decorated with Victorian furniture. The proprietors serve a full breakfast daily at 8:30. This includes homemade quiche, fruit, and other freshly baked goodies. If traveling with children, you should phone ahead of time to get approval; the B&B is selective about which children it allows as guests.

Local Flavors
Taste of the town—local cafés, restaurants, bars, bistros, etc.

SPRINGDALE

For having fewer than 500 residents, Springdale boasts a diverse and contemporary selection of restaurants. With more than 2.7 million visitors traveling through it into Zion National Park each year, this small town certainly has motivation to rise to the occasion. Cuisine in Springdale ranges from Italian to Asian and from formal to brown-bag lunches.

Whiptail Grill (435 Zion Park Boulevard; 435-772-0283) opens its doors seven days a week for lunch and dinner throughout the year. Operating out of a renovated gas station, this casual restaurant with a low-key look serves surprisingly creative southwestern- and Mexican-themed food. Here you won't just order a bean and cheese burrito; rather, you'll choose from fresh and inspired items like spaghetti squash and chicken enchiladas and habañero–peanut butter crème brûlée or classics like chile relleno. If possible, try to dine outside. One more thing: Vegetarians will enjoy the plentiful and tasty options here.

If you'd like to take lunch with you into the park, desire a delicious espresso drink in the morning, or crave a pesto pizza for dinner, stop by Café Soleil (205 Zion Park Boulevard; 435-772-0505), also right on the main drag of Springdale. This fresh little café serves three nutritious meals a day, made to order at the counter. Cheffing up a versatile and healthy selection of salads, wraps, sandwiches, burritos, quiche, and more, Soleil features locally grown produce when possible in addition to other organic and earth-friendly foods.

ST. GEORGE

Washington County is the most rapidly growing county in Utah and among the fastest growing populations in the entire United States. Located in the warmest and sunniest part of the state, it has become a popular place for Utahns to retire. Additionally, Dixie State College makes its home here, as well as many thriving industries. Skywest Airlines is headquartered here, and other businesses administer major distribution centers in St. George as well. Here you'll find the Utah Shakespeare Festival, as well as the 13th largest marathon in the U.S. All told, this is a thriving, active, and well-to-do community. Ergo, St. George also has quite a helping of restaurants.

If you haven't enjoyed Thai food or sushi in a while, you might think about stopping by Benja's Thai & Sushi (2 West St. George Boulevard; 435-628-9538; www .benjathai.com), located right in the Brickyard Village on historic St. George Boulevard. This dressed-up Asian restaurant offers classic Thai dishes and sushi rolls in a slightly upscale environment. If you arrive hungry on Monday through Thursday evenings, you can really go big at the sushi bar by ordering the all-you-can-eat option. This includes miso soup, vegetable

tempura, all rolls, and soda.

For a good cup of coffee and a cheap, hot breakfast, consider Jazzy Java (285 North Bluff Street; 435-674-1678). One of the larger cafés in St. George, this proffers much more desirable eats than the typical, overpriced coffee-shop pastries. Choose from eggs, hash browns, and more. The décor is quite unique and rather bizarre, but if you can't stand it, just sit outside and enjoy the sun.

If you like this . . . try The Bean Scene (511 East St. George Boulevard; 435-674-2237), a little, hipster coffee shop offering delicious, globally conscious brew and Wi-Fi. A small and basic joint, it has become a popular hangout for those with dark-rimmed eyeglasses and tight jeans.

CEDAR CITY

Cedar City gastronomy definitely can be classified as that of the small-town variety. Don't expect a lot of foreign words on the menus or any fusions of various continents. Still, Cedar City has a good selection of restaurants, especially in the lunch, pizza, and Mexican genres.

For lunch to go (or stay), steer slightly off Main Street and aim for the Pastry Pub (86 West Center; 435-867-1400; www.cedarcitypastry pub.com). This French-themed eatery began as a simple pastry shop and grew into more. Today, you can order soups, sandwiches, and salads. And many of these offerings deviate quite a lot from boring to-be-expected fare. The salads are delicious, creative, and nutritious. The menu also includes many hot dishes like ravioli and other filling options. They also provide wireless Internet access, so if you need to check your e-mail, this can be a good place to kill two birds with one tab.

Those with a hankering for Southwestern cuisine without the traditional food coma will enjoy

3 B's Coffee & Southwest Wraps (96 North Main Street; 435-867-8888). This interesting "not-Mexican" restaurant and coffeehouse gives customers a choice between traditional Southwestern fare and healthy, contemporary cuisine including salads, hand-held wraps, and smothered ones, too. All ingredients are fresh, and nothing here is fried. Open for breakfast, lunch, dinner, and any time for coffee in between, this restaurant has been going strong since 2002.

48 Hours

Two days in Zion will not suffice for seeing the entirety of the park, especially if you're a big hiker. But you can definitely take in a sufficient sampling of the highlights in just a few days. This representative itinerary will guide you to some of the area's classic spots. Those with more time and energy can pick and choose additional recreational, dining, and even cultural opportunities from the categories listed under "Extend Your Stay," below.

GETTING THERE

If you have just a few days to spend in the area, the best place to begin is in the "main" section of the park, Zion Canyon. Most people will travel to this southernmost portion of Zion on I-15, the most major

traffic artery in the area, connecting Salt Lake City to St. George and Las Vegas. Regardless of how exactly you arrive at the park's west entrance, you'll come through the town of Springdale on UT 9, also called the Zion–Mt. Carmel Highway.

Consider Springdale the last outpost before the park's entrance. But desolate it is not! Springdale, though roughly 450 residents in size, is a colorful and thriving town, at your service. If you are staying anywhere in town, you can simply park your car at the hotel and walk to the Bit & Spur Bar and Saloon (1212 Zion Park Boulevard; 435-772-3498; www.bitandspur.com). Those hungry enough may enjoy a first night's full dinner of fresh, contemporary Mexican and Southwestern cuisine. More serious entrées include spring lamb with polenta, grilled salmon with roasted vegetable couscous, and pollo relleno. Feel free to eat heartily, as you'll need the energy tomorrow. However, those desiring a lighter or less formal affair may choose from a variety of salads like smoked salmon Caesar. Or order a wrap, sandwich, taco plate, or burrito. Of course, the "saloon" part of the name means that you can simply opt to drink a beverage. Dining outside is available in front and in back of the restaurant. Play billiards or take a look at local art on display around the grounds.

If you're still not ready for bed, check to see whether there's anything going at the Bumbleberry Playhouse (897 Zion Park Boulevard; 435-772-3224; www.bumble berry.com). This local theater hosts a respectable number of acts hailing from around the region. Especially during peak season, odds are good that something will be running on any given weekend night. The shows vary quite a lot, so you may want to check online to see if the current offering tickles your fancy.

DAY 1

Sunrise in the Zion vicinity will be a sensational treat for anyone waking early enough to catch it. (If you prefer to sleep in, sunset in the area will provide equally spectacular colors, if not more so.) On the summer solstice, June 21, the sun rises just before 6:12 AM and sets just before 8:56 PM. On the equi-

nox, March 20 and September 23, the rise and set happens roughly at 7:30 AM and 7:30 PM. Though Zion's cliffs will stun you during any time of day with their staggering height and beauty, their reds, oranges, yellows, and whites enjoy especially poignant saturation in the first and last hours of daylight. Take a relaxed morning walk around town and enjoy the cool morning temperatures before the day's bustle begins.

Breakfast before You Go

Or stop by the Mean Bean Coffee House (932 Zion Park Boulevard; 435-772-0654; www.meanbean coffee.blogspot.com), the first to open in Springdale, and grab an espresso drink or an organic coffee and take a seat to watch the sun come up. This petite shop has earned a fine reputation among locals and tourists alike. Light fare such as pastries avail themselves, as well as heartier breakfast burritos and scurvy-fighting smoothies. Open all year, seven days a week, Mean Bean is a reliable spot for early risers, opening its doors at 6:30 every day.

Enter the Park

As breakfast makes its way toward your belly, you can begin making preparations to enter the park. Most visitors will arrive at Zion between April 1 and October 30 and will therefore be required to ride the shuttle bus on the Zion Canyon Scenic Drive (see "Zion's

Shuttle Bus System," earlier in this chapter). This free system, though it may seem restrictive, actually allows for much easier, hands-free viewing of the park. It also renders one-way hikes through the canyon much easier, eliminating a mandatory return to a specific parking spot. The one downside to this system is that you'll have to plan ahead for your entire day in the park, loading your backpack in the morning with whatever you'll require for the journey.

When packing your bag, don't forget sunscreen, a water bottle, some food, and shade-rendering clothing. Though you'll absolutely need more than one bottle's worth of water, the park has many taps scattered about, in operation during the warmer months of the year. If you plan to do a big day of hiking, it could be beneficial to carry an electrolyte drink of some kind to help your body stay hydrated in the dry desert heat. And bringing along an extra pair of dry socks isn't a bad idea, either. Believe it or not, a warm layer of clothing can prove useful too, particularly if you plan to stay out to watch the sunset. If you want to bring a sack lunch, swing by Café Soleil (205 Zion Park Boulevard; 435-772-0505; see Springdale's "Local Flavors" section of this chapter, above) before you get on the bus.

Lastly, do not forget to bring your wallet. Weekly passes to Zion National Park (435-772-3426; www .nps.gov/zion) cost $25 or $12 per person (if arriving as a pedestrian, motorcyclist, or bicyclist). If you own an Interagency Annual Pass, you'll still need to have that on hand, as well as a photo ID.

Once in the park, the first stop, logically and spatially, is the Zion Canyon Visitor Center (435-772-

The visitors center uses high-tech engineering to be ecofriendly.

Backcountry Desk

Anyone planning to sleep in the park anywhere but in the designated campgrounds or Zion Lodge must stop by the Backcountry Desk in person to speak with rangers and obtain a permit. Generally, backpackers and canyoneers on multiday trips or rock climbers sleeping on the wall or at the base of a climb will fall into this category. Canyoneers and anyone considering a journey in the Zion Narrows should also check the weather forecast posted here and discuss the potential for flash flooding with rangers at the desk.

You can also apply for all kinds of other permits at the visitors center, from those for wedding ceremonies to ash scattering and commercial filming. As a rule of thumb, if you think you might need a permit for what you're doing, it's a good idea to stop in and inquire. With the National Parks System, it's reliably better to ask permission than beg for forgiveness.

The Backcountry Desk is a mandatory stop for anyone requiring permits.

If you wish to stick exclusively to the Kolob Canyons portion of the park for backpacking or multiday rock-climbing routes, you may apply for these permits at the Kolob Canyons Visitor Center. Though not as large or flashy as the Zion Canyon Visitor Center, this too remains open year-round and is likewise staffed by rangers. It also carries a small selection of books and maps.

3256). This is an especially worthwhile detour for those unfamiliar with the area. This impressive building has been designed to function nearly off the grid. The building's design allows it to self-heat and -cool, and its solar panels provide nearly all of its electricity. Naturally the center also provides a great deal of information about the park, with photographs, brochures, a large 3-D map of the canyon, a gift shop, and a ranger-staffed information desk. The park's Backcountry Desk is also located in this building (see "Backcountry Desk," above).

If you've got the legs for it, now is the time to do Angels Landing, Zion's most famous and striking hike. This route, which seems completely unfathomable as a nontechnical, pedestrian journey, involves dozens of hairpin switchbacks, several ecosystem changes, and a final, very exposed section along a rock spine replete with hand chains. Those hiking the entire distance will find themselves at the top of a thin peninsula of cliffs, literally thousands of feet above the canyon floor below.

Access for Angels Landing is had by departing from the bus (or parking) at the Grotto, and then crossing over the Virgin River via a footbridge and heading up the canyon on the clearly signed trail. The entire trek has about 1,400 feet of elevation gain over 2.7 miles, rendering a roughly three- to four-hour, moderately paced hike and 5.4 miles of round-trip distance. Especially during the first two-thirds of the hike, the path more resembles a sidewalk than a hiking trail. Granted, this sidewalk climbs very steeply and zigzags up the hillside without delay. About halfway up, the trail enters Hidden Canyon, a cool and shady narrow slot with a momentary reprieve of steepness. Immediately following that, the trail enters a pinball-machine-like switchback section just before reaching an overlook.

Though the last section of this hike is indeed extremely exposed

and challenging, it actually requires no technical climbing at all. However, those afraid of heights or struggling with exposure should actually bypass the upper section; though not a technically difficult journey, it does feature sheer drop-offs of hundreds and even thousands of feet. Importantly, you should leave the last pitch alone in the event of current or impending winds, rains, or thunderstorms. This thin spine of rock presents enough of a challenge without being wet and slippery. And a rogue gust of wind or lightning bolt could easily bring the end to an overly imprudent hiker.

On your way back to the Grotto, don't forget to stop by the Virgin River to dip your feet in its cool waters. The pleasantly orange sandy shores of this river provide a tranquil place to unwind and stretch after a hike. If you find yourself with more energy to spare, you may consider some of the other in-park options listed in the recreation section toward the end of this chapter.

Stop for Lunch

After a hike like this, lunch will be calling your name loudly. If you complete your hike between 11 AM and 3 PM, you can catch a meal inside the park at the Zion Lodge's Red Rock Grille (435-772-7760; www.zionlodge.com). The lunch menu here consists of a fairly large selection of hot and cold sandwiches, salads, and other unexpected and healthy options like gourmet

The trail departing from the Grotto leads immediately over the Virgin River.

quesadillas and salmon cakes. If you miss this time frame, you may dine at 5 PM or visit the lounge, which remains open between meals. But reservations are required for dinner (only), and cell phones do not work in Zion Canyon.

Learn a Little

If you happened to pack a lunch, you can eat that at the Grotto's picnic area and then head straight back down the canyon and to the Human History Museum (435-772-3256), open year-round (with reduced off-season hours). Begin your visit with a screening of the museum's short introductory film. Though a screening takes only 22 minutes, it provides a general working background on the area's roughly 10,000-year history.

The museum also maintains a collection of roughly 290 thousand objects. Gathered from the area by rangers since 1909, these items represent the area's cultural and natural past and include plant, insect, animal, and paleontological specimens, as well as human artifacts representing prehistoric habitation, Mormon settlement, railroad work, and more. Obviously, not all of these are displayed permanently, but a good selection represents this massive anthology at any point in the year.

Dinner

Catch a westbound bus and head back out of the park for the time being. Hungry parties will enjoy a dinner at the Switchback Grill (1149 South Zion Park Boulevard; 435-772-3700; www.switchback grille.com), in Springdale. Offering a variety of satisfying selections with sophisticated and environmentally friendly twists on these, the

Switchback provides filling yet nutritious and gourmet meals. USDA prime beef, free-range chicken, fresh seafood, and wild game headline the menu, as does wood-fired pizza, nutritious and inventive salads, a savory variety of pastas, and a full bar with a fairly generous beer and wine list. Make sure to take a coffee with dessert if you plan an evening out.

Evening Out

After a strenuous hike and a satisfying dinner, a relaxing evening with a musical performance can prove to be one of the most pleasant ways to unwind and recover from a food coma. Catch a show at the O.C. Tanner Amphitheater (Lion Avenue, Springdale; 435-652-7994; www.dixie.edu/tanner). This 2,000-seat, outdoor amphitheater hosts numerous shows under the stars and is surrounded by the luminous cliffs of Zion National Park as they glow at sunset. Unfortunately, it's not possible to see a show every night, but nevertheless the amphitheater usually hosts about one show a week during the extended summer months. Check the online schedule; you may decide it's worth rearranging your trip a bit to arrive on a certain show date.

If you like this . . . and you're in the area at the right time, get tickets to the **Utah Shakespearean Festival** *(435-586-7878; www.bard .org), winner of the Tony Award for Outstanding Regional Theater. Taking place between the end of June and the beginning of September each year in Cedar City, this festival features the performances of William Shakespeare's play in three different theaters, including a replica of the famous Globe Theater. Not just one, but eight or nine plays come to life each season. In addition to these performances, another half-dozen or so miscellaneous sideshows accompany the festival. Known around the country for its high-quality performances, the festival is certainly worth a trip.*

DAY 2

Breakfast before You Go

Switch it up a bit on the second morning and sleep in before taking a slow cup of coffee at a new café. Those wanting to take in the early morning views of Springdale over a warm brew will have to wait until 8 AM to check out Oscars Café (978 Zion Park Boulevard; 435-772-3232; www.cafeoscars.com). With more than a dozen tables outside on the patio, the café provides plenty of space to look east into the park. Open all year, Oscars also serves breakfast, lunch, and dinner, providing a long list of burgers, sandwiches, and Mexican food for meat eaters, vegetarians, and vegans alike. If you do eat meat, you can do so with a good conscience here, as all beef on the menu has been grass fed and all chickens have been raised outside a cage.

Once the belly is full, pack the bags again and prepare to head into the park. Especially during the warmest months of the year, any kind of physical activity is definitely best taken during the morning, before the heat of the day. Assuming the first day's elevation gain has taxed your calves a bit, you may want to decrease the strain today and aim for a flatter trail. If you happened to bring a pair of sturdy, strap-on sandals (that won't detach themselves in water), a good second-day hike with very little elevation gain would be the Zion Narrows, located at the upper reaches of the Zion Canyon Scenic Drive (Temple of Sinawava shuttle stop). This journey actually follows the Virgin River upstream into the deep and narrow upper reaches of Zion Canyon. For those who aren't into canyoneering, this provides a similar environment and experience with absolutely no technical skill required at all—just as Angels Landing grants exposure to non-rock climbers.

Given that this hike actually follows the bed of the Virgin River, much of it takes place in water. It should not be attempted in spring or even early to midsummer, as this river carries spring runoff from the upper reaches of the Colorado Plateau. Relatedly, this river walk can be lethal if any major rainstorms take place in the drainages above. If you have any doubts about the regional weather, a pre-

hike discussion with a ranger is highly recommended. It might save your life!

Leaving from the trailhead at the terminus of the Zion Canyon Scenic Drive, you can walk upstream for hours and hours between ever-changing, shear sandstone walls. Often with no shoreline at all, the river is literally enclosed in this chute which it has slowly eaten into the rock over millions of years. The canyon's width ranges from only 15 feet to more than 1,000 feet high. Approximately 16 miles long (one way), this hike proves quite time consuming. Those wanting to walk the entire route should allow for at least 12 hours, as river-polished stones make passage slow.

Many people make a committed, one-way hike from top to bottom, descending approximately 1,400 feet as they go. If you're doing this, you'll need to have a full day's worth of food and water, along with walking poles and even rappelling gear and the wherewithal on how to use it. If you're considering this, you should at least speak with a ranger, if not a guiding service, to get a full understanding of this undertaking's scope. The starting point for this journey is located at Chamberlain's Ranch, about 80 minutes north of the park's southeastern entrance.

If you like this . . . and want to try more, or if the Virgin River is just too much walking, take a casual ramble along its shores, but not in its waters. The much more "civilized" Pa'rus Trail loosely follows along the banks of the Virgin River in the main section of Zion Canyon. With three main access points, this broad, open, and extremely well maintained trail can be enjoyed as a one-way hike in conjunction with the shuttle buses, as an out-and-back walk, or as an extension of the Watchman Trail. It also makes for an easy pedestrian commute from the visitors center to the Watchman Campground and Human History Museum. Its one-way total length is 3.5 miles and can also be a nearly flat one- or two-way jog.

Learn a Little

An alternate or supplementary activity to the Narrows hike would be to join in on one of the many ranger-led programs that take place during the summer. The availability, time, frequency, and nature of these change with the season and are listed in the "Zion Map and Guide" brochure, handed out at the tollbooth. Visitors in the canyon during peak season will find as many as 16 of these guided outings and discourses spread evenly throughout each day. Each program differs from the next in terms of length, scope, and age group. Many explore the park's hiking trails like Emerald Pools, while other talks and programs take place in the Zion Nature Center or Zion Lodge. Hikes involve more than just exercise and are enriched with out-of-the-ordinary features like GPS

units, animal habitat discourses, and discussions on water's erosive forces.

The indoor programs incorporate various media to explain the local animals' adaptations, describe the area's fantastic geology, and bring to light the regional history. Some even take place in the evening or at night and involve music and stargazing. If you would like to hook up with one of these programs, allow anywhere from 30 minutes to a few hours. The child-friendly offerings tend to run a bit shorter than those for the grown-ups. Most of the adult walks last at least a few hours, with the longest requiring 4.5 to complete. Talks last about half an hour. The park's brochure lists meeting places and reservation information for each.

Lunch before You Go

If you plan to leave the park by heading west through Springdale, stop at the Pioneer Restaurant (828 Zion Park Boulevard; 435-772-3009; www.pioneerlodge.com) part of the Pioneer Lodge. Right on the main drag, this establishment will be hard to miss with its old-timey wagon sign and raw wood porches. The restaurant portion of the lodge offers classic, hearty, diner-style lunches. The menu offers satisfying choices like chicken strips, ham and turkey club or Reuben sandwiches, numerous lasagnas, steaks, fish, soups, salads, many (oft-fried) starters, and a kids' menu. During your visit, you've probably worked

The Pioneer Lodge and Restaurant stands right on Main Street in Springdale.

heads eastward out of the park, it ascends quickly out of the canyon past numerous, scenic switchbacks, through the 1.1-mile-long Zion–Mt. Carmel Tunnel, and up among the white capstone domes of Zion National Park before reaching US 89 and the small village of Mt. Carmel Junction.

Pause here for lunch or dinner at the Buffalo Grill (9065 West UT 9; 435-648-2147; www.zmr .com) at the Zion Mountain Ranch. Offering spacious indoor and out-door seating, this restaurant does quite a good job of sticking to its theme, serving many selections of buffalo meat and providing views of its on-site herd to diners. Buffalo meat, which tastes much like beef with a pleasant hint of game flavor, has a delicious, savory essence but with a much healthier nutrition profile than cow beef. Additionally, the menu features many wood-fired or barbecue-style items and game meats like elk and venison, as well as pork, beef, and more. Though the restaurant's atmosphere might lower your guard with its informali-ty, its gourmet entrées will radically surprise your senses. A real gastro-nomical experience.

up an appetite and deserve a home-made cheesecake, brownie, or sundae.

Those preferring a quick pick-me-up before the drive can opt out of the full meal and visit the Inter-net café at the Pioneer Lodge. Tote in your laptop to access the wireless Internet, or pay a fee to use the café's computers. The café serves espresso drinks, drip coffee, crois-sant sandwiches, and pastries.

However, many leaving Zion National Park head east toward Bryce Canyon National Park or Cedar Breaks National Monument via Mt. Carmel Junction. As UT 9

Extend Your Stay
If you have more time, try to see these things . . . .

RECREATION

Scenic Driving

If you want to do more than "just" tour the Zion Canyon Scenic Drive, take a quick cruise on the Kolob Terrace Road, a 33-mile road that branches off of UT 9 to the northeast in the town of Virgin. Along its journey, pavement gives way to well-maintained dirt. The road meanders through the middle of Zion National Park and climbs in elevation from 3,606 feet at Virgin to 7,890 feet at Lava Point Campground, 25 miles up road, and beyond. As it climbs, the road leaves the hot valley floors below and enters higher, grassy flats among craggy and knobby sandstone domes and peaks. If you drive through the eastern entrance of the park later, you'll be reminded of the same colorful bands seen here—much like natural topographical lines.

Though Kolob Terrace Road departs from UT 9 quite near Springdale, it enjoys vastly less crowding than the Zion Canyon Scenic Drive. This piece of knowledge may come in quite handy between late May and early September, when Zion Canyon is filled with tourists. Beware: This road closes during winter and remains so until the snow has melted sufficiently. If you're curious about the current road conditions, you can call the Zion National Park's camping line (435-772-3256), which has up-to-date information about the accessibility of Lava Point Campground (see "Camping," below), 25 miles up this road from Virgin.

Kolob Canyons Road, toward the far northern end of Zion National Park, avoids the bulk of the main park roads almost as effectively as Kolob Terrace does. Departing from I-15 at exit 40, this road stretches for more than 5 uphill miles east and into the northern portion of Zion National Park. Like Kolob Terrace Road, this road has higher elevations and vastly less traffic than Zion Canyon, as well as numerous scenic pullouts along its length. Though the cliff bands in the area are not as dominating as in Zion Canyon, their closeness and variety render them equally beautiful—only with a different flavor. During any season, Kolob has a slightly lusher, more mountainous feel than Zion Canyon, with more evergreen forests, plentiful wildflowers in springtime, and more snow in winter. As the scenic drive winds through the area, the road's many intepretive signs point out the various nearby peaks, the Finger Canyons, and the Hurricane Cliffs. Look for Horse Ranch Mountain to the north, a broad mountain with huge, exposed cliff bands running its length; at 8,726 feet above sea level, this is the tallest point in the park.

Multiple hiking trails depart from different points along the road, including the La Verkin Creek Trail (accessing Kolob Arch) and a mile-long hike to the Timbercreek Overlook, from which you can see the Finger (or Kolob) Canyons. (For more information on these trails, see "Hiking," below.) This drive terminates at the Kolob Canyons Viewpoint, which has a parking and picnic area and pit toilets. Though plows clear the road throughout the winter, it sometimes will temporarily close during snow removal. If visiting during winter and after significant precipitation, call the park (435-772-3426) to ensure that the road is open.

The Lower Emerald Pools require very little hiking to reach.

Hiking

With just 23 miles of roadway and 229 square miles of land, the vast majority of Zion National Park must be explored off pavement and on foot. Luckily, the park service does an excellent job of trail maintenance, making the paths quite accessible to even the most hiking adverse. Typically, the shorter the hike, the broader and more domesticated the trail, so those with less experience and fitness can enjoy the tamer walks.

Among the more popular and accessible pedestrian destinations are the Emerald Pools (Zion Lodge Shuttle Stop, Zion Canyon Scenic Drive), of which there is a lower, middle, and upper. The lowest pool can be reached via 0.6 miles of a well-maintained but somewhat steep footpath. The upper pools require an extra mile of hiking along a more rugged trail with occasional steep grades, large steps, and oft-uneven footing. Youth will think nothing of these obstacles, but those with ailing or unpracticed bodies might find this upper destination somewhat tricky to navigate. The Emerald Pools themselves consist of round, shallow basins full of green-hued water. These were created and are still filled today by a small stream trickling down the steep hillside, terraced with sandstone cliff bands. As the stream has cascaded down these cliffs over time, it has created not only the pools but also eroded amphitheaters around them. The pools support oases of plant life, including moss and hanging gardens. As of the publication of this book, the (separate) trail leading to the middle pool was closed due to rockfall.

If you like this . . . hike for its lush environment and short walking distance, then you should also consider trekking to **Weeping Rock** *(Weeping Rock Shuttle Stop, Zion Canyon Scenic Drive). This extremely easy journey provides access to yet another off-road vista with just 0.2 miles of paved walking in each direction. Water from the plateau above Zion trickles down through the earth's surface, through fissures, and emerges here, painting a wet curtain of rock and hanging gardens. Here, this wetness seeps through an arching crack in an otherwise continuous, vertical sandstone cliff, creating a dark, streaked wall beneath a rainbow of green.*

Weeping Rock

The path leads right up and underneath the archway, providing a cool, up-the-skirt view of this feature.

For some serious bird's-eye views of Zion Canyon without the strain and extreme exposure of the Angels Landing Trail, take a walk along the 0.5-mile Canyon Overlook Trail (immediately east of Zion–Mt. Carmel Tunnel, Zion–Mt. Carmel Highway/UT 9). The Zion–Mt. Carmel Highway, which climbs past many steep switchbacks up and out of Zion Canyon, accomplishes most of the uphill work to earn the views afforded by the overlook—though it still leaves you with more than 150 vertical feet to climb. Once at the path's terminus, you will tower above the great and deep Zion Canyon below. The hugeness of this great and colorful chasm in the earth can be fully appreciated from this lofty viewpoint.

If you're hanging out in the northern Kolob Canyons–portion of the park and have a good set of legs under you, pack a sizable lunch and head out on the La Verkin Creek Trail to Kolob Arch. This 278.4-foot-wide rock window requires a 7-mile journey to reach, with the arch actually sitting about 700 feet lower than the trailhead, elevation 6,100 feet. Named by the Natural Arch and Bridge Society as the second largest arch in the world, Kolob Arch is only exceeded in size by Landscape Arch in Arches National Park. (To see more about the society's in-depth researching of these arches, check out their Web site: www.naturalarches.org.) Despite the relative lack of elevation change, the trail rolls a good bit along the way, passing over ridges and through sand, so don't pack for a speedy journey. But don't worry, you'll enjoy many more views than just that of the arch, including those of Paria, Tucupit, and Beatty points, as well as Gregory and Shuntavi buttes. En route you'll pass by 18 campsites; if you would like to turn this into an overnight trip, chat with the rangers at the visitors center and pick up a permit. The trailhead for this hike sits 3.5 miles up the Kolob Canyons Road from the visitors center at the Lee Pass Trailhead (before the terminus of the road).

An alternative, midlength Kolob hike is the 2.5-mile Taylor Creek Trail, likely the most popular in the Kolob Canyons region of Zion. This route follows along the bottom of one of the Kolob Canyons, also called the Finger Canyons. The journey begins by descending from the road to the namesake Taylor Creek, which it then follows upstream quite nearly. On the way, you'll pass two 1930s-era cabins, the first of which was built by Gustive O. Larson and the second by Arthur Fife. Larson worked at Branch Agricultural College (now Southern Utah University), where Fife was also employed as a geology professor. Both built their cabins prior to Kolob's inclusion in Zion National Park; after the land was brought into protection, they were forced to relinquish their claims on the cabins. Do not tamper with or attempt to enter these fragile structures. The trail terminates in Double Arch Alcove, a lush area where running water has cut into the sandstone, creating a cavelike indentation and habitat for plant life. Given its location in a creek bed, the trail is predictably less open and features fewer

Looking back down Zion Canyon from Angels Landing Trail.

gaping views than those in other parts of Zion. As the trail crosses over the stream quite often, you should expect it to be fairly wet during springtime. The well-marked and obvious trailhead for Taylor Creek is located about 2 miles up road from the visitors center.

Visitors with less time on their hands should take the 1-mile hike from the end of the Kolob Canyons Road to the Timbercreek Overlook, from which you can see the Finger Canyons and Lower Kolob Plateau. Just a minute's walk from the parking area, you'll run into a picnic area. Stop for a bite here if you wish, or hit it on the way back to the car. This short and easy trail leads you closer to the Kolob (or Finger) Canyons themselves. And though the view isn't spectacularly better than that at the parking area, it provides a quick stretch for the legs. If you have the luxury to choose your timing, come for sunset, as the complex west-facing cliff faces and peaks to your north and east will glow in the late evening light. This trail departs to the south from the road's end, or the Kolob Canyons Viewpoint.

Rock Climbing

Utah has a well-earned reputation for having some of the best, pure sandstone crack climbing in the world. With Indian Creek (see the "Nearby Areas" section; east of Canyonlands National Park, chapter 6) just six hours' drive away, many travel first to Indian Creek to learn the unique techniques required to climb splitter cracks.

With the requisite skills in hand, they then migrate to Zion to check out the similar but much longer climbs of Zion National Park.

Originally known for its aid lines, Zion has grown increasingly popular for its free routes. Most of these require 10 or more pitches to complete, but a few areas like the Touchstone Buttress (located at the northernmost point on Big Bend, Zion Canyon; Big Bend Shuttle Stop) feature several single-pitch climbs. Those who don't have the gear or time to spend on a big wall can simply crag for a day.

However, those with the time, skill, and gear should look into climbing either Shune's Buttress (Grotto Shuttle Stop, Zion Canyon

A belay station several pitches up Moonlight Buttress, a rock-climbing route.

David Sjöquist

A rock climber ascends a route at the Touchstone Buttress in Zion Canyon in January.

Scenic Drive) or Moonlight Buttress (Big Bend Shuttle Stop, Zion Canyon Scenic Drive), both class 5 climbs. Moonlight is possibly the canyon's most famous free (or aid) climb. At 5.12, this nine-pitch classic climbs a sustained and incredibly immaculate piece of rock more than 1,100 feet tall. Shune's Buttress, which logs in at 5.11, has a similar length and sustained nature as Moonlight, but at a gentler grade, with nearly every pitch boasting good or excellent quality.

The Kolob Canyons section of Zion National Park offers a good, though much reduced, selection of routes, including many of just one pitch. Some of these are even bolted and slightly overhanging. Try to locate a climb called Half Route, as this shares a wall with a handful of quite unique and fun sport pitches trademarked by massive *huecos*—some of which are even large enough to crawl inside midroute.

Those planning to aid climb—and thus in all likelihood sleep on the wall—must stop by the Backcountry Desk in the visitors center to obtain a permit. Rangers there can also advise you if anything fishy is afoot like rockfall or impending bad weather. Don't forget to check the shuttle bus schedule, too, as your day will suddenly get a lot longer if you miss the last bus out of the canyon.

For a more complete description of the climbing in Zion, invest in a copy of Bryan Bird's 2009 guidebook, *Zion Climbing: Free and Clean.* This book details free- and aid-climbing routes, from boulder problems (short difficult routes on boulders) to single-pitch climbs and the big-wall lines. If you look closely enough, you'll find a photograph of yours truly on the second crux pitch of Shune's Buttress.

Of course, many climbers come to Zion with the desire to enjoy some of its spectacular routes, but don't necessarily have all of the gear, multip-itching skills, or courage to attempt one of these quasi-big-wall routes. That's where guide services like Zion Rock Guides (435-772-3303; www .zionrockguides.com) come in handy. This group offers both guiding and instructional courses. Climbers and nonclimbers of all experience levels can be accommodated and will be treated at a level appropriate for their comfort and skill. You may choose to join a group for a guided trip or lesson, or make private arrangements. Group sizes typically top out around seven or eight people, so you won't get lost in the mix.

Biking

If you flew to the area, you most likely will not have your bike in tow. If you nevertheless wish to do some pedaling, stop by Zion Cycles (868 Zion Park Boulevard; 435-772-0400; www.zioncycles.com) in Springdale, open 9 AM to 7 PM every day (except January when they close for the month). Exclusively in the bike business, Zion Cycles offers a diverse spread of rentals, including road bikes, mountain bikes with various suspension options, tandem cycles, children's bikes, trailer bikes, vehicle racks, and even strollers. They also allow you to choose from a variety of rental period lengths so you don't end up shelling out more money than necessary. Maps and guidebooks can also be purchased in the shop, as well as accessories and clothing. If you don't feel much like mountain biking, you can simply ride a road bike through the park, as you'll notice many other people doing.

Though not as famous as Moab, the Springdale area actually holds some of Utah's finer mountain biking opportunities. Technically advanced riders must look into the Gooseberry Mesa Trail System, a classic and popular mix of single-track and slickrock riding atop an exposed plateau southwest of Zion National Park. Actually composed of several trails, this network allows you to ride as much or as little as you'd like. Weaving through sandstone nubs and domes, among ancient pinion trees and juniper bushes, across sandy flats, and over jumps and other obstacles, this circuit likens an adult playground. To access this trail, go to Rockville (west of Springdale) and turn south of UT 9 onto Bridge Road. Stay straight on this road as is crosses the Virgin River for about 1.5 miles. Bear left to stay on Bridge Road as it turns to gravel; do not follow signs toward Grafton. Instead, follow the dirt road as it ascends the obvious and huge plateau south of Rockville. This road is not recommended for vehicles with trailers. To get the most out of the experience on this rather complex trail network, it

Bridge Road leads up from Rockville to Gooseberry Mesa.

would be best to stop by a bike shop (above), pick up a map, and even chat with the staff about the current best rides for the season. Note: This area can also provide excellent, free camping for those not able to get a reservation inside the park, or simply not wishing to spend money on a site (see "Camping," later in this chapter).

Another option is Hurricane Rim Trail, a 7.5-mile section of pleasant single-track riding with open views of the surrounding landscapes. Though much of Hurricane Rim traverses buffed paths, some of it also crosses over rock surfaces and should be attempted by reasonably competent riders only. Though the trail's end is not much higher than its starting point, it does roll a lot, with elevation gains adding up over its course. This single stretch of trail can be taken in combination with other area bike routes like JEM Trail and Gould's Rim Trail to make a loop. You can also accomplish a circular journey by riding roads. Or simply double back on the trail, retracing your tracks. To reach the starting point, go to the town of Hurricane and head east out of town on UT 59. In less than a mile, you'll see a parking lot right off the road. It's best to carry a map in hand while taking this ride, especially if you plan to link into other trails along the way.

Some prefer to have an escort. These folks should get in touch with Red Desert Adventures (435-668-2888; www.reddesertadventure.com), a multifaceted guide operation with a mountain biking division. Offering two main categories of trips in the area, Red Desert can take you on a 2- to

12-mile tour of slickrock riding on either the Hurricane Rim or Gooseberry Mesa trails. Or if you prefer high-elevation riding, you can select a 6- to 16-mile route northeast of the park on the Navajo Loop Trail or Thunder Mountain Trail, near Bryce Canyon. Rides are offered to single persons and groups alike; per-person rates depend on group size.

Bird-Watching

Zion National Park estimates that 291 species live within its boundaries throughout the year. While many of these are quite common and unimpressive to most people, others like the peregrine falcon, bald eagle, and California condor have a special presence in the park. These species, once greatly threatened with extinction, have enjoyed a flourish of recovery and replenishment at home in Zion. As of 1970, the peregrine falcon species had been reduced to a mere 39 breeding couples in the contiguous 48 states, in large part because of the widespread use of the chemical pesticide DDT in farming. Research and activism led to the national ban of this substance, and today more than 4,000 pairs breed across the U.S.

Birdwatchers coming to Zion should first visit the park's Web site (www.nps.gov/zion) and print out the bird-watching list. Located in the nature and science portion of the site, this list includes not only a checklist of possible birds to see in Zion but also provides a general idea of where and when to expect each species. Also consider sitting in on one of the ranger-given talks (see "Learn a Little," Day 2 of this chapter, above) on animal species in the park, or joining one of the informative habitat walks. Though not specifically or exclusively covering birds, these will give you a foundational understanding of desert species' lives.

Horseback Riding

If your trip falls between March and October, you have the possibility to take a guided horseback trip in Zion National Park with Canyon Rides (435-679-8665; www.canyonrides.com). The only company permitted to operate within park boundaries, Canyon Rides gives the option of one-hour or half-day rides through the southern portion of the park. Surprisingly affordable, each option only costs $40 and $75, respectively. For the horses' health, certain weight restrictions apply. A minimum age of 7 is required for the shorter rides, and an age of 10 for the longer journeys.

ACCOMMODATIONS AND RESTAURANTS

Perhaps you plan to stay longer than a few days, or would like a bit more variety in accommodations. Zion Lodge (Zion Lodge Shuttle Stop, Zion Canyon Scenic Drive; 435-772-7771; www.zionlodge.com) presents the only in-park lodging option in Zion. This fact renders the lodge inherently exclusive, as it is the only hotel inside Utah's most popular national park. The establishment offers a variety of options, including 75 hotel rooms of various sizes, 40 cabins, and 6 suites. Despite the park-service-like external appearance of the structures, the interiors boast quite tasteful and modern furnishings, with appropriate mountain flourishes. Two dining options exist here, the Red Rock Grill (see Day 1, earlier in this chapter) and the Castle Dome Cafe.

High-end cabins and family lodges await short-term renters at the Zion Mountain Ranch (9065 West UT 9; 435-648-2147; www.zmr.com), just east of Zion National Park in Carmel Junction. Located at a higher elevation than the other, Springdale-area accommodations, this ranch provides cooler living conditions for its guests during the hot summer months. Many people come to this property just to eat at the Buffalo Grill (Day 2 of this chapter's 48-hours section, above). This first-rate restaurant serves plenty of local buffalo and game selections.

Zion Lodge: the only accommodation in the park.

The Zion Ponderosa Ranch Resort (Zion Ponderosa, Twin Knolls Road, East of Zion National Park; 435-648-2700; www.zionponderosa.com) offers much more than lodging. Those who want the full-on Utah outdoors experience and are willing to pay for guide services and/or equipment rental will find this place second to none. An all-in-one stop, the resort has a huge selection of accommodations, recreation choices, and multiple restaurants during the main season.

Zion Ponderosa Ranch's fanciest restaurant, the Blue Belly Grill (Zion Ponderosa Ranch, above; 1-800-293-5444), is open for business between the middle of May and into the first week of September. It serves fine, contemporary American and Southwestern cuisine with many choices of beef, pork, seafood, stream fish, and fresh vegetables from around the area. Also on the ranch is East End Pizza (inside the Zion Ponderosa Ranch Trading Post, near the eastern entrance to Zion National Park). Here, wood-fired ovens bake gourmet, thin-crust pizzas between the middle of March and late autumn. During pleasant evenings, you can savor these pizzas on the porch. This restaurant opens at 11 AM and closes at 8 PM daily.

CAMPING

The park itself has three pay campgrounds (camping information: 435-772-3256), two of which sit right in the heart of its Zion Canyon region. These are named South Campground (0.5 miles east of the southwest entrance, UT 9, Zion National Park) and Watchman Campground (adjacent to the visitors center, UT 9 in Zion National Park). You should expect these to be full to the brim every night between June and August. Knowing this, you can make advanced reservations for Watchman Campground for an additional fee. This pleasant area has 162 sites and is flat and sandy and polka-dotted with shade-giving trees. South Campground has 127 sites, all of which are doled out on a first-come, first-served basis. Both campgrounds offer a handful of wheelchair-accessible sites. Though South Campground has no hookups, Watchman offers some sites with electrical outlets.

Lava Point Campground sits out of the bustle of the park's main section, up north of Virgin (on Kolob Terrace Road, 25 miles north of UT 9). At nearly 7,900 feet, it sits at a much higher elevation than the other campgrounds and provides slightly cooler camping conditions during the heat of summer. Though subjected to less crowding, this primitive campground has only six sites. It offers no hookups, but does have a pit toilet. There is no water available at this campground. Be sure to call the park (435-772-3256) to verify that the access road to Lava Point is open and passable.

Zion Ponderosa Ranch Resort (Zion Ponderosa, Twin Knolls Road, East of Zion National Park; 435-648-2700; www.zionponderosa.com) offers out-of-park, established campsites with hookups, electricity, bathrooms, and amenities for recreation. With places for both RVs and tents, the resort offers wireless Internet, hot showers, barbecue grills, and access to the open-use activities and facilities offered at the ranch, including tennis, swimming, volleyball, basketball, and a hot tub. The ranch also provides a huge range of guide services like ATV rides, jeep tours, paint balling, and more. But these services cost money.

The South Campground, as viewed from the road to the visitors venter.

West of the park, the Zion River Resort (551 East UT 9), in the town of Virgin, serves primarily as an RV park, though it does also offer tent camping spots. RV sites feature hookups to propane, power, water, and even phone lines. All campers can access fire rings, wireless Internet, bathrooms, a game room, a pool and hot tub, a playground, and a camper kitchen. If you're traveling in an RV and obtaining such a site is crucial to your trip, you should call well ahead of time for reservations during the summer months.

Located dead west of the park and almost right off of UT 9, Mosquito Cove (south side of UT 9, by mile marker 24) offers free and unregulated camping within just 15 minutes of Zion. While the lack of fees or rules can be liberating, it also means that humans often leave behind litter and other, even more disgusting, waste. Nevertheless, Mosquito Cove can serve as a pleasant, sandy, and flat place to camp right near the Virgin River and among the cottonwoods. During springtime following heavy snow years, high runoff can cause the Bureau of Land Management to close this site; be sure to have a backup plan.

Gooseberry Mesa (as listed under "Mountain Biking" in the "Recreation" section, above), provides a free, less crowded and cluttered camping alternative to Mosquito Cove. Situated on a high plateau, these undeveloped campsites enjoy beautiful sunsets and sunrises. Because the area consists of mixed private and public property, it is best to seek and pitch camp in the daylight. As always, camp only at sites that have obviously been used before to avoid degrading the landscape further.

2

Bryce Canyon National Park

PARK OVERVIEW

In a state packed to the brim with spectacular geologic wonders, Bryce
Canyon stands on its own, a brilliantly unique specimen in the wild sandstone menagerie that is Utah. Whereas many of the other parks highlight
unfathomable, natural sculptures of solid rock, Bryce features somewhat the
opposite. Its showpiece is literally an amphitheater of eroding earth—earth
that has some of the most spectacular oranges, yellows, and reds imaginable. Here, the soft crust of the earth has been carved away by the wind.
What's left is a crumbling forest of vibrantly colored spires, fins, and
hoodoos.

The bulk of Bryce Canyon National Park, as well as all its infrastructure, sits on a wooded plateau, just back from the rim of this amphitheater.
Its roads, campgrounds, and buildings all enjoy the shade of pleasant and
thin high-elevation evergreen forests. Carving into the edge of the Paunsaugunt Plateau, headward erosion has created a series of adjacent bowls
full of thousands of peculiar, needle-looking spires and hoodoos. Headward
erosion differs from centralized river-style erosion; it eats away at the earth
from the bottom up instead of from the top down as in a canyon. Therefore,
Bryce Canyon is actually more properly called Bryce Amphitheater, as a
canyon, by definition, is caused by central stream erosion.

In total, this lofty park has just under 3,000 feet of vertical relief, with
its highest point, Rainbow Point, sitting at 9,105 feet. Its rim, as well as
most of its infrastructure, has an elevation of 8,000 to 9,000 feet. Those
hoping to explore the park on foot may access the Rim Trail, which traipses
along the top of this fantastic amphitheater system for 11 miles, overlooking

LEFT: The switchbacks of the Navajo Loop Trail are unlike those in any of Utah's other parks.

The infinite layers of Bryce Amphitheater's sandstone are visible in its many formations.

the spires and hoodoos below. From this path, several others extend down through rock and mud mazes, forming loops, which then reascend to the rim. Most of the trails descend less than 1,000 vertical feet, making the return journey reasonable for most to complete.

The park's scenic drive extends as far as 18 miles to the south (to Rainbow Point), with a major arm of it branching eastward to Bryce Point. A free shuttle makes frequent loops between early May and early October to Bryce Amphitheater; a bus departs just twice daily to Rainbow Point during these months. Bryce Canyon National Park sits nearly a vertical mile above the floor of Zion Canyon. Keep in mind that summer comes to this park much later than it does to Zion; even in July, you should bring a jacket in case a breeze comes up.

Pick Your Spot
Where to stay and what you'll find nearby . . .

RUBY'S INN/BRYCE CANYON CITY

Located immediately outside the park's northern entrance, Ruby's Inn provides the nearest amenities to Bryce Canyon National Park.

Technically called Bryce Canyon City, this cluster of buildings consists of a hotel, gas station, an RV park and campground, as well as a general store (selling local books), gallery, and a few restaurants.

Bryce Canyon Pines (Mile Marker 10 on UT 12; 435-834-5330; www.brycecanyonmotel.com), as suggested for dinner in Day 1 of this chapter's 48-hour itinerary, sits

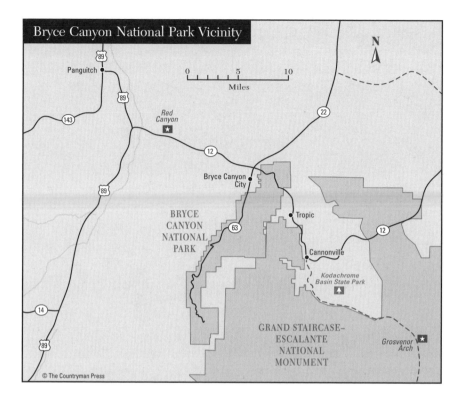

Bryce Canyon National Park Vicinity

© The Countryman Press

Bryce Canyon National Park has a general store within its boundaries.

6 miles west of the entrance to the park. Providing some of the higher-end lodging in the area, the hotel offers a choice among standard rooms, deluxe rooms, suites, and even cottages. Hand-selected bedding, wireless Internet, a hot tub, an on-site restaurant, and free HBO differentiate Bryce Canyon Pines from many of the other area lodging.

Ruby's Inn (26 South Main Street; 35-834-5341; www.rubysinn .com) itself operates under the Best Western franchise and has 370 guest rooms, as well as two suites. It offers wireless Internet, a post office, foreign currency exchange, a 24-hour Laundromat, a pool, a

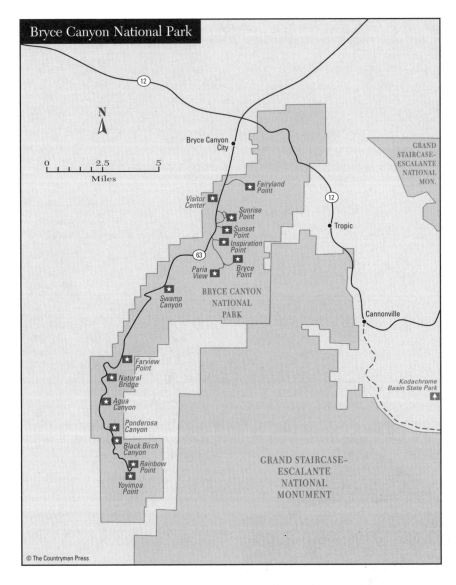

Bryce Canyon National Park

N

0   2.5   5
Miles

Bryce Canyon
City

Fairyland
Point

Visitor
Center

Sunrise
Point

Sunset
Point

Inspiration
Point

63

Paria
View

Bryce
Point

Tropic

GRAND
STAIRCASE-
ESCALANTE
NATIONAL
MON.

12

BRYCE CANYON
NATIONAL
PARK

Swamp
Canyon

Cannonville

Farview
Point

Natural
Bridge

Agua
Canyon

Ponderosa
Canyon

Black Birch
Canyon

Rainbow
Point

Yovimpa
Point

Kodachrome
Basin State Park

GRAND STAIRCASE-
ESCALANTE
NATIONAL
MONUMENT

© The Countryman Press

hot tub, and all of the standard hotel amenities. Established in 1916, this hotel has grown greatly and undergone many modernizing renovations rendering it a large, modern, and handsome lodging option. In addition to the guest rooms, they also provide tent and RV camping options.

TROPIC

The next closest town to Bryce Canyon's entrance, Tropic, expands your lodging options quite significantly, offering roughly a dozen hotels, motels, B&Bs, and rental homes. With a population just greater than 500, this town is a relative metropolis in the area.

Ruby's Inn sits just north of the park's entrance.

The Stone Canyon Inn (on Stone Canyon Lane, call or check online for directions; 435-679-8611; www.stonecanyoninn.com) offers a secluded lodging experience, offering just six rooms in a modern, mountain-style home. With a massive balcony, flower boxes, and large windows, this looks more like a luxury home than a bed & breakfast. Rooms vary in size, but all are new, immaculately clean, and well lit. Those traveling with families or larger groups should look into their private cottage rentals. In this case, *cottage* is hardly the appropriate word, as these, too, are modern, clean, and spacious homes with excellent amenities including air conditioning, flat-screen televisions, laundry facilities, and full kitchens. Surprisingly affordable, even the largest of these secluded homes tops out at around $300 per night in peak season.

If you want to keep it simple and stay in a motel, check into the Bryce Valley Inn (199 North Main Street; 435-679-8811; www.bryce valleyinn.com). Part of the America's Best Value Inn & Suites chain, this simple hotel provides clean rooms year-round, as well as free pancake breakfasts May through the middle of October. This hotel has a general shop with gifts and candy, as well as a restaurant. Though you probably won't have your pet with you—as pets aren't allowed most places in the park— pets are allowed (supervised, of course) at this hotel. Located just 7 miles from Bryce Canyon's entrance, this hotel is completely within commuting distance.

CANNONVILLE

Approximately 15 miles east of Bryce Canyon, Cannonville is a small town with fewer than 200 residents. The Grand Staircase Inn & Country Store (105 North Kodachrome Drive; 435-679-8400) is where you'll find the town's 26 hotel rooms. Simple, yet clean, this hotel provides a comfortable place to sleep without the extra costs and frills of a luxury resort. The Country Store portion of the establishment sells gasoline, coffee, breakfasts, and basic groceries.

If you prefer a private experience but don't require a large, luxury-home-style "cottage," consider staying at Kodachrome Basin Cabins (435-679-8536; www.red stonecabins.com). These cute freestanding log structures offer you an entire cabin to yourself but cost just a bit more than standard hotel rooms, even in peak season. Located inside Kodachrome Basin State Park (south of Cannonville by about 8 miles), they require a bit more of a commute to the park but provide an excellent and scenic place to sleep in one of Utah's more beautiful and secluded state parks.

PANGUITCH

To the west of the park, Panguitch is the largest town within reasonable closeness to Bryce Canyon and could be an ideal place to bed down for those en route from Zion or Cedar Breaks National Monument. Founded in 1864, this 1,600-resident town has an attractive, Old West-style, brick-laden Main Street. Its lodging scene is dominated by low-cost, locally owned motels, all offering quite inexpensive rates. About 28 miles northwest of the Bryce, those staying in Panguitch will drive 45 minutes to reach the park.

The New Western Motel (180 East Center Street; www.new brycewesterninn.com) has 55 guest rooms, making it one of the largest in the area. A slight price class above its competitors, this motel offers the most choice in room size. However, if it happens to be full, all you have to do is drive down Main Street to find any number of other, very comparable hotels.

Local Flavors
Taste of the town—local cafés, restaurants, bars, bistros, etc.

RUBY'S INN/BRYCE CANYON CITY

Ruby's Inn has two unabashedly pioneer-style restaurants. The first, Cowboy's Buffet & Steak Room (inside Ruby's Inn main building, 26 South Main Street; 435-834-5341; www.rubysinn.com), serves just what the name would have you expect: basic American food in a sit-down restaurant with an optional buffet bar. Don't expect a fancy affair, but if you're hungry, you can pick and choose, eating heavily from the well-stocked salad bar.

The Canyon Diner (next to Ruby's Inn; www.rubysinn.com) serves fast-food-style meals that can be eaten there or taken away. This smaller restaurant primarily cooks up burgers, fries, and their typical accomplices.

TROPIC

Not to be confused with the Bryce Valley Inn, the Bryce Canyon Inn's Pizza Place (29 North Main Street; 435-679-8888; www.bryce canyoninn.com) has an on-site pizza restaurant. Perfect for large groups, this restaurant focuses on simple, fresh, homemade pizzas that please children and adults alike. During the summer months, the restaurant opens its doors seven days a week, serving a full breakfast, lunch, and dinner menu. In the afternoon, you can also choose from hot and cold sandwiches, pasta dishes, salads, and more. Though it remains open during winter, the Pizza Place reduces its operation times to just Friday and Saturday dinners. Call ahead if you have doubts. Indoor and outdoor dining is available during pleasant conditions.

Panguitch's streets offer a variety of fast-food and convenience-store-style eateries. The Cowboy's Smokehouse BBQ (95 North Main Street; 435-676-8030; www.cowboys smokehousecafe.com) represents the full-service exception to this cluster. Though it specializes in mesquite grilling, it also offers other entrées, salads, and a children's menu. Don't forget: You're in cowboy country, so remember to calibrate your expectations accordingly.

48 Hours

GETTING THERE

Bryce Canyon has but one entrance and is quite far removed from any interstate highway. That said, it sits precisely in the center of Utah's western national parks and just off UT 12, one of the state's most scenic roads. If coming from the southwest, as from St. George and Zion National Park, you'll arrive by way of US 89, a decently straight and speedy roadway when considering the region's topography. Those coming from Cedar Breaks National Monument should check the Utah Department of Transportation's Web site (www.udot .utah.gov) to be sure the high-elevation roads between Cedar Breaks and US 89 are even passable. These roads close during winter and during heavy snow years

can remain impassable until the second half of June. Those coming from the east will arrive via UT 12, passing through Boulder and the slightly larger town of Escalante along the way.

Regardless of your trip's origin, allow plenty of time for slow driving caused by tourist traffic on these curvy and hilly roadways. Also, supply yourself ahead of time with plenty of food and any other necessary items. Though many convenience stores do business in the area, you'll be hard-pressed to find a proper supermarket.

The area around Bryce Canyon has seen rather little development, aside from small, tourist-friendly shops, restaurants, and lodging options, so don't even try looking for a movie theater. However, if you can tolerate Western music, buy tickets (available at Ruby's Inn; 26 South Main Street; 435-834-5341; www.rubysinn.com) for a dinner

Meat Alert: Veggies Come Prepared

Bryce Canyon, despite its vivid beauty, has about a third fewer visitors than Zion National Park coming to see it each year. Though this number is still greater than 1.5 million people every year, the vicinity of Bryce hasn't quite seen the culinary renaissance that the Zion area has—likely due to its increased remoteness and much longer and more severe winters. The added difficulties of bringing in food and the short tourist season limit the dining options near Bryce Canyon. Especially those with specific dietary restrictions should plan ahead and bring their own gluten-free, vegetarian, or vegan cuisine in a cooler. Though Bryce Canyon does enjoy the companionship of some restaurants, these tend to serve meat-heavy, hearty, classic American cuisine.

and show at Ebeneezer's Barn and Grill (also located on the Ruby's Inn campus). The menu offers four main dinner options, among them fresh-baked salmon, rib-eye steak, or barbecue chicken. These massive, heart-menacing meals accompany Western musical performances by the house band, the Bar G Wranglers. If you're planning to go on a big hike the following day, these protein bombs and accompanying Dutch oven potatoes, baked beans, cornbread, and dessert will more than suffice to fuel your body.

DAY 1

Breakfast before You Go

Many hotels in the area offer complimentary breakfasts. But if for some reason yours isn't to your liking, you can always stop in at the Ruby's Inn (listed above, in Bryce Canyon City) and grab a simple and filling breakfast. Call ahead to be sure their serving times line up with your schedule. Better yet, if you happen to be satisfied with a picnic breakfast, hurry into the park before dawn and take the hike recommended below; an easy mile into the suggested journey, the route comes to Sunrise Point, a highly recommended location for this daily event and an excellent place to enjoy a sack breakfast.

Enter the Park

If you aren't there already, you'll need to locate Ruby's Inn (or Bryce Canyon City, as it's officially called). Departing south from UT 12 on UT 63, drive only 2 miles before encountering this cluster of buildings comprising Bryce Canyon City. Keep your eyes fixed on the eastern (left) side of the road and look for a National Park Service building; this

The green of Bryce's conifer trees contrasts with the park's reds year-round.

is the Shuttle Boarding Area. Though you are still about 2 miles from the park's entrance (and 3 miles from the visitors center), you may want to park your car in the sizable lot there. Here you can purchase your day pass—or show your Interagency Annual Pass with photo ID—and board the park shuttles. (See "Bryce's Shuttle Bus System," below.) Especially in summer, this is recommended, as parking in the park often surpasses capacity, making it literally impossible to park legally.

Once inside the park, take the time to stop by Bryce Canyon Visitor Center. Though this park's installment really is not much different than its peers, it nevertheless offers an abridged overview of Bryce Canyon's layout, geology, and history. As in most other national parks, it has bathrooms, water, books, and informative rangers available to answer questions. Make sure to use the restroom, as Bryce Canyon's facilities are rather widely spread, with little natural cover beneath the canyon rim behind which to "go."

Take a Hike

You won't have to drive or board a bus to reach this morning's hiking trail. From the visitors center, walk directly across the road (to the east), following signs to the North Campground. Though the many dirt roads in this campground can seem convoluted and confusing, continue on this due-east trajectory, following visibly worn footpaths. Doing so will lead invariably to the Rim Trail and your first viewing of Bryce Amphitheater.

From here, the Rim Trail stretches north for 2.5 miles to Fairyland Point and south for 8.5 miles to Bryce Point, with numerous side trails along the way (as well as an extension, the Under the Rim Trail, at its southern point). For now, take a right and head south, following signs to Sunrise Point, about a mile away. Look to the northeast to see the Sinking Ship and Boat Mesa, two obvious landmarks standing above their surrounding landscapes. Though this viewpoint offers beautiful vistas during any time of day, the early morning light paints them particularly well, bathing the landscape in glowing, warm hues.

Look for signs for the Queen's Garden Trail, departing from the

Bryce Canyon Visitor Center stands near the park's entrance.

northern end of this viewing platform. This 0.9-mile trail descends gently down the mud and rock shoulders and slopes of Bryce Amphitheater's side, reaching what's called the Queen's Garden. From here, a 0.8-mile section of

Sunrise Point, along the Rim Trail, is the starting point for the Queen's Garden Trail.

Bryce's Shuttle Bus System

Unlike in Zion, riding the buses in Bryce Canyon National Park is not mandatory—even in summer, the peak visitor season. However, the park does provide a robust and free bus system, with shuttles running primarily between Ruby's Inn and Bryce Point. In operation between the first week of May and the first week of October, buses come as frequently as once every 10 minutes and roughly between 8 AM and 8 PM (with reduced hours beginning the second half of September). These times are approximate and do change every year. Bryce Canyon also operates buses that travel to the southernmost point of road, Rainbow Point. During most days of the bus season, two bus tours depart to this area from the Shuttle Boarding Area (just north of the park) and from the visitors center. To familiarize yourself with the exact current schedule, refer to your park-issued "Map, Shuttle, and Hiking Guide," handed out at the park's entrance.

Park your car here for cost- and hassle-free touring within the park.

Though the buses are not mandatory, they come highly recommended. Especially for those planning to do a one-way hike along the Rim Trail, buses remove the headache of retracing your route to your car. The bus system offers several stops, so you have plenty of options for deboarding. Additionally, they allow for unlimited gawking as you cruise along the park's scenic drives. If you do find yourself waiting for a bus, most stops have shady benches—even though you must only wait 10 minutes or less.

trail weaves among and through the hoodoos, spires, and fins you have just seen from above. Kids love this trail, as it penetrates through rock fins numerous times by way of man-made arches and tunnels. Along the way, the rock and mud has beautiful pastel shades of pink, ivory, orange, and yellow. The occasional bristlecone, pinyon pine, or juniper dots the landscape, providing a photogenic contrast with the soil colors.

At the southern end of the

Looking north across Bryce Amphitheater from the Rim Trail

Queen's Garden Trail, two paths head back westward and uphill to meet the rim. (Another heads east toward the eastern border of the park and does not reconnect with the park's main area.) Together, these two rim-bound trails form the Navajo Loop Trail. The slightly shorter of the two options climbs up past Thor's Hammer; the other zigzags incredibly through a narrow chasm called Wall Street. (As of the publication of this book, the Thor's Hammer section of trail was closed due to rockfall.) Both trails reach the rim in roughly 0.6 mile. Don't discount them because of their shortness; both ascend approximately 600 feet, requiring a bit of fitness, water, and blood sugar to complete. Once back at the rim, you're now at Sunset Point.

The Queen's Garden Trail leads down into Bryce Amphitheater.

High Elevation: Thin, Dry Air

Almost the entirety of Bryce Canyon's commonly visited portions sits between 7,200 and 9,115 feet. Though this height might not seem excessively lofty when compared with true high-altitude mountain ranges, you should still anticipate the thinner air affecting you, even if you stick only to easy hikes. Thin, dry air has a remarkably dehydrating effect on people, especially those hailing from sea level and more humid habitats. To best mitigate these effects, increase water consumption and simultaneously decrease caffeine and alcohol intake. Allow for extended hiking times and possibly shorter distances than you would normally expect of yourself. Also, don't forget to apply plenty of sunblock; the opportunistic sun, unmitigated by clouds and thick atmosphere, will happily toast you in no time at all.

Assuming this hike took just an hour or two to complete, it's probably closer to lunchtime than it is to bedtime.

Stop for Lunch

At Sunset Point, you're less than half a mile from the Bryce Canyon Lodge (1-877-386-4383; www.bryce canyonlodge.com). To get there, either walk north along the Rim Trail (toward Sunrise Point), taking a left after just 0.2 miles toward the lodge, or walk back toward the road and take a northward-trending trail paralleling the road and leading toward the lodge. The first option is slightly shorter. The dining room in this lodge is open for breakfast, lunch, and dinner and serves upscale, American cuisine. If you happened to skip breakfast in the interest of catching the sunrise, you can also take a full, morning meal here after your morning walk.

Take a Ride

When you finish lunch, take a post-meal, digestive stroll (or bus ride) back north to the visitors center to meet up with the afternoon Rainbow Point bus tour (departure times vary per season). Those who missed the afternoon's trip, or who simply prefer to drive, may do so. From the visitors center, head south past Sunrise and Sunset points. Do not turn left for Bryce Point; rather stay right as the road bends westward toward Rainbow Point, 13 miles from this junction.

Along the drive, the road offers pleasant and subtly changing views, as well as many pullouts from which to take photographs. At the end of the road, Rainbow Point stands higher than any other place in the park at 9,115 feet, and affords pleasant views in all directions. A very short, wheelchair-friendly trail leads to the viewing platform, from which you can see the many steps of the Grand Staircase, including the Aquarius Plateau, its uppermost tier. In this southern end of the park, you'll still see some of the Bryce Canyon rainbows, but through many more evergreen trees than in the northern section. About a mile of Bryce Canyon National Park stands to your east, followed by a sliver of Dixie National Forest. Beyond that, the vast Grand Staircase–Escalante National Monument (see chapter 4) stretches for 1.9 million acres.

Dinner

Driving back out of the park, you'll likely have enough time to hop quickly in the shower before your

Man-made tunnels and doorways ease the way through the bottom of Bryce Amphitheater.

evening meal. If your hotel is located west of the park, or if you're willing to take a slight detour in that direction, consider commuting to Bryce Canyon Pines (Mile Marker 10, Bryce Canyon City; 435-834-5330; www.brycecanyonmotel.com). The short drive will potentially reward you with lessened crowding and a likely better dining experience than you could expect at the restaurants immediately adjacent to the park's entrance. Bryce Canyon Pines serves hearty, home-style, and totally calorically indulgent meals rich in the meat and potatoes department. If you have a sweet tooth, save room for dessert; this restaurant bakes numerous treats including classic pies and other less traditional versions like banana strawberry.

Evening Out: Learn a Little

While city nightlife is completely absent in the region, Bryce Canyon's rangers do a bit to make up for it by offering a variety of evening programs. Especially in the summer, these occur after the sun sets. Consider joining a ranger-led, full-moon hike. Though these do not run every day, the park offers two or three of these events each month during the summer and fall. Early reservations are not accepted; free tickets must be obtained the morning of the hike at the visitors center. Group size is restricted to 30 people (at least six years of age), and no headlamps or flashlights are allowed. For safety, the park only grants tickets to those with lug soles (aggressive traction) on their shoes.

*If you like this . . . and you happen to be in the park during winter (November through March), ask rangers about the current winter astronomy offerings or the moonlight winter hikes. These **astronomy nights** occur each Saturday evening (with some additional holiday programs), taking advantage of the park's excellent celestial views, rendered especially visible by the cold, dry air. **Moonlight snowshoe treks** go by the light of a full moon. The park provides snowshoes and poles for this, but you must come with your own snow boots. Though the hikes are free, they're restricted in size, so you must obtain a ticket from the visitors center the morning of the hike. Locations are not announced publicly, so inquire at the center when booking your spot.*

DAY 2

Breakfast before You Go

If you liked your breakfast yesterday, it's best to just repeat that meal and move onto the finer part of the day: the outdoor portion. If you'd like to change your venue and wake up quite hungry, stop by Ruby's Inn (Day 1, above), as their culinary strength certainly is in their portion sizes. Those craving a more deluxe meal should hold out until

the Grand Staircase–Escalante portion of their trip, if possible. Together, the towns of Escalante and Boulder offer a much broader selection of cafés and restaurants than those in Bryce's vicinity.

Take a Hike

On day two, head to Bryce Point either by bus or by car, for the Peekaboo Loop (Bryce Point Parking Area/Shuttle Stop). This quite steep trail passes through accordion-like switchback sections, past smooth mud banks, through narrow flutes and fins, and by the Wall of Windows, a large fin of rock pillars connected at the top by natural rock arches. The initial trail accessing loop is just longer than 1 mile; the actual Peekaboo circuit has a length of 3 miles. Those returning to Bryce Point after hiking the loop only will cover more than 5 miles of terrain and more than 1,000 vertical feet, taking into account the rolling sections of trail.

To access the Peekaboo Loop, you'll depart from the northern end of the parking lot, heading east at first, and then looping back north and west as the trail descends into the core of Bryce Amphitheater. Hikers on taking this trail have the option to return to Bryce Point or to link up with the Navajo Loop and/or Queen's Garden trails (see the park's "Map, Shuttle & Hiking Guide" for an overview). Both of these eventually lead back up to the Rim Trail, and you can connect with these paths quite easily via a

A surprising Dr. Seuss landscape along the Queen's Garden Trail

connector trail at the northern end of the Peekaboo Loop. If you take the bus, you have the luxury of deciding your route on the fly; those driving will have to return to their car.

Lunch before You Go
As mentioned earlier in this chapter, the Bryce Region's best assets are found outside any building. If you finish your morning hike and hunger is eating through your stomach, stop in at Ruby's Inn on the way through town. Or if you're heading east and can hold out, wait to grab lunch in any of the fun and funky cafés in Escalante.

Extend Your Stay
If you have more time, try to see these things . . .

RECREATION

Scenic Driving
Bryce Canyon National Park's scenic drive extends for 17 miles from its northern end to Rainbow Point, with an additional two-mile spur extending eastward toward Bryce Point. As with all other park infrastructure, this road maintains a high position atop the plateau, roughly following a path parallel to the rim of Bryce Amphitheater. As it heads south, the road climbs rather imperceptibly, from just under 8,000 feet to 9,115 feet, ascending through subtly changing ecosystems. Rainbow Point, at the terminus of the road, is the highest place in the park. The route has 15 scenic lookouts along its path, counting the

two at the road's southern terminus and some on the spur roads. While some of these, like Ponderosa, Yovimpa, and Rainbow Point lookouts, serve to display the vast stretches of the Grand Staircase, others, like Aqua Canyon and Natural Bridge lookout, showcase peculiar or otherwise remarkable arches, towers, and hoodoos. Along the drive, be sure to read the interpretive signs; these point out key items of interest and help you to piece together an educated understanding of this area's geology and ecology. Though the road is maintained all 12 months each year, extreme winter conditions can force temporary closures.

Just north of the park's entrance, UT 12 extends westward to US 89 near Panguitch and eastward through Escalante and Boulder, up north and over the Boulder Mountain Plateau, before it terminates at UT 24 in the town of Torrey, just west of Capitol Reef National Park. This incredibly scenic route plunges from the high elevation of Bryce Canyon, down through the layers of the Grand Staircase, around sandstone domes, into valleys, and up fins as it traverses the northern girth of the Grand Staircase–Escalante National Monument before ascending Boulder Mountain. About 125 winding and rolling miles in length, this drive would be a rather serious undertaking as a short trip. But as a connector between national and state parks, as well as the towns of Escalante and Boulder, this road will be a highlight on your trip. (For more information on this route and the recreation opportunities lining its path, look in chapter 4.)

Hiking

Bryce Canyon National Park's network of interconnected paths can form many choose-your-own-adventure loops. If riding the free shuttle buses, you can get really creative with the hikes, stringing together any number of trail segments and ending at a completely different point than where you started. The best general tip for hikers is to carry a map with them on the journey. Being able to see the layout and length of these trails will greatly assist in decision making based on time, hunger, and energy levels.

One notable outlier of the network is the standalone Mossy Cave Trail, whose trailhead is located along UT 12, 4 miles east of its junction with UT 63. Located away from the scenic drive and in the northeastern portion of the park, this easy trail follows a stream as it ascends quite gradually though Water Canyon for a total of 0.5 mile. A garden of pines and Bryce-style rock spires sits on the step just above the creek bed, making for cozy scenery. At a fork in the trail, you can either opt to hike to a cave with year-round moss or to a waterfall. The waterfall is small and picturesque; the cave is more of a wet hollow in the rock than a proper tunnel. Either path is quite short, so it takes little time to see both. Any way you decide to do it, it will be a short journey, the summer heat somewhat mitigated by the waterfall.

If you like this . . . try the Bristlecone Pine Loop, inside the main portion of the park. Also a short journey, this mile-long loop passes through forests, past cliffs, and among bristlecone pines. This species of tree is thought to live longer than any other thing on earth, reaching estimated ages of greater than 5,000 years. The "young" specimens in Bryce Canyon have an approximate age of 1,600 years. Still, these were alive when the Franks were first making a home in Denmark and Rome was sacked by a Visigoth army. Along this trail you'll also catch views of the surrounding Grand Staircase, including the Pink Cliffs and the Aquarius Plateau.

Inside the main section of the park, and linked directly into its central trail network is the Under the Rim Trail. To get one of the best views of hoodoos in the park, take a hike along this trail from Bryce Point to The Hat Shop. This 2-mile, nonloop trail descends slightly more than 1,000 vertical feet through pleasant Bryce Canyon scenery to this gathering of hoodoos. More resembling ocean floor life than a collection of hats, these hoodoos consist of white capstone blocks atop thin, mudlike, orange phalanges.

The Under the Rim Trail extends quite a distance beyond the Hat Shop, stretching all the way from Bryce Point to Rainbow point and covering almost 23 trail miles along the way. Those wanting to lengthen this journey into a two- or three-day backpacking trip must first stop at the visitors center to discuss backcountry permits and camping access. Campers can choose from more than half a dozen sites along this trail, but must have a reservation to do so. As the extreme majority of visitors stick only to the roads and short hikes, anyone taking this hike in its entirety will likely enjoy a great amount of solitude, especially toward the trail's midsection. That said, hikers here should prepare themselves to be self-sufficient and safe. Carry a seemingly excessive amount of water and pack first-aid gear, including antivenom in case of an unfortunate rattlesnake encounter. Remember that cell phones do not work in the park.

From North Campground (across from the visitors center), the northernmost portion of the Rim Trail meanders for 2.5 miles to Fairyland Point. The vista at this overlook (and those along the way) is first class, with one of Bryce's richest collections of tall, exposed rock spires. Given its location slightly off the main road, it enjoys a touch less congestion than Bryce, Sunset, or Sunrise points. The 8-mile Fairyland Loop departs from Fairyland Point and descends more than 1,700 vertical feet, passing first through Fairyland Canyon and then climbing back up through Campbell Canyon (or vice versa). The trail approaches within 0.5 mile of the Sinking Ship, a tilted mesa that indeed appears to be disappearing into the drink. A short spur trail also leads from this loop up to Tower Bridge. This rock formation absolutely resembles its name, containing two natural bridges as well as the namesake turret. The loop also passes by the China Wall, recognizable as a long, very even sandstone fin. The length of this loop guarantees that you will enjoy many more views of natural points of interest than seen along the shorter hikes.

Park Tours and Educational Offerings

Bryce Canyon National Park (435-834-5322; www.nps.gov/brca) maintains a year-round calendar of lectures and ranger-led programs. During the summer, these include geology talks, rim walks, and evening astronomy events. Even though winter visits the area aggressively, programs continue, but usually on snowshoes. Check their online events calendar, under the "Things to Do" portion of their Web site for exact offerings and times during your visit.

The Bryce Canyon Natural History Association (435-834-4782; www .brycecanyon.org) serves as one of the park's major stewards, established to assist and promote science and education in Bryce Canyon. Their schedule is restricted to just a few items each year and includes events such as the Geology Festival, which takes place over a few days in July. If you are interested in learning more about the park, check online before your visit to see what's happening, or stop by the visitors center. As a way to extend their mission and raise funds, the association sells books, maps, games, posters, DVDs, and more in the bookstore there, as well as online and at other vendors.

Biking

Given the number of hikers and horses on Bryce Canyon's trails and their steepness and fragility, it shouldn't come as a surprise that mountain biking within the park is prohibited. However, road biking along the park's scenic drive is allowed. Those riding from the entrance station to Rainbow Point will climb more than 1,200 feet over 17 miles, making for an excellent, reasonably long ride with only moderate elevation gains. Add the Bryce Point spur road, and the total distance increases from 34 miles to 38. The only downside to biking within the park is that you're guaranteed to share the road with a zoo of RVs, cars, and buses. To avoid the worst of the traffic, wake up early, put on a few extra layers, and beat the crowd.

Those simply dying to mountain bike in the area will have to excuse themselves from the actual national park and head to Thunder Mountain (on UT 12 in Red Canyon, east of US 89). Though not actually in Bryce Canyon, this ride certainly offers thematically similar views and warm color schemes. This single-track trail switches back and forth across open, smooth mud slopes, among rock pillars and hoodoos, and betwixt sparse ponderosa pines and occasional shrubs. This can be taken as a primarily downhill, roughly 8-mile ride, leaving one car parked at the lower parking lot (Thunder Mountain Trailhead) to function as a shuttle vehicle. You can also do it as an out-and-back, nearly 16-mile journey, keeping in mind that the uphill portion demands a fairly high level of fitness. Or ride it as a 15-mile loop, in conjunction with the Red Canyon Trail (below). The ride does occasionally feature exposure and somewhat technical sections, so take an honest inventory of your skill and comfort level on a bike before committing to this one.

If your skills and/or fitness inventory fall short of the Thunder Mountain requirements, take it a bit easier on the 5.5-mile, paved bike trail of Red Canyon. This new, completely paved bike path roughly parallels UT 12. Wide, smooth, and built-up, it rivals even the finest of golf cart paths in Green Valley, Arizona. As the path heads eastward, it climbs approximately 1,000 feet.

When riding downhill on Thunder Mountain, keep your speed in check for the safety of yourself and the poor souls ascending this great trail. And if you do the Thunder Mountain/Red Canyon loop, watch out for families on the paved Red Canyon bike path. The lower parking area, Thunder Mountain Trailhead, is located about 3 miles east of US 89. The upper lot, Coyote Hollow, is reached by a dirt road heading south from UT 12, about 8.5 miles east of US 89. The paved Red Canyon trail parallels UT 12 between Thunder Mountain Trailhead and the turnoff for Coyote Hollow.

Bird-Watching

Bryce Canyon and its immediate vicinity provide habitat to at least 210 species throughout the course of every year. Of these, more than a dozen are extremely rare. In fact, if you happen to spot the bohemian waxwing, American pipit, or Tennessee warbler, the park requests that you provide a detailed report of your sighting. For a complete list of the birds, rare and common, visit the nature and science portion of the park's Web site (www .nps.gov/brca), where you'll find a PDF compiled by the Resource Management Division.

Horseback Riding

Unlike many other national parks, Bryce Canyon actually has a trail, fittingly called Horse Trail, designated for riding and offers two-hour or half-day trips on it or the Peekaboo Loop Trail, guided by a wrangler from Canyon Trail Rides (435-679-8665; www.canyonrides.com). Both rides depart twice daily, and each has a maximum weight of 220 pounds for the sake of the horses. The short rides have a minimum age requirement of 7; the longer rides take people ages 10 and up only. Riders of all experience levels are welcome, novice and expert. Call ahead for meeting place and reservations.

Skiing and Snowshoeing

Those lucky enough to visit Bryce Canyon during winter will find it to be a completely different place, its infrastructure much less crowded than during

Horse Trail has been appropriately named.

the warm half of the year and its natural features—poking out from a beds of snow—even more visually striking. For this reason, many Utah locals make the drive to the park for a weekend of snowshoeing or cross-country skiing. Though it is possible to hike the park during these months, you should consider snowshoes an excellent choice for walks down into the amphitheaters, as generally steep trails often bear a cover of packed snow and ice. If you want groomed skiing trails and a full Nordic skiing center, head to Ruby's Inn.

Sleigh Rides

Adding to the already compelling list of reasons to visit Bryce during winter—such as reduced crowding, beautiful snow, and lower lodging rates—are the sleigh rides offered at Ruby's Inn (26 South Main Street; 435-834-5341; www.rubysinn.com). These cozy outings last 30 minutes and depart four times daily (with the possibility to schedule other times). Group and charter rates may be arranged if you wish to enjoy a private tour. Call the inn to schedule reservations.

CAMPING

The North Campground sits across the road from the visitors center.

Bryce Canyon National Park offers two campgrounds, Sunset and North. Both share the same type of lightly forested shade cover and relatively flat terrain—with level tent and parking spots, of course. The park accepts reservations (435-834-5322) for 20 spots at Sunset Campground only. All other sites at that campground, as well as the entirety of North Campground, are assigned on a first-come, first-served basis. Both campgrounds offer RV spots; though you won't find hookups here, you can pay to dump toward the southern side of North Campground.

The park also has a handful of backcountry campsites. These are found along some of the park's longer hiking trails, such as Under the Rim Trail. The park service requires permits and fees of anyone planning to sleep out in the wild, so stop by the visitors center to discuss backpacking, permits, and available sites.

Just north of the entrance, Ruby's Inn (26 South Main Street; 435-834-5341; www.rubysinn.com) devotes a large chunk of its property to providing tent and RV spaces. All told, it has 240 sites, all with access to restrooms, showers, a pool, and drinking water. The inn also has the closest restaurant to the park (not including the Bryce Canyon Lodge, inside the park).

Bryce Canyon Pines (Mile Marker 10 on UT 12; 435-834-5330; www.brycecanyonmotel.com), just 6 miles northwest of the park, has both RV and tent spots. Campers all share access to restrooms and showers. This is also the site of a hotel, as well as one of the better restaurants in the immediate vicinity.

KOA, the familiar national brand (215 North Red Rocks Drive; 435-679-8988; www.koa.com/campgrounds/cannonville), operates a tent and RV campground in Cannonville. It has a pool, electrical hookups, a camping kitchen, and pavilion. There they sell firewood, munchies at a snack bar, and propane. They also offer bike rentals.

To the east, the Grand Staircase–Escalante National Monument (www.ut.blm.gov/monument) has nearly 2 million acres available for wild camping. However, this spacious area also falls under special government protection, and unlike in most other BLM lands across the nation, anyone camping here must first stop at any of the four monument visitors centers to obtain a permit. Be aware that visitors center hours are quite restricted (closing as early as 4 PM, even during peak season), so plan ahead to ensure yourself a legal night's sleep. Though the nearest center to Bryce is found in Cannonville, you can find another in Escalante just to the east, as well as in Kanab and Big Water, on the monument's southern side. All towns are small enough that the visitors centers are easily spotted. (See chapter 4 for more information on the Grand Staircase–Escalante National Monument.)

3

Capitol Reef National Park

PARK OVERVIEW

Capitol Reef National Park centers around the Waterpocket Fold, a 100-mile-long stretch of incredible uplifting and folding in the earth's crust. Because of its distinct complexity and beauty, this geologic feature has borne many names given to it by the people encountering it. With its vibrant hues of red, brown, yellow, and orange, this area was called Land of the Sleeping Rainbow by the Navajo. The name *Waterpocket Fold* comes from the area's many natural water-catching tanks that have been carved into the sandstone by erosive winds. Forming a nearly impenetrable barrier to east–west travel, early traders and settlers considered it to be a "reef" on land, hence the name Capitol Reef National Park.

Caused by major tectonic activities beginning roughly 60 million years ago, the Waterpocket Fold is a monocline; that is, a steeply folded section of crust in an area otherwise dominated by flat strata. Since its uplift, the fold has undergone vast amounts of erosion. And though this has robbed it of much of its vertical relief, it has also exposed 270 million years' worth of colorful geologic history. Not to be underestimated, this fold still towers above the nearby landscape today as a gnarled and raw bulge in the earth. Cliffs and mesas soar high above the surrounding landscape, while deep gorges slice into the bellies of vast and steep domes.

As a national park, this is not nearly as popular as some of Utah's higher profile parks, receiving only 750,000 visitors annually, compared with Zion's 2.7 million. However, this desolate and stunning phenomenon certainly is one of the most beautiful places on the planet. In addition to its extreme

LEFT: The sun gets ready to set on the west-facing cliffs of the Waterpocket Fold.

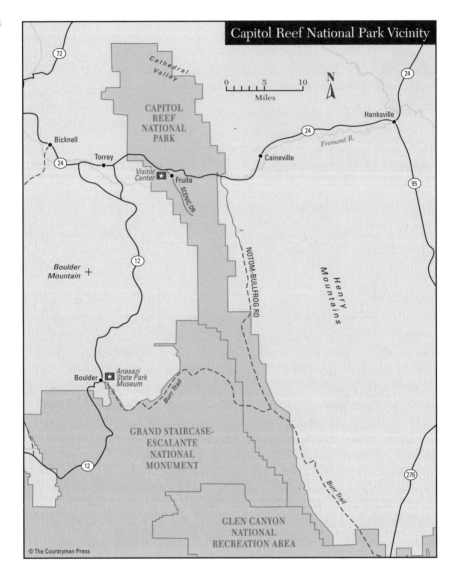

natural splendor, the park also showcases pictographs, ruins, and artifacts left behind by the Fremont Indians, as well as an early 1900s Mormon village with orchards called Fruita.

Capitol Reef National Park (435-425-4111; www.nps.gov/care) itself is a very long and thin sliver of land, primarily centered around the spectacular Waterpocket Fold. The park service maintains a 16-mile road called Scenic Drive, which extends south from UT 24 and runs parallel to, and in the middle of, the fold. In the park's central portion, you'll find the visitors cen-

The Capitol Reef glows at dusk.

ter, several hikes departing from Scenic Drive, and the historic town of Fruita. Founded by Mormon families in the early 20th century, this historic and picturesque village has been preserved, with its remaining structures standing scattered among idyllic cottonwood trees and its historic fruit orchards still producing fruit. Today, these former homes and farming buildings and a schoolhouse can be found clustered around the junction of UT 24 and Scenic Drive. A few of these buildings house the living history of these early pioneers, with staff crafting pies, preserves, and other edibles made from the fruit trees of the old orchards.

And while the park service collects a fee from those touring the scenic drive, there is no cost to travel along UT 24; if you feel like driving quickly through this incredible area, you may cross through the park on this state highway at no charge. UT 24 cuts a roughly 15-mile path through the park's northern lobe; from the high plateau of Torrey, it plunges down into the park, sweeping past many of the Capitol Reef's more spectacular features, like Chimney Rock and Castle Rock, Fruita village, a petroglyph panel, and Behunin Cabin.

The northernmost and least-visited portion of the park, Cathedral Valley, is accessed exclusively by dirt roads departing from various points along UT 24. Many of these roads can only be traveled by vehicles with four-wheel drive and/or high clearance, which heavily filters the number of visitors to that area. Those determined and able to reach Cathedral Valley will find themselves in a flat, grassy valley out of which orange Entrada sandstone pillars protrude, capped by ivory-colored Curtis sandstone—an area not dissimilar to Kodachrome Basin State Park, only larger.

A scenic and historic road called the Burr Trail crosses through the southern tip of Capitol Reef as it makes its way from Boulder to UT 276, near Lake Powell (see "Scenic Drives" in the "Extend Your Stay" section of this chapter, below). This vaguely developed and irregularly maintained road contains a mixture of dirt and pavement and is not advised for vehicles pulling trailers. This road connects with the Notom-Bullfrog Road, which

Around 1900, more than 20 students attended the Fruita Schoolhouse.

heads north through a portion of the park and up toward the town of Notom (just south of UT 24). Each of these byways consists primarily of dirt and should be considered backcountry journeys; if attempting any of them, prepare your vehicle with a spare tire and a preemptive tune-up.

Pick Your Spot
Where to stay and what you'll find nearby . . .

TORREY AND TEASDALE

Located west of Capitol Reef National Park and north of Boulder Mountain, Torrey and Teasdale are both small and relatively undeveloped towns surrounded on all sides by natural beauty. South of them, Boulder Mountain rises to an elevation of 11,313 feet at its tallest point, Bluebell Knoll. Roughly 80 small alpine lakes cover this broad and massive plateau. To the north, Fishlake National Forest covers 1.5 million acres of central Utah, including the high alpine terrain of the Colorado Plateau and Basin and Range. This area provides habitat to aspen groves and evergreen trees, deer, black bears, elk, moose, and wild turkeys and is also the location of Utah's largest mountain lake, Fish Lake. And of course, Capitol Reef National Park sits just 5 miles east of Torrey. Despite their rich milieu, these towns, founded in the 1880s, have maintained an authentic essence and a combined

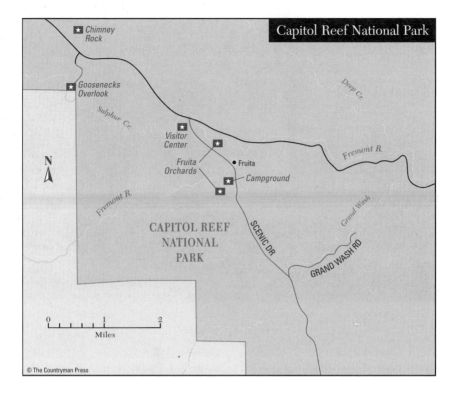

population of just a few hundred people.

The Red River Ranch (2000 West UT 24, Teasdale; 1-800-205-6343; www.redriverranch.com) provides the area's finest lodging. This Western-style luxury cabin has just 15 unique rooms outfitted with fine bedding, antique furniture, a private patio (or balcony), and in-room music. The lodge itself is situated on 2,000 acres and is also the site of the Cliffstone Restaurant, which serves breakfast, lunch, and dinner daily. Those wishing to purchase a sack lunch to take into the park may put in a request at the restaurant the evening before and pick it up the following morning. Though you don't have to be a guest to dine here, you should place a reservation to enjoy an evening meal. Cliffstone serves contemporary Western American cuisine, which includes fresh fish, buffalo, various grilled entrées, and vegetarian dishes. Those who want to explore the ranch grounds may request a horseback-riding tour, or fish along its five private river miles. You may even arrange for hunting trips on the property. These outings are offered year-round, and the ranch has all the necessities for hunting pheasant, chukar partridge, and big game.

Torrey, Utah, has a tree-lined main street.

In town, Austin's Chuckwagon Motel (12 West Main Street, Torrey; 435-425-3335; www.austin schuckwagonmotel.com) offers guest rooms and small rental cabins. Most rooms are of a quite normal size and offer very simple amenities; however, you have the option of booking a large suite. Cabins typically accommodate up to six people and contain a living room and small kitchen. Locally owned, this motel has a basic, albeit tidy and well-kept feel and provides lodging for affordable rates. AAA-approved, this establishment also offers a pool and hot tub, free wireless Internet, and cable television with HBO. Here you'll also find a sandwich deli, bakery, and general store proffering groceries, sporting goods, ice, and other essentials like batteries and film.

The Red Sands Hotel (670 East UT 24, Torrey; 435-425-3688; www.redsandshotel.com) provides another basic lodging option right in Torrey. Offering a pool, hot tub, Wi-Fi, cable television, and a variety of guest room sizes, this hotel has décor that is a slight notch up from other Torrey hotels. Red Sands guests enjoy free breakfasts that include waffles, fruit, toast, boiled eggs, and more.

CAINEVILLE

Just 10 miles beyond Capitol Reef's eastern border lies the town of Caineville, on UT 24. This tiny village, located near the confluence of the Fremont River and Sandy Creek, sits more than 2,000 feet beneath the town of Torrey. Eighteen miles farther east is the slightly larger town of Hanksville; to the southeast, the massive Henry Mountains tower over the landscape.

If you find yourself sleeping here for the evening, check into the Rodeway Inn (25 East UT 24; 435-456-9900; www.cainevilleinn.com). Much like the other national-brand hotels of desert Utah, this modest, yet modern lodging option provides Internet, a pool, and a continental breakfast every morning. A very typical roadside hotel, it fits nearly any budget while providing a clean place to rest your head.

BICKNELL

Just 8 miles west of Torrey stands Bicknell. With a population of just over 350, this is nearly double the size of Torrey. Though not a

metropolis by any means, this town does contain a few additional lodging and dining options. The Sunglow Motel (91 East Main Street; 435-425-3821; www.aquariusinn.com) is a locally owned, modern hotel with a desert color scheme, wireless Internet, exercise room, and family-style restaurant serving standard American and Southwestern cuisine. Inn guests are privy to free coffee in the restaurant when they wake up. Rates are quite low—sometimes less than $50.

Or you can check out the Aquarius Inn (292 West Main Street; 435-425-3835; www.sunglowmotel.com), another lodging-and-dining combination in the area. This motel offers very basic small-town-style rooms in a variety of sizes, from standard hotel, up through large family, and suites with kitchenettes.

Local Flavors
Taste of the town—local cafés, restaurants, bars, bistros, etc.

TORREY AND TEASEDALE

For genuine gastronomical pleasure, swing by the Cafe Diablo (599 West Main Street, Torrey; 435-425-3070; www.cafediablo.net), one of the area's most high-profile joints, recognized in publications like *1,000 Places to See before You Die* and more. Focusing on Southwestern cuisine, this kitchen runs under the leadership of certified executive

chef Gary Pankow. Though indoor seating exists, the outdoor seating predominates, exposing diners to views of red cliffs in the distance and much nearer wildflower beds. Entrées on the menu include crown rack of glazed ribs, pecan chicken, and fire-roasted pork tenderloin. Additionally, a few delicious fish and vegetarian options are available to excite vegetarians and those adverse to red meat. A large selection of beers and tequilas complement the cookery. If you dine out only once in the area, make reservations for this restaurant.

48 Hours

Capitol Reef National Park contains 242,000 acres of wild and rugged lands. Called a reef because of its hindrance to travelers, it has historically presented a major obstacle to all forms of overland journeys. Even today, its lands are crossed by only a few modernized motorways: UT 24, the 16-mile Scenic Drive, and the partially paved Burr Trail and Notom-Bullfrog roads. Thus, trips to the park can either be brief and contain a simple out-and-back car tour, or they can be lengthy and include long days of hiking the park's numerous trails and exploring it backcountry roads in vehicles suited for their ruggedness.

GETTING THERE

Everyone coming to the park's main section will arrive via UT 24. If coming from the west (as from Boulder Mountain and the Grand Staircase–Escalante National Monument), try to arrive at the park near sunset. The low-angle light cast upon the park's west-facing sandstone walls paints the landscape in utterly fantastic and memorable hues of red, yellows, purples, and oranges.

An easily reached, first-arrival destination is Sunset Point. From this overlook, look to the east and watch the rocks as they glow in the late afternoon light. Though the park has stunning, wild beauty dur-

ing any time of day, these natural features are greatly enhanced by the richness of low-angle sunlight. As this lookout stands some miles back from the major cliffs of the Waterpocket Fold, it affords a sweeping view of its entire relief, including more than 20 varieties of rock. From the top down, the layers include ivory domes, sheer and deep-red cliff bands, talus piles, and rust-colored Moenkopi sandstone. To get there, head south from UT 24 on Panorama Point Road, about 1 mile east of the park's western border. This overlook requires about five minutes' walking to reach.

Sulphur Creek continues deepening its canyon 800 feet beneath the Goosenecks Overlook.

If you like this . . . but don't have the energy or time for the walk, consider instead viewing the area from Panorama Point, which is accessed by the same road but requires less than a minute's walk to reach. Here, you can also check out the Goosenecks of **Sulphur Creek** *from a lofty, though mostly fence-enclosed viewing station. Beneath your feet, this unimposing creek has been slowly meandering for millions of years. Holding its snaking path as the Waterpocket Fold was thrust upward, the creek has eaten its way through several hundred feet of rock.*

If you have the desire to grab a bite in town, Red River Ranch's Cliffstone Restaurant (see Red River Ranch, in "Pick Your Spot," Torrey and Teasdale, above). Though you may already be staying at the ranch, you'll need reservations to dine here. Though the ranch may look like an oversized cabin at first glance, it provides some of the finer dining and most luxurious lodging in the area. The menu offers a range of contemporary Western American cuisine, ranging from less spendy (but still delicious) items like buffalo burgers to more pricey and intricate entrées like potato-crusted trout and buffalo tenderloin. Situated on 2,000 private acres, the establishment provides a truly relaxing resort-style experience—even to those just dining there for a few hours.

DAY 1

Breakfast before You Go

Castle Rock Coffee and Candy (junction of UT 12 and 24; 435-425-2100; www.castlerockcoffee .com), in Torrey, combines a café, breakfast bar, bakery, and dessert shop into one. Here, you can purchase anything from breakfast sandwiches made with farm eggs to espresso drinks, fudge, and croissants. This presents an opportunity to enjoy a light-and-fast artisan bite before a day in the park. Make sure to pick up some goodies to go, as they won't taste finer than during or after a hike. Castle Rock also provides wireless Internet.

Enter the Park

Marked by a classic National Park Service sign, Capitol Reef's western boundary lies just a few miles east of Torrey. However, you won't see a visitors center (or any kind of fee station) until after you turn off UT 24. If you need a restroom, keep an eye out for pit toilets, found at some of the trailheads along the highway. For the first day, try to bring a sack lunch; there are no proper restaurants inside the park. However, you can stop by the Gifford Homestead (on Scenic Drive) during peak season and purchase a homemade pie, crafted from fruit grown in the Fruita orchards.

Take a Hike

Open your first day with a somewhat casual but scenic stroll up to Chimney Rock (trailhead located on UT 24, west of Scenic Drive). This dominant red spire, once part of the greater mesa behind it, now stands alone. The hike ascends about 300 vertical feet through a broad and open basin, before reaching a loop trail, just south of this pillar. The entire outing, including the loop, requires just less than 3.5 miles of hiking and a little more than an hour for experienced hikers. From here, it is possible to vastly extend the trek into a 10-mile (or more) hike, by heading farther north and east through Chimney Rock Canyon. To do this, you'll need to carry a detailed map and drop off a shuttle vehicle ahead of time.

*If you like this . . . and are arriving from the eastern side of the park, consider a stroll to the **Hickman Bridge** (trailhead located 1.9 miles east of Scenic Drive on UT 24). Just 2 miles of round-trip hiking lead from the parking area, up to this natural bridge, and back. The trail ascends through varied landscapes, first rolling along the Freemont River, then ascending a switchback section, dropping down into a wash, and finally climbing back up and into quite open and exposed country. On the way, it passes a Freemont Indian pit house and granary, as well as the smaller Nels Johnson Natural Bridge. It eventually reaches a loop at the base of the Hickman Bridge. This 300-foot-wide arch, solid and pale, can provide an excellent spot to pause and nibble on some pastries*

The trailhead for Chimney Rock

purchased at Castle Rock Coffee and Candy earlier in the morning.

Learn a Little

Once you've completed your morning's hike, head toward the Capitol Reef National Park Visitor Center (Junction of UT 24 and Scenic Drive; 435-425-4111). Immediately upon arrival, you'll notice that Capitol Reef has a much lower-key feel than Utah's busier parks like Zion. This small center features several display cases illustrating the area's geology and human history through images and artifacts. Its centerpiece is a massive, three-dimensional relief map of the Waterpocket Fold. Showing in great detail the area's natural features, this map helps you comprehend the complex landscape and all the features within its context. Pick up a park brochure and hiking guide here; in addition to providing trail maps and information on local flora and fauna, the center also gives current open times and activities for Fruita orchards and the Gifford Homestead. Talk with a ranger if you're interested in picking fruit, have any questions about the weather, or require a permit for backcountry camping.

Stop for Lunch

Heading south from the visitors center along Scenic Drive, you'll notice pullouts for shady picnic areas. Pull over and pluck your lunch out of the cooler. You can enjoy your food in the shade some of the roughly 2,500 fruit trees planted by the Mormons of Fruita around the beginning of the 20th century. Try to save some room in your belly, because if you arrive during fruit-harvesting season, you'll want to swing by the Gifford Homestead (1 mile south of the visitors center on Scenic Drive) and pick up a home-baked pie and some handmade ice cream for dessert. You can also purchase period household goods, crafts, and kitchen implements here, as well as preserves, dried fruit, and other snacks. Take your time here; up next is a tour of the park's Scenic Drive, and you'd be most pleased to experience some of this route near sunset, when the cliffs colorfully radiate in the evening light.

The Capitol Reef National Park Visitor Center has a dated, laid-back feel.

Fruita and the Gifford Homestead

Founded in 1880 under the name *Junction,* this historic village stands at the confluence of Sulphur Creek and the Freemont River. Given its reasonably warm climate and abundant water supply, its early Latter-day Saints homesteaders were able to grow quite a variety of crops, including sorghum, alfalfa, and numerous vegetables, in addition to their fruit-bearing apple, orange, and cherry trees. By 1896, the settlers erected a one-room school-house. Twenty-four years after its founding, the town's name changed to reflect its vast orchards and eliminate confusion with many other villages sharing the name *Junction.*

The interior of the schoolhouse has been preserved by the National Park Service.

In 1908, the Calvin Pendleton family built the Gifford Home, along with a barn and a smokehouse. Containing just two bedrooms and one front room, the small house provided quite narrow quarters for this polygamist family, and they remained in it for just eight years. The Jorgenson family lived there next, but sold it after just 12 years to the namesake Gifford family, who lived there from 1928 to 1969. It was this family that greatly expanded the home, adding a carport, utility room, kitchen, and bathroom to it.

By the early 1930s, people from around Utah and the nation had heard rumors of the area's beauty and begun traveling along a narrow access road to visit. In 1937, Capitol Reef National Monument was created, and the local industry shifted to cater to the ever-growing flock of tourists. Though visited by many between 1937 and 1971, when the monument became a national park (and the government purchased the entire town), Fruita never grew to be the kitschy tourist trap that it could have become.

Today, Capitol Reef maintains a uniquely isolated flavor, different from that of any other national park in Utah. Its history and quiet beauty remain seemingly untouched and unaltered, and the hand of preservation—though effective—has worked rather invisibly to keep the area pristine.

Take a Drive

After lunch, the heat of the day will be setting into Capitol Reef. And if you're visiting the park during summer, as most people do, this means you would be wise to avoid hiking during the early afternoon hours. Not to worry; afternoon can be a perfect time to tour Scenic Drive. This route begins at the visitors center near UT 24, passes the Guifford Home, and runs down the center of the Waterpocket Fold for 16 miles. Those who wish to do so may purchase a self-guided driving tour brochure for $2 at the visitors center. (You may also print it out at home for no cost by visiting the "Plan Your Visit" section of the park's Web site, www.nps.gov/care.) This pamphlet points out the changing rock types and other points of interest that might otherwise go unnoticed, in the format of an 11-stop journey.

After leaving the visitors center and heading south for a mile, you'll come across a self-serve pay station. If you don't already have an Interagency Annual Pass, stop by and feed the tube. If you do have this pass, be prepared to show it to rangers who occasionally perform random checks. However, you do not need to display it on your dashboard if parking. Speed limits can be quite slow, so be sure to allow at least two hours to complete the round-trip 32-mile distance. Expect to be stuck behind the inevitable RV, which will crawl slowly over this rolling narrow ribbon of pavement.

The many layers of the Waterpocket Fold are visible from the Scenic Drive.

Though a handful of signs and pullouts point out and interpret various geological features along the way, the first major turnout is that of the Grand Wash Road. This dirt lane winds down the mouth of an ever-narrowing gorge. Where the road ends in a parking lot, the Grand Wash Trail (see "Take a Hike," in Day 2, below) begins and leads into the famous and fittingly named Narrows Section. After just a few miles of walking, the wash pinches down to a girth of just 15 feet and a sheer-walled height of greater than 700 feet. This same parking area serves as the starting point for the Cassidy Arch Trail (see "If you like this . . ." in Day 2, below). This arch, visible to the north of the road, stands more than 1,000 feet above ground level. Butch Cassidy, famed outlaw and partner of the Sundance Kid, reportedly used this area frequently as a hideout.

Traveling farther south along Scenic Drive, you'll notice the landscape first rising and then descending. The crest, called Sliprock Divide, casts water either to its north and into the Grand Wash, or to its south and into the Capitol Gorge. Here, you can see parallel curving lines in rock that was originally ancient sand dunes. Just before the next junction, the road begins snaking abruptly. Turning left at this intersection leads east into Capitol Gorge. This chasm, running roughly parallel to Grand Gorge, actually held the main through highway of Capitol Reef National Park for decades. However, regular flash flooding and washouts rendered this road too tedious to maintain. This old road, originally constructed by the Mormons, was replaced by today's UT in 1962. If you head into the Navajo sandstone confines of Capitol Gorge, you will be able to spot a collection of defaced petroglyphs, carved by the Fremont Indians who occupied the area until around 1300 A.D. Turning right leads to the less-visited Pleasant Creek area.

Dinner

To catch a proper evening meal, you must again leave the park. Located right on UT 24 in Torrey is the Rim Rock Inn (2523 East UT 24; 435-425-3398; www.therimrock.net). A hotel-restaurant combination, it offers fine dining in its main restaurant and more casual dinners at the Rim Rock Patio. The restaurant menu features the best of contemporary American and Western cuisine, using locally grown vegetables, regional meats and fish, and a grill when relevant. Reservations for a table in this two-fireplace main dining room are suggested but not mandatory. The Patio provides meals from a separate, self-described "spaghetti western" menu, which blends Italian and Western cuisine. This equates to barbecued items, pizza, pasta, salads, and more. The atmosphere on the Patio side is much more casual, replacing the fireplaces with a flat-screen TV.

Evening Out

Whether or not you had dinner at the Rim Rock Patio (see "Dinner," above), consider spending an evening here to catch live music on the weekend. If you happen to miss Friday or Saturday night, this still provides a viable place to unwind and catch a game on the television.

DAY 2

Breakfast before You Go

Austin's Chuckwagon Motel (12 West Main Street; 435-425-3335; www.austinschuckwagonmotel.com) in Torrey makes for a perfect prepark pit stop. The motel operates a deli and bakery, in addition to its grocery store, gas station, and motel. On the bakery side, you can pick up a number of items throughout the day, such as doughnuts, cinnamon rolls, Danishes, other pastries, cakes, pies, and several varieties of fresh bread. Handy for those planning to spend most of the day hiking in the park, this deli prepares made-to-order sandwiches from a large selection of cheeses, breads, meats, and vegetables. Salads and other sides are available, as well. A perfect all-in-one stop, Austin's provides you with a light and tasty breakfast, snacks for the trail, and gas for the car. A small grocery store can also fill in the gaps if you require any goods not offered at the deli or bakery.

Take a Hike

A classic and totally manageable hike for the second day is the Grand Wash to the Narrows (trailhead at the end of Grand Wash Road; approximately 3 miles south of the visitors center on Scenic Drive). Park where the road ends in a spacious lot; simply continue downstream into the wash, following the almost-always dry riverbed as it gradually descends to the east. Though the trail begins as a separate entity than the streambed, it very soon interlocks with it for the remainder of the hike. The farther you go, the more the wash pinches down on itself, eventually reaching a section called the Narrows, where the canyon walls are more than 700 feet tall and the distance between them is no wider than 15 feet. Keep your eye out for bighorn sheep, as they reside high on these complex, rounded cliff walls and domed slabs. Though the hike is

The Grand Wash can be hiked during any dry time of year, when flash floods do not threaten.

only 2 miles each way and has only 50 feet of elevation loss, you should allow plenty of time; walking on river cobbles is time consuming and unpleasant when rushed. Be very careful to avoid this hike in the event of significant rain; as one of the few water channels penetrating the Waterpocket Fold, the Grand Wash is no stranger to flash flooding.

If you like this . . . area, but want to gain a bit more elevation, take a hike instead to the **Cassidy Arch** *(trailhead at the end of the Grand Wash Road). This hike begins by descending into the Grand Wash along the Grand Wash Trail, but quickly cuts back west and uphill. This trail is just a bit shorter than that for the Grand Wash, but at only 1.75 miles in length, gains nearly 1,200 feet of elevation. This sometimes exposed trail terminates at Cassidy Arch, named after famous outlaw Butch Cassidy, who roamed the Wild West around the year 1900. If you don't have the energy or time to make this hike, look for the arch high on the hillside to your north as you drive Grand Wash Road.*

Lunch before You Go

After this hike, you can head back to Torrey and grab a bite at any of the restaurants there (as listed earlier in this chapter). Don't expect to find anything in Caineville; if you're heading east, your best bet is to drive straight to Hanksville.

Extend Your Stay
If you have more time, try to see these things . . .

RECREATION

Scenic Driving

Nearby UT 12 heads south from Torrey and rapidly ascends the lofty shoulders of Boulder Mountain, the tall plateau dominating the landscape southwest of Capitol Reef National Park. Standing between the Waterpocket Fold and Grand Staircase–Escalante National Monument, Boulder Mountain is less talked about, but nevertheless a worthy destination. Even if you simply must cross over the mountain to reach the monument, you will have a hard time resisting the scenic pullouts. These signed, broad parking areas overlook the great and complex landscape below. From these perches, you can see straight over the aspen trees and down to various cliff bands, mountain ranges, plateaus, and other features that the illustrated signs identify for you. Particularly in summer, when the rest of the region endures sometimes sweltering daytime highs, Boulder Mountain—which tops out at 11,313 feet above sea level—offers a cool escape. Though you won't see them from the road, this plateau has roughly 80 lakes that provide opportunities for fishing, as well as pleasant camping venues and backpacking destinations.

Slicing through the southern tip of Capitol Reef National Park, a road called the Burr Trail spans approximately 70 miles, stretching from the town of Boulder, through Capitol Reef, and eastward to UT 276, near the northern end of Lake Powell. Namesake John Atlantic Burr, who was born on a ship crossing the Atlantic Ocean, grew up in Salt Lake City during the second half of the 1800s. He moved south to the area in 1876 and began ranching cattle. Requiring a route to bring his herd between low- and high-elevation pastures with the changing seasons, he constructed a trail to navigate the otherwise impassable Waterpocket Fold. This most famous section of the Burr Trail road today is called Muley Twist Canyon, said to be so folded it could twist a mule. Because this portion of Burr Trail is incredibly steep and winding, this road is not recommended for trailers and large vehicles. In addition to this wild stretch of road, the Burr Trail crosses some of Utah's more wild and remote lands, with views of the Circle Cliffs, Waterpocket Fold, and Henry Mountains. This backcountry road has a surface alternating between pavement and dirt and should likely be avoided in winter. The town of Boulder (detailed in chapter 4), on the western end of this route, has various lodging and dining options; the eastern terminus of the route leaves you in quite a remote area. The nearest large town is Hanksville, to the north via UT 276 and 95. However, if you have decent clearance and/or four-wheel drive, consider camping up in the utterly remote Henry Mountains.

Hiking

Like Grand Wash, the Capitol Gorge Trail (located at the end of Scenic Drive) ventures into one of the few waterways that actually penetrates the

Pictographs located south of Escalante, along the Smokey Mountain Road

Waterpocket Fold. This hike takes you past pictographs, alongside historic pioneer engravings dating back to 1871, by some of the park's namesake waterpockets or tanks, for a total of 1 mile eastward. Until 1962, this gorge actually contained the only highway to cross through the park; since its replacement by UT 24, this route has been retired as a throughway. The route's exposure to traffic is likely the reason the petroglyphs alongside the trail have been vandalized. The gorge bears the heavy responsibility for draining the area during rainstorms—and so it is quite susceptible to flash flooding. Keep this in mind, in case you visit the park during a rare rainstorm.

Park Tours and Other Educational Offerings

The Fruita orchards (centered around the junction of UT 24 and Scenic Drive) date back to the 1880s, when this area was settled by Mormons. Though no more than 40 people lived in the town at any given time, this group planted a total of roughly 2,700 trees. Bearing mostly apples, pears, cherries, peaches, and apricots—as well as a few mulberries, plums, almonds, and walnuts—the trees can still be harvested today by park visitors. Check the harvest dates and rules (listed online under the "History and Culture" section of www.nps.gov/care). Generally speaking, you may walk into any open, unlocked orchard and pick as much fruit as you desire. Simply give the appropriate amount of money for it on the way out at the self-pay stations. If you don't have the time, consider picking up dried fruit, preserves, or pies at the Gifford Homestead.

Rock Climbing

Looking around the park, it's not surprising that the area contains more than a few rock-climbing routes. However, climbing does not have nearly the presence in Capitol Reef as it does in Zion National Park, as the placement of new bolts (and therefore bolted anchors) is prohibited. Permits for day climbs are not required, but anyone planning to bivouac at the base of a climb and sleep on the wall must obtain a backcountry permit at the visitors center. For more information on the routes here, pick up a copy of Stewart Green's *Rock Climbing Utah* or Eric Bjornstad's *Desert Rock*, sometimes available for purchase at the visitors center. The best seasons to climb here are during spring and fall. All routes are sandstone, which are traditionally protected; however, the park also has some bouldering. In the interest of preserving the rock's aesthetics, the park service requires all climbers to use colored chalk that camouflages with rock color.

Biking

While cycling is allowed in the park, bikes—much like pets—must be kept on existing roads at all times. Because of regular vehicle traffic on Scenic Drive and UT 24, not too many cyclists ride in the park. Though the speed limit remains fairly slow for the entire length of Scenic Drive, the road is quite narrow and provides no real shoulder for safe riding. However, if you happen to have your mountain or cross bike and are spending some time in the southern or eastern portion of the park, you can spend quite a lot of time bicycling along the Notom-Bullfrog or Burr Trail road. The northern portion of the park, Cathedral Valley, also receives very little human and vehicular traffic, rendering its dirt roads quite pleasant for cycling.

The park service maintains a 71-site mixed tent and RV campground among the shady trees of the Fruita orchards. Located just off the western side of Scenic Drive, this spot offers easy access to the visitors center and Gifford Homestead. Much less expensive than other park service campgrounds, these sites cost just $10 per night. Though there are no individual hookups for RVs, the ground does have a dump site. This is the only developed camping within the park, and though it commonly fills to capacity during peak season, the campground does not accept reservations.

Capitol Reef National Park also contains a large number of primitive campgrounds and backcountry sites, proportionate to its large expanses of wildlands. The park's two primitive campgrounds go by the names of Cathedral Valley and Cedar Mesa. Cathedral Valley Campground stands north of the park's main section, in the region of the park of the same name, on the Cathedral Valley Loop Road. This small camping area has six sites and a pit toilet and an elevation of roughly 7,000 feet. Cedar Mesa Campground sits toward the eastern border of the park's central section, roughly 35 miles south of UT 24, on the Notom-Bullfrog Road. This has an elevation of 5,500 feet, and makes for a great overnight spot. No fee is required to stay at either area, and no reservations are accepted.

Boulder Mountain, to the south of Torrey, is a massive plateau reaching a height well above 11,000 feet and is largely managed by the Dixie National Forest. UT 12 cuts a winding path up the eastern flank of this high-elevation area, providing access to developed (i.e., "pay") campgrounds and other backcountry roads along the way. After the deep snowpack melts out, this beautiful area provides excellent summer camping, given that its temperatures are much cooler than those of lower elevations. Additionally, the mountain contains roughly 80 lakes, so is an excellent area for fishing.

Some of the state's most scenic, free, and unregulated camping can be found directly outside the park on Bureau of Land Management property, approximately 2 miles west of the park boundary, on UT 24. As you leave the park (or approach it), keep your eye out for an unmarked dirt turnout heading directly to a number of visibly obvious campsites north of the road. Here, roughly 20 tent spots are separated perfectly by occasional shrubbery, rock domes, and hillocks. Located on the cusp of the Waterpocket Fold, this campground affords both fantastic views to the east and into the increasingly complex topography of the lands in Capitol Reef, as well as west and toward Torrey. If you need a restroom, you must simply drive a few minutes eastward into the park, where free pit toilets exist by the trail-head for Chimney Rock. As always, when wild camping, be sure to occupy already established sites and clean up after yourself.

4

Grand Staircase–Escalante National Monument

MONUMENT OVERVIEW

The Grand Staircase–Escalante National Monument is a vast and complicated landscape in south central Utah governed by the Bureau of Land Management. The monument, with 8,000 feet of vertical relief, contains every imaginable variety of desert: sweeping planes, sandstone slot canyons, high plateaus, and sheer cliff bands. Nearly three times the size of Rhode Island, it contains a wealth of cultural, historical, recreational, and scenic offerings. From paleontologists to photographers, backpackers to RVers, everyone can find their own private niche in this landscape.

The Grand Staircase portion of the name comes from its location on what's known as just that—a massive, geological stairway, descending in Utah from the Paunsaugunt Plateau in its northern portion, with elevations higher than 11,000 feet, down to the Colorado River in the Grand Canyon, roughly 3,000 feet above sea level, to the south. Between these two points, natural erosive forces have cut into this massive uplift, exposing southern Utah's gems, from the upper showpieces of Bryce Canyon and Cedar Breaks, down past the Pink, Grey, and White cliffs, Kolob and Zion canyons, the Kaiparowits Plateau, and a number of other major cliff bands and mountains. The monument itself sits roughly between scenic UT 12 on its northern side, Lake Powell to its east and south, US 89 to the south, and Capitol Reef National Park to its west. Along UT 12, the towns of Boulder and Escalante service the many visitors to the area; its southern visitors are serviced mainly by the towns of Kanab and Big Water.

LEFT: The Devil's Garden, located along Hole-in-the-Rock Road, is a colorful maze of spires.

143

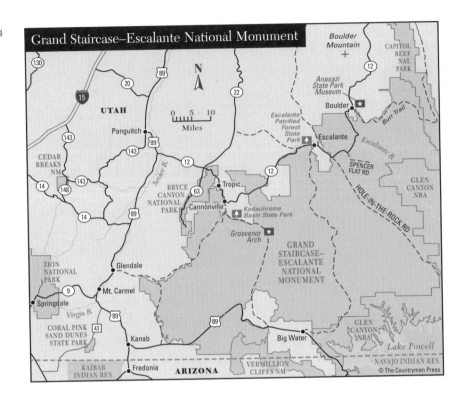

Grand Staircase–Escalante National Monument

UT 12 winds through fantastic country between Escalante and Boulder.

The Escalante segment of the name honors early Franciscian priest and explorer Silvestre Vélez de Escalante. Seeking a viable land route between their missionary in Santa Fe, New Mexico, and Monterrey, California, Escalante and his partner, Francisco Atanasio Domínguez, are believed to have been the first white men to arrive in the area in 1776. To this day, the vast majority of this landscape has undergone little or no change in those subsequent 235 years; only two paved roads venture into the monument: one on its northern perimeter and one on its southern.

Established as a national mon-

The majority of the monument's 1.9-million acres have hardly been altered by people.

ument in 1996, this 1.9-million-acre protected area has a unique blend of essences. Vast and largely untamed, it seems, on the one hand, like an unregulated, unpopulated, high-desert playground on a planet all its own. Yet with its numerous—though hugely spread-out—attractions, its four monument-specific visitors centers, and its own fleet of rangers, it also comes off somewhat like a national park. Though much of the scenery within the park competes strongly with that found in Arches, Canyonlands, or Capitol Reef, nearly all of the roads accessing its vistas are dirt.

A huge variety of people come to the monument to play—though, except in a few of its more popular places, they rarely see each other in large quantity. These include dirt bikers, whizzing down the long and open roads; canyoneers exploring the vast network of oft-technical slot canyons; sightseers checking out its state parks like Anasazi, Kodachrome Basin, and Petrified Forest; and history buffs rediscovering uncounted petroglyphs, pictographs, and pioneer registers on the rock. Perhaps the most populous user group, hikers can find numerous well-developed and popular trails, as well as infinite backcountry exploration.

Given the hugeness of this region, this chapter has two separate 48-hour sample itineraries. The first is based in its northern end, along UT 12, and around the towns of Boulder and Escalante. Most people coming to the monument will end up in this region, especially in conjunction with Capitol Reef National Parks and the Anasazi, Kodachrome Basin, and Petrified Forest state parks. The second itinerary centers around the monument's southern area, US 89, and the Kanab area. Most people visiting this area will likely come in conjunction with a trip to the Grand Canyon or Lake Powell.

Visitors Centers

Appropriate for such an enormous and decentralized national monument, the GSENM has not one but four visitors centers. Along UT 12, in the monument's far northern swath, you'll find one in Cannonville and one in Escalante. To the south and along US 89, one is in Big Water and another in Kanab. Though technically not even inside the monument at all, the town of Kanab is also home to the main headquarters for this system. Those wishing for information or seeking a permit (mandatory for wild camping within the monument, as well as for boating and other such activities) will need to stop by one of these outposts. Beware: Most of these operations keep quite limited hours, closing well before sunset even during peak season. Though these towns are so tiny that each visitors center is readily located, a list of addresses follows. Kanab Monument Headquarters deals with monument administration and issues special permits for boating and more. The other four centers distribute information and permits to people entering the monument.

A visitors center in the monument much resembles that of a national park.

Kanab Monument Headquarters 190 East Center Street; 435-644-4300

Kanab Visitor Center 745 East US 89; 435-644-4680

Big Water Visitor Center 100 Upper Revolution Way; 435-675-3200

Cannonville Visitor Center 10 Center Street; 435-826-5640

Escalante Visitor Center 755 West Main Street; 435-826-5600

Pick Your Spot
Where to stay and what you'll find nearby . . .

ESCALANTE

The coolest town in the vicinity, Escalante clusters itself around the very scenic highway, UT 12, on the northern border of the monument. Serving as the area's headquarters for recreation, Escalante offers a gear shop, a handful of outfitters, some restaurants, hotels, and cafés, and a campground.

Escalante Outfitters (310 West Main Street; 435-826-4266; www .escalanteoutfitters.com) provides a little of every relevant service. From selling books and gear to providing guide services and a small restaurant and café, this warrants a stop just for those reasons. Additionally, though, it offers campsites and rustic cabins, both with access to shared, hot showers. All accommodations are pet friendly: A good piece of knowledge, as pets are fully welcomed in the Grand Staircase–Escalante National Monument, unlike in national parks. Guide services for hire include those for fly-fishing, canyoneering, and even natural history tours. You can additionally rent mountain bikes at the Outfittters to take away on your own exploratory missions. While here, you can purchase any number of espresso drinks and baked goods, pick up a guidebook or literature covering local subject matter, and pick up the sunscreen you forgot to bring. Also, this shop is a licensed Utah State Liquor Store and sells a variety of spirits and full-strength beer to go.

BOULDER

Much smaller than Escalante, Boulder has fewer amenities to offer. But it also has some of

Escalante Outfitters is one of the most popular businesses in town.

southern Utah's finest lodging and excellent contemporary dining. The best lodging in Boulder (and in the vicinity, actually) can be found at the Boulder Mountain Lodge (20 North UT 12, Boulder; 435-335-7460; www.boulder-utah.com). Rooms at the lodge range in size from standard, queen-size-bed affairs, through various degrees of bed sizes and room arrangements. All are appointed with contemporary Western-style furnishings and, despite their elegance, do not break the bank. During the low season, rooms start around $100; during high season, they cost about 50 percent more. Located on a spacious lot, the lodge shares land and ownership with the Hell's Backbone Grill (see "Dinner" in Day 1 of the suggested itinerary for Northern/UT 12, below). In addition to these two businesses, the proprietors operate many spacious gardens from which they craft many of their restaurant's dishes. For both dining and rooms, it is a good idea to call fairly well ahead of time for a reservation.

Another, slightly out of town option is the Boulder Mountain Guest Ranch (3.5 miles up Hell's Backbone/Salt Gulch Road, northwest of Boulder; 435-335-7480; www.bouldermountainguestranch .com). This ranch-style guest house offers a variety of rooms, ranging from six-person bunk options, through various allotments of queen-size beds within the lodge, as well as three private cabins. Despite the log cabin feel and presence of bunk beds, the accommodations here are quite nice, clean, and well kept. You'll find that all rooms, even those with bunk beds, are handsomely and simply decorated in Western style and are as modern as possible, given the nature of the structure. Be sure to make reservations; limited rooms make it difficult for this lodge to provide beds on short notice. The guest ranch additionally provides a variety of guide services, which include any length of hiking, backpacking, or horseback-riding outing, in combination with meals or lack thereof, equipment rental, and more. Essentially, all trips are customizable depending on your time frame, desired spending, equipment needs, and personal desires. Finally, consider dining here—whether or not you sleep here. Though slightly out of town, an evening meal on the ranch warrants the drive. (See "Local Flavors," below.) Check online or call for exact directions to the property.

KANAB

Compared with its regional peers, Kanab is a thriving metropolis with more than 3,500 residents. In addition to its heavily Mormon history, this far-southern Utah town has quite a place in film history, as many Hollywood Westerns were shot on location here. These include classics like *Gunsmoke*, *El Dorado*, and *The Lone Ranger*, as well as *Planet of the Apes*. Here you'll find a number of lodging options, ranging from national chains to locally owned establishments.

If you like family-run establishments with self-described "classic style and contemporary comfort," call for reservations at the Quail Park Lodge (125 North 300 West; 435-215-1447; www.quailpark lodge.com). Suites, standard rooms, and variations therein are appointed with tasteful modern furnishings, providing you with plenty of color, cheer, and open space for a pleasant experience. Additionally, the lodge offers wireless Internet and guide services. Trips range from tours of movie sets to journeys through slot canyons, hikes to petroglyphs, and full-day expeditions in the Grand Canyon. Dogs (but not cats) are allowed in designated guest rooms only and must meet certain criteria to stay here.

The Bob-Bon Inn (236 North US 89; 435-644-3069; www.bob boninn.com) is another locally owned favorite in Kanab and costs a bit less than the Quail Park Lodge. This safely Old West–themed motel offers friendly service and allows pets. Newly remodeled, this log-cabin-style building indeed has wireless Internet and offers a choice between single- and queen-size bedrooms.

Local Flavors
Taste of the town—local cafés, restaurants, bars, bistros, etc.

ESCALANTE

Inside Escalante Outfitters, you'll also see Esca-Latte Internet Cafe and Pizza Parlor (310 West Main Street; 435-826-4266; www .escalanteoutfitters.com). More than just a pizza parlor, this offers a menu full of delicious sandwiches and other items for breakfast, lunch, and dinner, like pesto and chicken calzones stuffed with red onions and served with a salad of baby greens and house raspberry vinaigrette. If hungry, you can opt for larger entrées or full pizzas and a local beer. Sometimes you'll even luck out and run into evening live

The town of Escalante has a rather genuine Old West feel.

music on the weekends. This restaurant is small, but limited patio dining is available. Order espresso drinks or good coffee any time of day.

BOULDER

This small town has but a few restaurants, but the quality of those certainly does more than compensate for the lack of quantity. The most touted and talked about restaurant in the area is the Hell's Backbone Grill (see "Dinner" in Day 1 of "48 Hours: Northern /UT 12," below), which sits right in the center of town, along UT 12. However, if you forget to make a reservation and can't get a table, the other best option in the area is the Boulder Mountain Guest Ranch's Sweetwater Kitchen (see "Pick Your Spot," in Boulder, above). This restaurant draws on the area's Anasazi history, as well as Western settler heritage for inspiration, crafting its dishes from local organic pork, chicken, and beef, as well as homegrown produce when possible. These are used to create entrées with modern touches based on daily availability. Breakfast and dinner are served in the restaurant; boxed lunches can be ordered to take with you into the monument. Each evening has three distinct seating times; though reservations are not required, they are encouraged for your sake and that of the kitchen.

Another in-town alternate for less fancy dining is the Boulder Trail Grill & Outpost Store (junction of Burr Trail road and UT 12; 435-335-7503; www.burrtrailgrill .com). With its central location and long front porch, this restaurant is the most visually obvious in town.

As you might expect based on its name, the Boulder Trail Grill serves many burgers and sandwiches, as well soups, salads, and a selection of heartier entrées in combination with beer and wine if desired. The restaurant is open for all three meals of the day, seasonally only; guests may choose either indoor and outdoor tables. Any meal can be made to take away. The Grill accepts, but does not require, reservations.

KANAB

Rocking V Cafe (97 West Center Street; 435-644-8001; www.rocking vcafe.com) is the most popular dining option in the mighty town of Kanab, serving three meals a day of contemporary American cuisine. The menu offers healthy and varied gourmet entrées with a creative and eclectic touch. Various meats, fish, legumes, fresh vegetables, and herbs combine to form a variety of Southwestern entrées, pasta dishes, grilled selections, and more. As the menu draws heavily on seasonally and locally available ingredients when possible, the options change regularly, but can include tenderloin, trout, seafood, polenta cakes, fish tacos, and numerous artisan salads. Vegans and vegetarians can eat quite well here, unlike in most other rural Utah locations. Check the menu for Utah beers; though the state has a deservedly bad rap for its liquor laws, its breweries certainly know how to produce a fine

Rules of the Monument

The Grand Staircase–Escalante National Monument, neither a national park nor an ordinary parcel of BLM land, has a special set of regulations. Though typically much more relaxed than a national park, the monument's rules still do not provide for a free-for-all. The first major difference between this monument and national parks is that **pets are allowed** within the monument almost without restriction. In the Calf Creek Falls Recreation Area, dogs must be leashed; dogs may not enter Coyote Gulch at all, as this is a particularly sensitive example of the monument's fantastic geology and ecosystems.

Just as within the national parks, all **backcountry campers** in Grand Staircase–Escalante National Monument must obtain a permit prior to their camping out. Permits may be obtained at any of the four monument visitors centers (see "Visitors Centers," toward the beginning of this chapter). Campers may only stay in already disturbed areas; the creation of new sites is prohibited. Use preexisting fire pits. All human waste must either be buried at least six inches deep or carried out, along with toilet paper and other refuse. Any special permits must be applied for by calling the monument (435-644-4305). Beyond that, the land may be used at your respectful whim.

variety of microbrews. The restaurant encourages you to dine comfortably while casually dressed and has a fun ambience replete with local art on display. Given the Rocking V's remote location and specialized ingredients, you can't fault it for its slightly inflated prices.

For breakfast, lunch, or dinner, head to the Rewind Diner (18 East Center Street; 435-644-3200), a '50s-style eatery with classic American food. For reasonable prices, you can choose from a regular or vegetarian/vegan menu and consume a filling meal without spending a lot of time or money. Its large selection for every time of day

pleases people of all tastes, including those with pickier palettes—even children. Quite popular among locals and tourists alike, the diner can get rather crowded on the weekends.

Mexican cuisine can be quite fitting for calorically drained hikers in the Desert Southwest. Escobar's Mexican Restaurant (373 East 300 South; 435-644-3739) serves three meals a day throughout the year (except on Saturdays and holidays). Affordable, classic dishes crafted with fresh ingredients contend with even the biggest of appetites without breaking the bank or requiring too much time or frills.

48 Hours:
Northern/UT 12

GETTING THERE

UT 12, one of the state's most scenic and spectacular byways, is one
of just two paved highways to penetrate this great landscape. It skirts
along the northern periphery of the
Grand Staircase–Escalante National
Monument, originating in the west
at US 89, near Panguitch and
Bryce Canyon National Park. As it
travels to the east, it cuts a broad
swath across the top of the monument before arching steeply toward
the north and ascending the Boulder Mountain Plateau before dropping down into UT 24 at Torrey
and near Capitol Reef National
Monument.

 Regardless of which way you
arrive, come prepared with extra
time, as the desert landscape
through which this road winds up,
down, and around will require
you to stop multiple times and
take photographs. Especially in the
warmer months of the year, the
happiest travelers here will be
those building extra driving time
into their schedules; happy RV
drivers sharing the topographically
rich roadway will certainly slow
driving time. The morning's itinerary begins in Escalante, but if you
prefer to sleep in Boulder, no worries: A mere 29 miles of the most
incredible scenery separate the two.

 If staying in Boulder, look at
"Pick Your Spot," above; if you seek

a hotel in Escalante, the Padre
Motel (20 East Main Street; 435-
826-4276; www.padremotel.com)
sits right in the center of town and
offers simply decorated rooms
ranging from a single queen bed to
a two-room suite. The hotel,
though basic, offers wireless Internet, more than 150 channels of dig-
ital cable, and five-star Serta
mattresses. This clean and locally
owned establishment provides a
comfortable place to sleep without
the extra expense of a posh resort.

Sunrise paints the fields lavender in early
summer south of UT 12.

If you like this . . . area around Escalante, but prefer luxurious accommodations a short drive from the town's center, call the **Slot Canyons Inn Bed & Breakfast** *(northwest of Escalante via NF 17, call or see Web site for details; 435-826-4901; www.slotcanyonsinn.com). Located very near town but at the mouth of a private canyon, this modern outfit features a lodge built in 2006 with eight guest rooms, as well as a historic private cabin. This cabin, originally constructed in 1899, underwent a thoroughly modernizing renovation in 1999, simultaneously preserving its original flavor and updating its infrastructure. All accommodations of this establishment feature contemporary Western design. Breakfasts, prepared fresh daily, feature special bonuses like homemade jam. Pets, as well as children under the age of six, are not permitted here.*

After you're settled into your hotel, grab a bite to eat at the Escalante Outfitters' Esca-Latte Pizza Parlour (as listed in Escalante's "Local Flavors," above). Offering much more than pizza, this small, all-inclusive operation offers a large selection of hot and cold sandwiches, salads, and calzones in its restaurant, as well as everything from books to outdoor equipment, camping, lodging, and guide services outside its dining room. They even brew their own beer, so you can enjoy a cold one with dinner if you'd like. Or if you

want to purchase a bottle of wine for a romantic evening, the Outfitters also operate a Utah state liquor store—the only place in Escalante where you may purchase full-strength beer and other spirits outside a restaurant. It's possible you might run into some live music here on a summer weekend night. If you have any doubts or questions about your upcoming day or how to locate your B&B, inquire with your server or the staff manning the store's front desk.

DAY 1

Breakfast before You Go

Waking up in a town of just 800 residents, you're not going to have a huge sampling of choices, and the best one here—even for breakfast—is the Escalante Outfitters (described above). Begin the day with a steaming, organic, fair-trade drip coffee or espresso drink, or possibly with some tea or orange juice. Sit out on the small patio to enjoy a light breakfast of baked oatmeal with fruit, a bagel with cream cheese, some homemade granola, or strata. Those planning to be active during the day should start with a heavier meal like eggs Benedict (either their standard or a special southwestern variety), a breakfast sandwich with red potatoes, or an egg burrito with red onions, pinto beans, and green chilis. Not only does Escalante

Outfitters dish up the best breakfast in town, but their staff is also among the most knowledgeable about the recreational possibilities within the monument. In fact, this business also operates a guiding service, so if you would like some serious direction, you may speak with the personnel here about arranging a trip.

Enter the Monument

Once you finish breakfast, your options broaden enormously. Perhaps you would like to check out a petrified forest, take a scenic drive, witness the unique sandstone features and petroglyphs of the Devil's Garden, or even go canyoneering. For simplicity and readability, we'll take a linear journey through time. But if any of these options don't excite you, or you find time to do more, see the "Extend Your Stay" section toward the end of this chapter.

Learn a Little

The first logical step for anyone arriving at this corner of the Grand Staircase–Escalante National Monument is to stop at the Escalante Interagency Visitor Center (755 West Main Street/UT 12; 435-826-5600), on the western outskirts of Escalante. Morning is a good time to do this, as your daytime activities will probably keep you occupied much longer than this center stays open, which is sometimes only as late as midafternoon. One of the first things you'll want to

pick up here is a map of the monument. This free handout features an overview view of the entire GSENM and highlights major trails, campsites, roads (and their BLM number), picnic areas, towns, visitors centers, and other points of interest. It also briefly discusses monument regulations and fees (of which there are few).

Take a Hike

The visitors center is quite near the Escalante Petrified Forest State Park (710 North Reservoir Road; 435-826-4466; www.stateparks.utah .gov), the turnoff to it just 1.2 miles west of the center. This state park, as you might guess, is centered around a massive natural collection of petrified wood. Departing just north of the park's entrance station, a footpath leads up a steep hillside to the Petrified Forest Loop Trail, with the 0.75-mile Trail of Sleeping Rainbows, a U-shaped extension. Taking the trail in its entirety means walking about 4 miles. Though the initial trail and the Sleeping Rainbows extension are challenging for their length, the 1-mile-long loop trail in the middle is almost completely flat. Hiking this trail not only leads you past massive chunks of petrified trees, but it also gives you a more expanded view of the surrounding area. In addition to this hiking trail, the park also contains a shorter walk, the Petrified Wood Cove, and approximately 25 campsites. If it's warm enough, consider taking a dip

The hiking trails of Esclante State Park overlook the Wide Hollow Reservoir.

after the hike in the Wide Hollow reservoir.

Take a Drive and Stop for Lunch

If you have just 48 hours to check out the northern portion of the monument, the next logical thing to do is drive eastward along UT 12 (www.scenicbyway12.com) toward Boulder. Prepare to be amazed as this road leads away from Escalante and across a seemingly implausible route of sandstone domes and deep canyons of the Escalante River. The road begins rather tamely, passing by Hole-in-the-Rock Road (see "Extend Your Stay," below), but then quickly enters into vastly more complex and colorful terrain. From the first major pullout on the road, the Head of Rocks Overlook, 160-million-year-old red- and ivory-

colored sand dunes are visible in the foreground. From here, the massive Henry Mountains, reaching 11,506 feet at the summit of Mt. Ellen, can be seen to the east. This range, much like the La Sal Mountains near Moab, is also characterized by laccoliths. These stone domes formed as igneous intrusions in the earth's crust, which solidified underground and were exposed by subsequent erosion. To the north, Boulder Mountain, which contains the Aquarius Plateau, dominates the landscape. Farther along the UT 12, the Boynton Overlook provides an aerial view of the Escalante River and its riparian lushness below.

Keep your eyes open for the turnout to the Kiva Coffee House (Mile Marker 73.86 UT 12;

435-826-4550; www.kivacoffee house.com), on the northern side of the road. This structure, perched loftily on a knoll, should be fairly difficult to miss. Here you can enjoy a lunch of some of the area's better homemade and artisan goods, including soups and breads. Afterward, take a coffee and check your e-mail. The restaurant is open April through October for breakfast and lunch, except on Tuesdays.

Continuing eastward, you'll next cross over the Escalante River. Drive carefully as you make the steep descent; at the bottom of this pitch lies the Escalante River Trailhead. This serves as a popular pullout for hikers heading toward the Escalante Natural Bridge and Natural Arch, as well as for those picnicking along the cottonwood-lined, sandy-banked river. If you want to explore the area yourself, look for a pullout to the north, just after crossing the river. (See "Extend Your "Stay," later in this chapter.)

The road now enters a sandstone-walled canyon as it reascends onto higher terrain. Keep your eyes peeled to see the pullout for the Calf Creek Recreation Area (see "Take a hike," Day 2 of this chapter's 48-hour itinerary). Though this trailhead-and-campground combination is one of the singularly most popular destinations within the monument, it sits a bit downhill and away from the highway, rendering it a bit inobvious. If you're still on UT 12 as it ascends a long, steep

segment, you've gone too far.

This next portion of the drive represents the highlight of the 29 miles between Escalante and Boulder. Called the Hog's Back, this section of UT 12 climbs quickly to the top of the nearest ridge. Once there, it follows along the crest of a tall sandstone fin, winding back and forth and up and down. Though vivid scenery calls for your attention here, make sure to keep your eyes on the road; large pullouts serve as safe sightseeing areas. The final pullout before Boulder is the Homestead Overlook, from which you can again see the Henry Mountains, as well as the Waterpocket Fold and Navajo Mountain.

If you like this . . . drive, have extra time, and perhaps a vehicle with extra clearance (depending on road conditions), inquire at the Escalante Interagency Visitor Center about the current state of the Pine Creek/Hell's Backbone Road. Taken as an alternative to UT 12 between Escalante and Boulder, this dirt road circuit stretches more than 44 miles and takes about three hours to navigate. Built in 1933 by the Civilian Conservation Core as the only motorway between Boulder and Escalante, it is now driven as a matter of novelty. Skirting alongside the Box–Death Hollow Wilderness area, this unlikely dirt road crosses through some spectacularly wild scenery. The Hell's Backbone Bridge, near Boulder, carries 109 feet of road up a spectacular height above Sand Creek before heading into town. Washboarding on this dirt road can become rather severe and persistent; speak with a monument ranger to find out whether the route has recently been graded. If you don't feel like making the entire 44-mile drive, you can sample just a bit of this road by making a shorter out-and-back journey from the town of Boulder to the Hell's Backbone Bridge. This road is closed during winter for obvious reasons. To access this road from Escalante, head north from town on Pine Creek Road, bearing east at the junction by Posey Lake.

Dinner

After this day of exploration, you should arrive in Boulder rather hungry. Stop in at the Hell's Backbone Grill (20 North UT 12; 435-335-7460; www.boulder-utah.com), which shares its location and ownership with the Boulder Mountain Lodge (listed in "Pick Your Spot," toward the beginning of this chapter). This restaurant has been a favorite among critics and guests statewide and has even won recognition across the nation. Drawing from its on-property gardens, the Grill crafts creative, contemporary American and southwestern-influenced dishes in compliance with the current availability of produce, herbs, and locally raised meats. In addition to these satiating meals, your evening's enjoyment will include the relaxed atmosphere of the beautiful grounds. If you think of it ahead of time, call for reservations—otherwise, because of the restaurant's popularity, you may have to wait as many as a few hours

The Hell's Backbone Grill is likely the most famous restaurant in southern Utah.

to be seated during busy nights. Remember that cell phones do not work out of town.

DAY
2

Breakfast before You Go

If staying at the Boulder Mountain Lodge, you'll be able to dine at the Hell's Backbone Grill again. Here, the kitchen crafts breakfast with delicious farm eggs and garden vegetables raised right on the property. Relax with a cup of coffee before heading back out for another day of undertakings.

Take a Hike

If you don't mind a little backtracking, head back along UT 12 toward Escalante to the Calf Creek Falls Trailhead (Calf Creek Falls Recreation Area, 15 miles west of Boulder, 14 miles east of Escalante on UT 12). Here, a 3-mile trail leads up to the namesake waterfall. As it gradually climbs, the path roughly follows Calf Creek, rolling up and down small hills. At its end, a 126-foot-tall, narrow ribbon of water cascades into a broad and cold idyllic pool. The Grand Staircase–Escalante National Monument's most popular hike, this accessible journey is popular among people of all ages. Along the way, keep your eyes open (and binoculars out) to spot rock art panels and an 800- to 1,000-year-old granary (at the trail's halfway point). Brave persons can

conclude their uphill trek with a dip in the pool beneath the falls. Despite the hike's roughly streamside location, this trail is quite exposed to sun and gets pretty warm during the day. Additionally, a lot of deep sand covering sections of the path render it somewhat strenuous, despite is relative lack of elevation change. Come prepared with plenty of sunblock and water.

Learn a Little

If time allows after your hike (or if you'd rather give your legs a break and skip the hike all together), head to Anasazi State Park (460 North UT 12; 435-335-7308; www.state parks.utah.gov). Located on the northern side of Boulder, this provides a completely relaxed way to learn about the indigenous peoples of the area and to see some of their ruins. The state park is centered around what's called the Coombs Site; this ancient village was occupied from approximately 1160 to 1235 A.D. Home to as many as 200 people at a time, this site was one of the largest Ancestral Puebloan communities ever to have existed on the western side of the Colorado River. Begin your visit with a stop at the museum, where exhibits teach you a bit about these people and help you contextualize the ruins you'll see outside. On display here is a selection of the many thousand artifacts left behind at this archaeological site. From the museum, a short trail tours the excavated

Calf Creek is lush with vegetation in early June.

portions of the ruins, which include stone and mud homes and other structures. Major excavations of the area began in 1958 and have unearthed nearly 100 rooms and 10 pit structures; to date, only about half of the known site has been uncovered. The park is open year-round during normal business hours, except on major holidays; slightly reduced hours during winter. Interagency Annual Passes are not accepted here.

Lunch before You Go

Head back into Boulder for a quick bite at the Boulder Trail Grill (listed above in "Local Flavors"). Or if you're heading north and over Boulder Mountain, you can wait until you arrive in Torrey to eat (see "Local Flavors" in chapter 3). Though UT 12 climbs and descends an enormous plateau to reach the next town, the highway is quite well built here, and the 36 road miles do not take very long to cross.

48 Hours:
Southern/US 89

Two days in the southern portion of the Grand Staircase–Escalante National Monument will leave you with just a taste of what the area has to offer. Much less trafficked than the monument's northern section, this area has a much wilder atmosphere and more diffuse attractions, usually accessed by more involved hikes and complicated route finding. For these reasons, the southern portion of the monument is most popular among backpackers, canyoneers, and others into exploring nature away from the beaten path.

GETTING THERE

US 89, which roughly parallels the Utah-Arizona border, connects the town of Kanab to Lake Powell. Along its path, it crosses into the Grand Staircase–Escalante Monument and teases alongside the Vermilion Cliff National Monument and the Paraia Canyon–Vermilion Cliffs Wilderness before plunging headlong into the Glen Canyon National Recreation Area. Here, it crosses into Arizona and over the 710-foot-tall, 1,560-foot-long Glen Canyon Dam and finally into the town of Page. Near the highway are a few established campgrounds, the Coral Pink Sand Dunes State Park (west of Kanab), and a whole slew of the Grand Staircase's natural features such as the Chocolate Cliffs to the south and the Vermilion, White, and Grey Cliffs to the north.

DAY 1

Breakfast before You Go

For being such a small middle-of-nowhere town, Kanab really has a lot to offer food-wise. For your first meal in the area, head to Houston's Trails End Restaurant (32 East Center Street; 435-644-2488; www.houstons.net). This simple and casual American restaurant serves some of the town's most popular and filling breakfasts over red and white, checkered tablecloths. The cowboy ambience fits well its hearty, simple meals. Classic breakfast options such as pancakes, egg plates, and the like come at an affordable price and without much to-do. Consider coming back for lunch or dinner; all meals at this place are popular among locals and tourists alike.

Enter the Monument

To begin an educated exploration of the area, you should stop in at the Kanab Visitor Center (190 East Center Street; 435-644-4300). Here you can gather free maps and purchase more specialized guidebooks if you're planning to head out for a true backcountry or technical adventure. Because the Bureau of Land Management requires anyone camping within the monument to

Lunch on the Trail

One thought before you leave town: Once you leave Kanab and enter the monument, you won't run into any restaurants. So if you plan to spend the entire day outside, you should either order a sack lunch at ·one of the restaurants in town or stop at a grocery store. Kanab has two main food shops, **Glazier's Family Market** (264 South 100 East; 435-644-5029) and **Honey's Marketplace** (260 East 300 South; 435-644-5877). If you don't feel like paying restaurant prices for trail food, simply pack your cooler with sandwich fixings, granola bars, and fruit. Don't forget water—or electrolyte beverages—if you'll be hiking a lot during the heat of the day.

have a permit, pick one up during your morning visit if you plan to sleep out.

Take a Hike

While in Kanab, you're not that far from the Great Western Trail. To reach this national treasure, which crosses right over US 89, head about 15 miles east from town to a large parking area. This vast and complicated trail system stretches from Mexico to Canada and is much less streamlined than the Appalachian Trail, often with two or more trails running parallel to each other and in the same direction. It traverses 4,555 miles through the states of Montana, Wyoming, Idaho, Utah, and Arizona. Within Utah alone, this trail covers more than 1,600 miles, many sections of which are quite popular hikes in their respective locations. If heading to the north of US 89 on this section of trail, you hike up toward the Vermillion Cliff and

then the White Cliffs. Longer afield, the trail crosses over the entire western portion of the Grand Staircase–Escalante National Monument and ends up in Bryce Canyon National Park Park.

Stop for Lunch

After your hike, head back west to Kanab. If you don't have a lunch in the car, stop at Laid Back Larry's (98 South 100 East; 435-644-3636). A pleasantly healthy and earth-friendly surprise, this café serves all kinds of ecosavvy meals, including an excellent vegetarian and vegan selection. In addition to espresso drinks and coffee, you can order nutritious smoothies, filling and protein-rich salads, eccentric sandwiches, wraps, nachos, and other lunchtime items and snacks to take away.

See a Little

After lunch, head north on US 89, as toward the Coral Pink Sand

Dunes State Park (7.5 miles north of Kanab on US 89, then 10 miles southwest on Hancock Road; 435-648-2800; www.stateparks.utah.gov). The only significant field of sand dunes in the Colorado Plateau, this striking area looks much more like a scene from a Middle Eastern or African desert than that of the Rocky Mountain West. Here, grains of iron-rich sand originating from Navajo sandstone have oxidized, rendering them a brilliant pink color. Winds passing over the Moccasin and Moquith mountains are funneled through a narrow gap between the two. As the winds pick up speed, they erode the sand grains and carry them away. Once through the notch, these winds slow down, depositing the sands into this massive field. At an elevation of approximately 6,000 feet, these dunes receive snow cover during the winter, rendering them an even more bizarre sight. In spring, when the snow melts into water, the resulting ponds provide homes to amphibians, insects, and other creatures.

Dinner

After your day outside has come to a close, head back to Kanab for a meal at Spurs Grill (36 North 300 West; 435-644-8080). Given its name, you might properly assume that the menu contains a proper helping of ribs, steaks, and burgers. But vegetarians can also dine well here, so shouldn't be discouraged. In addition to the meal, you can also enjoy a microbrew or bottle of wine. Don't be deterred by its low-key appearance. A large and well-stocked salad bar provides an excellent supplement to any meal—or can function as a meal all by itself.

DAY 2

In Town, before You Go

Grab a quick bite to eat at your favorite restaurant from yesterday. Consider the Rewind Diner or Rocking V Cafe (as listed in Kanab's "Local Flavors," near the beginning of this chapter). After breakfast, animal lovers should consider a stop at the Best Friends Animal Sanctuary (5001 Angel Canyon Road; 435-644-2001; www.bestfriends.org). This nationally famous animal rescue shelter houses dogs, cats, horses, pigs, parrots, waterfowl, and even rabbits. This safe house serves as a home to sick, old, injured, abused, and otherwise cast-out animals. Much bigger than most shelters, Best Friends has about 1,700 critters living there on a daily basis. This open and pleasant campus provides a home to these formerly unfortunate souls, making sure they will never be roofless again. The cheery and positive center attracts visitors and volunteers from around the nation and is largely responsible for the presence of so many veggie- and vegan-friendly restaurants in Kanab.

Take a Hike

Located just on the northern end of Kanab is Squaw Trail (trailhead on northwestern side of town, north of Jacob Hamblin Park). This dirt path climbs more than 800 feet from its starting point, up a massive red rock plateau and to a town overlook, after approximately 1 mile of hiking. Though the trail continues uphill, the pitch lessens for the next 0.5 mile before reaching a Grand Staircase Overlook. You can hike as far as 6 miles on this scenic trail, past picturesquely carved sandstone knobs and domes and even occasional small arches. As the hike continues on past the Grand Staircase Overlook, it bends first toward the west and then to the south to its terminus at the Bottles Overlook.

Lunch before You Go

If your tour must end here, revisit your favorite restaurant in Kanab. However, if you're traveling onward to Zion National Park or to the northern portion of the Grand Staircase–Escalante National Monument, grab a sack lunch to go and dine at a scenic pullout along the way. Though Kanab has surprisingly hip eateries for its size and location, some of Utah's finest scenery awaits you.

Extend Your Stay

If you have more time, try to see these things . . .

RECREATION

Scenic Driving

No trip to the northern portion of this great monument would be complete—or possible—without a tour of UT 12 or its alternate and predecessor, the Hell's Backbone Road (see Day 2 of 48 Hours: Northern, above). If you have come to the monument with time to spare, think about adding a drive down Hole-in-the-Rock Road (turnoff just 5 miles east of Escalante center, on UT 12). The entirety of this road consists of (sometimes) graded dirt and actually serves as one of the monument's main arteries. Departing from UT 12 in the north (just east of Escalante), it plunges headlong toward the far southeastern corner of this national monument, often laden with severe washboards for its entire length. Along the way, it passes by several points of interest, including the Harris Wash Trail, Devil's Garden, Twenty Mile Wash Dinosaur Track Site, 25 Mile Wash Trail, Dry Fork Slots with Peekaboo and Spooky canyons, and Chimney Rock. The last 4 or so miles of road deteriorate greatly, making them impassable to most vehicles. But many people bike or hike to the end of this "road" to see the namesake Hole-in-the-Rock, a notch through which a pioneer train of Mormons traveled down to the Colorado River en route to establishing a new community on the other side of the river in early Utah history (see sidebar). The popularity of this

Hole-in-the-Rock Road: Along the Way

In 1879, just 32 years after the Mormons arrived in Salt Lake City, a troupe of 236 of them set out from Escalante to establish a direct overland route to Bluff. They headed to the southeast in a nearly straight line toward the Colorado River. After crossing 40-some miles of reasonably passable land, they encountered Glen Canyon, a chasm thousands of feet deep in the earth and lined with sandstone cliffs. Not to be deterred, these industrious people set about improving this piece of cliff so that it could be traveled by wagon trains, livestock, and civilians. This required 1.5 months' worth of chiseling and dynamiting, as well as the creation of various pulley systems and other items of reinforcement. Though the road miraculously supplied passage to all members of the crew—including livestock and wagons—the group faced an equally, if not more, tedious journey to reascend the southern banks of the river. Though today the waters of Lake Powell cover much of this former "shortcut," the sight will still impress even the most jaded of onlookers.

Today, a roughly improved and sometimes graded dirt road stretches 90 percent of the way from UT 12 (5 miles east of Escalante) to the Hole-in-the-Rock. Along the way lie numerous other sights and side roads. Beware: Though most two-wheel-drive vehicles can pass over even the majority of these routes, high clearance is sometimes mandatory. Additionally, these roads should be avoided when covered with snow, as well as during and after heavy rains.

The first turnout to the west is **Cedar Wash Road** (about 3 miles from UT 12, and on the west side of the road). Parking slightly less than 5 miles down this road, on its shoulder, you can wander northeast approximately 2.4 miles up a wash to a pair of accessible slot canyons called Zebra and Tunnel. These fork from the same place, with Zebra heading almost due north 0.6 miles and Tunnel continuing 1.2 miles to the northeast. These should best be attempted with a proper topographical map and water-friendly clothing (especially for Tunnel Slot, which usually contains running water).

Harris Wash Road (roughly 9 miles south of UT 12) departs to the east of Hole-in-the-Rock Road and goes on for about 4 miles. Where the road ends, a trail begins, and extends more than 11 miles to the Escalante River. Though the distance is quite generous, the elevation loss is only 300 feet to that body of water.

The most accessible and popular attraction along the Hole-in-the-Rock Road is the **Devil's Garden** (12 miles south of UT 12). Taking a signed and short spur road to the right (west) leads you to the parking area for this extraterrestrial sandstone landscape. In this miniature valley, densely packed hoodoos and arches form a maze through and upon which you can walk around and explore. Among the formations you can even spot petroglyphs occasionally. There is no trail in this area; keep all foot traffic to already worn

When hiking through the Devil's Garden, walk only on existing trails.

areas and try not to get lost. Though many people stick near the parking lot, you can venture quite a distance to the south and west of the parking area.

Continuing south along Hole-in-the-Rock, you'll see a turnout to the east for the **Twentymile Wash Dinosaur Track Site** (turnoff located 14 miles south of UT 12), where more than 800 naturally preserved tracks of three-toed theropods can be seen petrified in a 400-meter-long Entrada sandstone shelf. These two-legged ancient animals were meat eaters and lived approximately 160 million years ago.

The **25 Mile Wash Road** (16.5 miles south of UT 12) heads to the northeast, reaching the 25 Mile Wash Trailhead in just 2 miles of driving, and then the Egypt Trailhead nearer its end. This and the next side road, **25.0,** feed into a number of the monument's best and most easily accessed slot canyons, including a series of canyons called Egypt, Peek-a-boo, and Spooky. As some of these require technical gear and know-how to navigate, it is best to speak with a ranger and/or pick up a detailed trail guide before attempting to navigate these on your own. Alternatively, you can contact a guide service like **Grand Staircase Adventure Guides** (435-826-4122; www.grandstair caseadventureguides.com) and enter the area with an expert.

Continuing farther south, you'll pass a number of side roads like **Forty Mile Ridge Road** with the **40 Mile Water Tank** and **Crack-in-the-Wall** trailheads, as well as the **Hurricane Wash** and **Willow Gulch** trails, which originate rather near the road. From here, many hikes and established paths head out into the wild; those with a good sense of direction should explore on their own. But others, or those heading out on particularly long treks, should strongly consider carrying a detailed topographical map and a GPS unit.

Once you pass by the parking for **Willow Gulch,** only a handful of road miles extend before the way deteriorates too much to be passed by most vehicles. Needless to say, this remote corner of the world is not the best place to test your vehicle's clearance. Park as necessary and continue on a mountain bike to the historic Hole-in-the-Rock. It is possible to reach this area by foot; but it just requires more time to do so. Once there, imagine 80 wagons passing down this unlikely passageway and look for remnants of the pulleys and other structures that allowed them all to do this with no casualties.

Hole-in-the-Rock Road heads south into the monument from UT 12.

road renders it frustratingly washboarded as often as not; so if you have the option, riding in a truck would be preferable to a passenger car.

Those visiting Kodachrome Basin State Park (see "Overview of Southern Utah: Its History, Parks, and Monuments"), south of Cannonville, will already have driven the first 9 miles of the 46-mile-long Cottonwood Road to reach this picturesque valley lined with colorfully striated walls and filled with deep orange Entrada and Carmel sandstone spires. South of the park and back on Cottonwood Road, another 10 miles of (now) dirt road surface leads to the turnoff for one of the monument's more famous landforms, Grosvenor Arch. Actually comprised of two adjacent rock windows, this structure stands approximately 150 feet above its surroundings, its largest opening spanning approximately 100 feet in height. Those not particularly into hiking might enjoy this one, as the footpath leading up to its base is paved and takes but a minute or two to walk. The main road continues toward the south, passing the Cottonwood Narrows, accessed by a northern and southern trailhead. This approximately 1.75-mile hike takes you through a fun and accessible slot canyon (see "Hiking and Canyoneering: Southern," below). Next comes the Cockscomb, a prominent and serrated feature that officially divides the Kaiparowits Plateau, to the east, from the Grand Staircase, to the west. What it lacks in colors, it makes up for in form! About two-thirds of the way to US 89, the road passes the trailheads for Lower Hackberry and finally the Paria Box, two of the most popular hikes in the monument (see "Hiking and Canyoneering: Southern," below). Cottonwood Road terminates in US 89, about 10 miles west of Big Water (and its GSENM Visitor Center) and about 46 miles east of Kanab.

Drive to where UT 12 crosses over the Escalante River (14 miles east of Escalante, 13 miles southwest of Boulder) to park at the Escalante River Trailhead, on the northwestern side of the bridge. From here, approximately 15 river miles lead very gradually uphill through cottonwood trees, past occasional natural bridges, and across the sandy river. Because this hike requires that you ford the river multiple times, you should wear sturdy sandals and take this hike during the summer or fall. Because this hike is often shady and wet with fewer hikers, it can present a better summer alternative to hiking Calf Creek Falls (see Day 2's "Take a Hike" section, in the 48-hour itinerary, above). That hike, though scenic, tends to be much sunnier and with fewer encounters with water. Alternatively, you can park at the Escalante Town Trailhead and take this walk downstream for its 15-mile one-way distance. (This trailhead is reached by driving into the town cemetery on the eastern end of Escalante, turning quickly east for 0.25 miles, and then left for 0.25 miles.)

The Boulder Mail Trail, typically taken as an overnight trip, follows a historic actual mail trail that was used to forge contact between the towns of Boulder and Escalante before vehicle roads existed. On the way, the trail

Flash Flooding

Hikes in the canyons of the Escalante River and the greater Grand Staircase–Escalante National Monument take place, as often as not, in slot canyons. These narrow, sheer-walled passages, though extremely beautiful and fun to navigate, can turn into lethal death traps in the event of significant rain. Given the general sparseness of vegetation in the area, the landscape does very little to absorb rapidly falling precipitation. This water, having nowhere else to go, rushes into streams and rivers. Slot canyons, which by nature are narrow and walled with sheer, sandstone cliffs, turn into channels filled with rushing water. There are no feasible escape routes for hikers caught in them during such an event. If planning to take a slot canyon hike, or any type of hike through a narrow gulch, you should proactively check the local and regional weather and stay away if rain threatens. It could save your life.

passes through three distinct canyons of the Escalante River and stretches for 16 miles. It originates at the Boulder Landing Strip (located on the Hell's Backbone Road, just northwest of Boulder) and crosses diverse and wild terrain, including slickrock slabs, river bottoms, and high desert plateau on the way to the Upper Escalante River Trailhead (about a mile east of Escalante, reached by way of the town cemetery; see "Escalante Town Trailhead," above). It is possible to link this trail into other major trails and wild side hikes; those interested in doing so should pick up an in-depth hiking guidebook and topographical map. In fact, maps are not a bad idea for just the basic hike as it, like many in the monument, is scarcely improved and can be difficult to follow in places. If you have time, consider taking multiple days to complete the entire journey, to add some exploration of the colorful and diverse wilderness of the Box-Death and Phipps-Death hollows.

Driving east of Boulder about 6 miles on the Burr Trail road leads to the Deer Creek Trailhead and Campsite. With four tent spots, this small campground is a good base for those wishing to explore this northeastern portion of the monument on foot. Deer Creek crosses directly through this area, flowing from the north, down into the Escalante River to its south. The campsite itself is somewhat vegetated, compared with many other spots in the vicinity. The canyon through which Deer Creek runs, though not as spectacular as some of the other canyons of the Escalante, is extremely pleasant, with gently flowing water and trees and other vegetation lining its way.

Running parallel to, and just a few miles east of Deer Creek, The Gulch also flows from the north to the south, originating just north of the monument's boundaries and pouring into the Escalante River after its short course. Another choose-your-own-adventure, stream-side hike, you can either hike upstream or downriver, and for as long as you'd like to explore yet another of the beautiful, sandstone canyons in the area.

Hiking and Canyoneering: Southern

Drive east of Kanab about 47 miles (or 10 miles west of Big River) to reach Cottonwood Road. Turn north and drive north about 13 miles to reach the parking for the Paria Box Trailhead. Yet another stream-based hike, this heads up the Paria River. However, in addition to its natural beauty, this hike also features the Pahreah Town Site, a ghost town originally founded by Mormon settlers in the late 19th century. Though just a few buildings stand here, they are quite intact, and the overall site is forlornly scenic, with cottonwood trees in the foreground, and brightly colored, striped sandy bluffs in the background. Nearby and to the south is a 1962-era abandoned set from the Western movie Sergeants 3, a film graced by Frank Sinatra, Sammy Davis Jr., Peter Lawford, Dean Martin, and Joey Bishop. Though you can easily walk there from the actual ghost town, you can alternatively reach the site via FS 585, a dirt road departing north from US 89, 13 miles west of Cottonwood Road.

For an easy hike that requires a bit more driving, head to the Cottonwood Narrows, reached by way of the Cottonwood Road. The hike through this Navajo sandstone slot canyon runs for 1.5 miles, parallel to the road and just west of it. Though most of the hike is accessible for almost all abilities, a few meters' drop toward its northern end does strain out some of the less agile hikers. Two trailheads exist for this hike, neither of which are marked. The northern one sits about halfway down the length of this road: 23 miles south of UT 12, and 23 miles north of US 89. The southern one can be found about a mile south of that. Though an easy hike with very little elevation change, the sandy and stony floor of this canyon make for relatively slow going; bring some water along. The drop at the northern end of the canyon ensures that most hikers travel from north to south.

One of the more difficult established hikes in the monument—if taken its entire distance—is the 20.5-mile Lower Hackberry Trail. This can be taken either as a day hike or as a full-bore, multiday backpacking trip. As with many of the hikes in the monument, the trail follows a creek rather than a proper trail and features stream crossings; plan your footwear accordingly. As you climb up the canyon carved by Hackberry Creek, you'll cross through the Cockscomb, the properly named geological feature separating the Grand Staircase to the west and the Kaiparowits Plateau to the east. The trailhead for this hike sits about 31 miles south of UT 12 and 14.5 miles north of US 89, on Cottonwood Canyon Road.

Even those desensitized to Utah's richly diverse sandstone sculpture garden will still get a kick out of the Wahweap Hoodoos. An exceptionally striking set of formations, this Valley of the White Ghosts is comprised of three subareas: the White Hoodoos, Hoodoo Center, and the Towers of Silence, the most prominent group of all. Topped by rust-red Dakota sandstone boulders, these extremely thin and elongated rock filaments consist of bone-white Entrada sandstone that more resembles

A subtly colorful wash bottom in the northern portion of the monument.

sugar towers than rock. As you hike into the hoodoos, don't stop once you see the first groupings; continue into increasingly rich terrain for a total of approximately 4.6 miles (one way). To get to the parking area, head north from Big Water on Ethan Allen/Nipple Creek Road and park at the Wahweap Hoodoos Trailhead, approximately 3 miles beyond US 89. The road can become impassable to two-wheel-drive vehicles; park as appropriate and walk from there.

If you like this . . . but don't have a lot of time to spend driving and hiking, consider a shorter outing. The **Toadstools** *is yet another grouping of hoodoos; that is, boulders perched atop thinner rock pedestals. However, these are much more accessible than the Wahweap Hoodoos, as the trailhead sits immediately off US 89 (12.5 miles west of Big Water and about 2 miles west of Cottonwood Road), and the well-defined path itself stretches just 0.8 miles to the formations. Like the Wahweap Hoodoos, the Toadstools formed when boulders of Dakota sandstone fell onto the more easily erodible Entrada sandstone below. The harder Dakota boulders protected their underlying pedestals as the elements ate away at the surrounding bedrock.*

Biking

The Grand Staircase–Escalante National Monument has very little pavement and no established biking trails. That said, biking in the monument can be a popular alternative to walking some of the rougher sections of dirt road in the monument, including the final stretch of the Hole-in-the-Rock Road. Bikes are not permitted on backcountry hiking trails and, like vehicles, must stay on established roads only. Though dirt road riding might not sound that exciting, it can provide an environmentally savvy means to explore broader stretches of the monument than you could cover on foot, given the same amount of time. If you require a rental, Escalante Outfitters (310 West Main Street; 435-826-4266; www.escalanteoutfitters.com; also listed in "Pick Your Spot," toward the beginning of this chapter) carries a variety of mountain bikes in their fleet. A good place to stop anyway, the Outfitters not only offers a guide service but also has a generally active staff who can give personal recommendations on where to ride.

CAMPING

Within the park, there are three developed campgrounds, approximately 18 primitive campgrounds, and infinite wild camping sites. The number-1 requirement from the BLM is that everyone camp exclusively in already disturbed areas; as you tour the monument, you inevitably will come across a preexisting, viable campsite and absolutely do not need to (and should not) create another. All campers staying outside developed grounds must have a permit. To obtain one of these, stop by a visitors center (see "Visitors Centers," this chapter, above). But beware: They typically keep quite limited hours. All in-monument campers must abide by the 14-day limit. Though primitive grounds may be found all around, the developed sites are clearly signed and located off of UT 12 and US 89. For more information and crude maps, visit the monument's Web site: www.blm.gov.

The most popular hiking trail and campground in the monument both center around the Calf Creek Falls Recreation Area (15 miles west of Boulder/14 miles east of Escalante on UT 12). This developed campground has 14 sites, as well as running water and small restrooms. Located right off Scenic Byway 12 and roughly halfway between Boulder and Escalante, this is a convenient and central place to sleep for a few nights. Though the parking area is rather small, RVs can generally find a place to park.

Deer Creek Campground (6 miles southeast of Boulder on the Burr Trail) contains pit toilets and just four sites. Though no reservations are accepted for this campground, fees are required. A bit off the main drag, this site stands in the eastern corner of the monument and serves as a great base for exploration of Deer Creek and The Gulch, as well as the Burr Trail historic road itself (see the "Scenic Driving" portion of "Extend Your Stay," above).

Whitehouse Campground (43 miles east of Kanab on US 89) provides nine campsites located among small sandstone domes and desert shrubbery just north of the Paria Canyon–Vermilion Cliffs Wilderness Area. Each has its own picnic table and fire ring. Though the area has pit toilets, no running water is available.

Ponderosa Grove (15 miles west of Kanab on Hancock Road) is the other option for developed camping in the southern vicinity of the monument. Though technically outside the monument, this BLM-operated campground is within just a few miles of the Coral Pink Sand Dunes State Park ("See a Little," in Day 1 of the "48 Hours: Northern," above).

Kodachrome Basin State Park (see "Overview of Southern Utah: Its History, Parks, and Monuments"), about 9 miles southeast of Cannonville, is another of the more popular camping areas within the monument for RV drivers and tent sleepers alike. In a cozy, desert valley surrounded with bluffs and filled with 67 sandstone spires and numerous hiking trails, this 25-site campground is quite often full.

Escalante Outfitters (see "Pick Your Spot," under "Escalante" near the beginning of this chapter) offers tent and RV camping, in addition to its general store, restaurant, guide services, and rental cabins. Campers have access to showers and drinking water, as well as a large fire pit and communal pavilion.

5

Arches National Park

PARK OVERVIEW

Driving along US 191 from I-70 to Moab, you'd be hard-pressed to guess the location of Arches National Park without a map or road signs. Tucked uphill and east of the highway, this iconic park—though quite near US 191 and the town of Moab—remains completely hidden from view to all but those entering the park itself. With more than 2,000 documented natural arches within its boundaries, the park claims the densest collection of these peculiar features on the earth. Arches also contains varied landscapes filled with rock fins, spires, and hoodoos, as well as petrified sand dunes and unadulterated views of the surrounding mountain ranges.

The entirety of Arches is contained within one contiguous section. Arches Entrance Road originates at US 191, passes the visitors center, and climbs steeply uphill to enter the heart of the park—where it continues north for a total of roughly 19 miles. Additionally, the park contains two paved side roads, and many miles of graded and four-wheel-drive dirt byways. Its southernmost paved spur branches 2.5 miles to the east, reaching from Balanced Rock toward the North and South windows and Double Arch. Just north of this, another side road of the same length stretches eastward past Wolfe Ranch and to viewpoints of the famous Delicate Arch. Beyond the pavement, you'll find dirt roads of varying quality and many dozen miles worth of hiking and backpacking trails. Your experience in Arches will primarily be a self-guided adventure; don't expect to find the same amount of structure and developed programs here as in other parks.

Despite Arches' location directly north of and just five minutes from

LEFT: Balanced Rock sits just south of the turnoff to the North and South Windows. Gordon McArthur

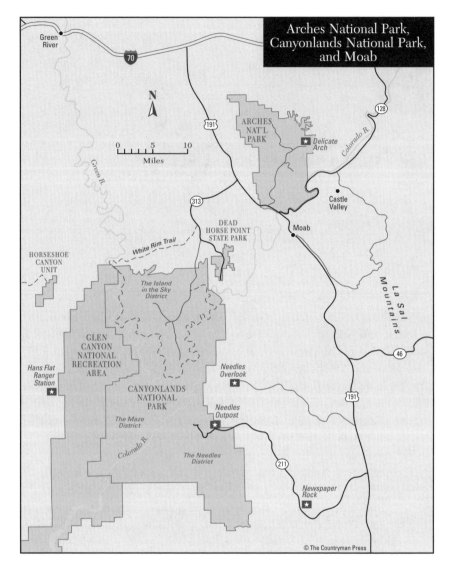

Arches National Park,
Canyonlands National Park,
and Moab

© The Countryman Press

one of Utah's most famous outdoorsy towns, it receives just more than 1 million visitors each year—hardly a third of Zion National Park's tourist load. Because of this, it maintains somewhat of a low-key feel, with open expanses of land and relatively little infrastructure. However, because Arches has limited roadways and because the bulk of its visitors arrive during the year's warm half, it endures notable vehicular congestion, particularly in its parking areas and trailheads. If at all possible, consider visiting Arches during the off-season; Arches' natural features are quite beautiful under a blanket of snow. Or wake up early in the morning to beat the crowds. Doing either will cleanse your experience of crowding and related stress.

The famous Delicate Arch   Gordon McArthur

48 Hours

GETTING THERE

Arches occupies 120 square miles in the east central portion of Utah and is among the most easily accessible national parks for those traveling by vehicle. Located just 27 miles south of I-70 and right off US 191, this park's entrance stands just 245 miles of southeast of Salt Lake City and 365 miles west of Denver, Colorado. Those planning to sleep in a hotel will stay in or around the town of Moab (detailed in chapter 7), whose lodging options range from basic motels to spendier, more luxurious establishments.

After checking into your room or pitching your tent, head to the Moab Brewery (686 South Main Street; 435-259-6333; www.the moabbrewery.com) for dinner. Open seven days a week, this brewery-slash-restaurant provides you with the chance to take a full dinner, a casual snack, or a fresh beer at a clean bar. Offering a modern, pub-style menu, the kitchen crafts a range of foods, including creative and satisfying salads, diverse sandwiches and burgers, and entrées featuring fish, poultry, beef, and vegetarian-friendly staples. You can also sample many of their beers, which are crafted right on the spot.

DAY
1

Breakfast before You Go
The Moab Diner (189 South Main Street; 435-259-4006; www.moab diner.com) serves high-quality,

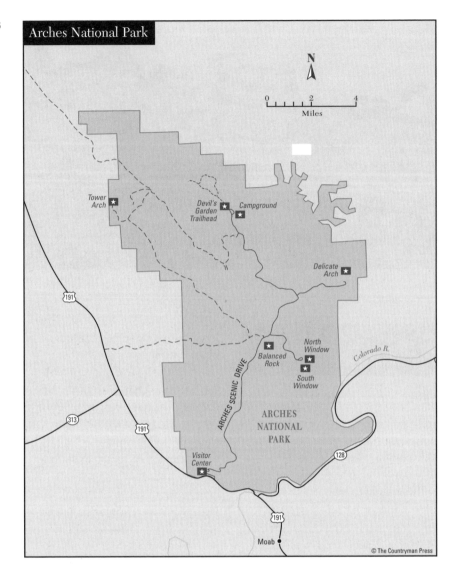

no-frills, classic American-style breakfasts. Simple meals and fast service provide quick nourishment at a low cost. Choose from 11 house specialties based on various combinations of eggs, pancakes, French toast, and meat sides. Or pick one of their six omelets.

Before paying your tab, talk to your server about ordering a take-away lunch at the diner. If spending the day in the park, you'll need to bring your own food; once you leave Moab, you will see no restaurants or shops of any kind until you return. The Moab Diner prepares simple and easily portable brown bag–style lunches that include a

Accommodations and Restaurants in Moab

Moab, just 5 miles south of world-famous Arches National Park, provides the area's best—and only—accommodations and restaurants. Moab is also surrounded by equally notorious mountain biking, rock climbing, river running, and other outdoor activities, rendering it Utah's most famous outdoorsy hub. Appropriately, it contains a generous amount of related services. For more information on this town and what to do here, see chapter 7.

choice of sandwich, potato chips, fruit, a candy bar, and a drink. Beware: The Moab Diner closes on Sundays.

Enter the Park

From Moab, drive north on Main Street/US 191 as it heads out of town and crosses over the Colorado River. Less than 5 miles from the center of Moab, the clearly signed turnoff to Arches National Park stands on the east side of the highway. It doesn't take long for Arches Entrance Road to arrive at the entrance station and Arches National Park Visitor Center (435-719-2299; www.nps .gov/arch). Here, rangers can answer any questions you may have, as well as issue backcountry permits to those planning to sleep outside the park's developed campgrounds. In addition to its staff, the visitors center offers a predictable number of brochures and illustrative displays, which provide an overview understanding of the park's geology and history, lending

a bit of context to the day's sights.

Once past these buildings, Arches Entrance Road doubles back to the south and makes a leap for the canyon rim. Near the top of this ascent, stop at the scenic pullout on the right side of the road. Anyone traveling to Arches National Park must have at least some interest in geology, and this first pullout provides a glimpse into some of the tectonic activity responsible for Arches' creation. From the parking area, look back west into the canyon through which US 191 runs. Visible here is a massive fault line caused by severe tectonic restlessness in the area. Called the Moab Fault, this is a north–south running, extensional fault. About 6 million years ago, the earth's crust broke here, unable to stretch between two plates moving apart from one another. After this fracture formed, the eastern (Arches) side of it sat approximately 2,600 feet lower than the western side. Subsequent erosion has greatly leveled the two opposing sides.

Avoiding Traffic

Arches National Park does *not* offer a shuttle bus system, and all parking areas there contain a limited number of spots, delineated by painted lines and enforced by traveling rangers. It is therefore possible that during busy days you may not find a parking space for your car at a particular trailhead or point of interest. If you have a flexible schedule, consider traveling to Arches outside its busiest season, summer. If you must come during the park's most popular months, you can mitigate this traffic issue by experiencing the park during the early morning or late evening. After all, sunset and sunrise present the best light for photographs.

Take a Hike

Driving farther into Arches, the first major pullout and parking area along the roadside is that for the Park Avenue Viewpoint and Trailhead. From here, a 1-mile trail heads down into a miniature canyon lined with solid, squared-off, sandstone fins. As the path leaves the parking lot, it descends rather steeply to the depths of this scenic valley. Be prepared for a somewhat laborious return trip; though the trail meets back up Arches Entrance Road at the Courthouse Towers Viewpoint, you'll have to retrace your steps if you haven't parked a shuttle vehicle there already.

The Scenic Drive climbs steeply into Arches National Park. Gordon McArthur

Though winter can sometimes be drab in Arches, it does keep the crowds away.

Stop for Lunch

Back at the car, you can either take lunch there, or drive on a bit farther to eat in front of a new vista. Just a few minutes up the road stands the Courthouse Towers Viewpoint, a familiar site if you just hiked the entirety of the Park Avenue Trail. Farther along Arches Entrance Road stands the Petrified Dunes Viewpoint, which looks out over ancient dunes. The original sand drifts were gradually buried under layers of sediment and compressed and hardened into Navajo sandstone. Later, the overlaying layers eroded away, exposing the dunes as a reminder of the sea that once occupied this place. If you haven't already stopped to eat, pull over at Balanced Rock, immediately before the turnoff for the Win-

dows Section of this park. Here you'll find picnic tables, pit toilets, and the 128-foot-tall namesake rock pillar. This natural rock sculpture features a 58-foot, tear-drop-shaped boulder perched precariously atop, and slightly off-center, a thin pillar.

Take a Hike

Once finished with lunch at Balanced Rock, turn east and drive about 2.5 miles toward the North and South windows region of the park. Along the way you'll pass by a handful of other signed features, such as Ham Rock and Cove Arch. This road ends in a large loop adorned with parking spaces, pit toilets, and numerous trails leading off to the nearby arches. To see three massive arches with one easy hike, look for the Windows Trail,

Geology of Arches

Though all of Utah's national parks feature the creative capabilities of geologic activity and erosive forces, the shaping of Arches National Park is likely the most difficult of all to understand without a bit of insight from experts. While Zion's mighty canyons and Bryce's spectacular amphitheaters can readily be understood as products of water and wind erosion, the origin of 2,000 rock arches requires a little more background information to grasp.

Sandstone, the general rock type of Arches, is sedimentary—meaning that it forms when grains of sand or mineral crystals are deposited and then cemented together. The sandstone of Arches was formed roughly 300 million years ago when seas covering the area evaporated, leaving behind sandy beaches and an enormous salt bed. Subsequent millennia saw repeated flooding and evaporation of the same area and, later, the gradual deposition of debris atop this salty layer. Over time, these upper layers became as much as a mile thick, compressing the layers beneath into stone.

Much less sturdy than rock, the underlying salt layer eventually yielded under the mounting weight of the upper layers, liquifying under pressure, which created widespread instability. The upper rock layers floated on this slippery salt layer, shifting, fracturing, and tilting. The nearby Moab Fault, which provided for a 2,500-foot vertical displacement of rock, further destabilized the local crust, causing even more breaking and shifting of sandstone blocks.

Over time, erosive forces ate into the fissures caused by all of this upheaval, broadening the gaps and sometimes forming fins and spires. Weaker salt deposits in these outcroppings yielded much more easily to erosion than heartier sandstone. Gradually, these weaknesses became arches and windows in the rock that would later be buffed smooth by the wind. What remains today is a snapshot of the park's ever-changing natural sculpture garden of fins, spires, hoodoos, and arches.

located at the eastern edge of this parking lot. This 1-mile gravel trail loops past the North and South windows and Turret Arch. North Window consists of a 90-foot-wide and 48-foot-tall oblong opening in a smooth fin. South Window Arch forms a soaring bridge between two globular mounds of sandstone. The origin of the name *Turret Arch* should be quite clear upon first sight of this feature. Because of the

South Window   Gordon McArthur

trail's shortness and intimate views of these impressive features, it is likely the most popular one in the entire park.

*If you like this . . . hike, but don't feel quite satisfied with its distance, tack on another short journey from the same parking area to **Double Arch***. *Just half the distance of the Windows Trail, this hike requires only 0.5 mile of total walking and can serve as a pleasant supplemental hike. Though Double Arch can clearly be seen from the parking area, the view of its massive double span is much more impressive from a point-blank distance. Classified as a "double pothole natural arch," Double Arch was formed when the walls and floor of a pothole ruptured. Subsequent wind and water erosion have eaten away all of this rock basin, but for the two remaining arms of Entrada sandstone spanning from one cliff to another. The larger of the two arches is 148 feet across and 104 feet tall; the other opening is roughly 70 feet across and 90 feet tall.*

Dinner

After completing the hikes in the Windows Section of Arches, consider this day's exploration done and head back toward the visitors center; tomorrow's trip will focus on the northern portion of the park. Having completed two or three hikes, you should feel your stomach rumbling as you head back south on US 191.

To enjoy dinner and a bottle of locally made wine away from the bustle of town, turn east on UT 128 (2.1 miles south of Arches National Park), just after crossing the Colorado River. Continue down east on this road as it winds through the

Double Arch   Gordon McArthur

sheer-cliffed canyon carved by the Colorado. As you head east, you'll trace along the southern border of Arches for much of the 14.2 driving miles along UT 128 required to reach a picturesque, riverside campus containing the Castle Creek Winery (Milepost 14 UT 128; 435-259-3332; www.castlecreekwinery .com) and Red Cliffs Lodge (435-259-2002; www.redcliffslodge.com).

It's in the lodge itself that you'll find Red Cliffs Restaurant (435-259-2002). There you can enjoy a full dinner heavy with Western accents and a bottle of wine made by the Castle Creek Winery. Choose a salmon entrée or perhaps beef prepared on the grill. Though the restaurant offers excellent surroundings and cuisine, it maintains a casual atmosphere—inviting to those who have just spent the day outside. Call ahead for reservations.

Learn a Little

After dinner, you won't even have to move your car to check out the Moab Museum of Film and Western Heritage (in the Red Cliffs Lodge; 435-529-2002). Situated on a historic ranch, the museum depicts the area's early ranching and pioneer lifestyles. In more modern decades, many films and over 100 commercials have been shot on location right at this ranch; accordingly, the museum displays photographs and artifacts documenting the filming of *Son of Cochise, Cheyenne Autumn, Rio Conchos, and Wagon Master* and their silver screen stars, Henry Fonda, Maureen O'Hara, Rock Hudson, and Anthony Quinn, among others. The museum is open daily and charges no admission. Take an hour here to digest your food and the glass of wine you had at dinner before driving in to Moab—if you're not staying at the Lodge, that is.

DAY 2

Breakfast before You Go

If you're waking up in Moab, roll on over to the Jailhouse Cafe (101 North Main Street; 435-259-3900), which specializes in breakfast foods. Its morning meals offer much better quality and creativity than standard, greasy-spoon establishments. Imagine sitting outside (or inside) and eating berry waffles, ginger pancakes, or eggs Benedict. Located right on Main Street, this petite restaurant can get crowded, so stack the odds in your favor by arriving early—or by building extra time into your schedule in case you have to wait for a table.

Pack a Lunch

Don't forget to buy a lunch before you head back into Arches; as you witnessed yesterday, the park offers no restaurants or food of any kind. If you already tried and liked the lunch at the Moab Diner (Day 1, above), head back south a few blocks and pick up a lunch to go. Or continue another minute or two down Main Street to the City Market (425 South Main Street; 435-259-5181). This full-service supermarket has all the fixings to help you assemble an affordable and nutritious lunch of your liking—including a deli and salad bar. The market also operates a gas station with some of the best fuel prices in town.

Clouds settle in over the southern part of Arches in February. David Sjöquist

Edward Abbey

Edward Paul Abbey, famous essayist and author of *Desert Solitaire* and *The Monkey Wrench Gang,* came into this world in Indiana, Pennsylvania, in 1927. At age 18, he set off for the Desert Southwest, making the journey by hitchhiking, walking, train hopping, and bus riding. He fell in love with the Four Corners region, but was immediately drafted into the army and served two years in Italy. Upon his return to the U.S., he hurried back west and attended the University of New Mexico. There, his sometimes radical, environmentalist ideas began to surface as he developed into a writer and a social thinker. Though he returned to Europe to study in Scotland, he maintained an attachment to the Four Corners region and returned again, this time to work as a seasonal ranger in Arches during 1956 and 1957. Between April and September of those years, while performing duties like collecting camping fees, speaking with visitors, and maintaining trails, Abbey collected most of his sketches and notes for what would become *Desert Solitaire.*

Take a Hike

Drive back north, toward and into the park. Along the way, you'll pass by yesterday's vistas until you reach Balanced Rock and the Windows turnoff. To the north lies new territory. One of the first destinations in this portion of the park is Delicate Arch. No trip to Arches National Park can truly be considered complete without a sighting of it. Despite this arch's fame, it actually cannot be seen from the roadside and requires everyone to walk at least a short distance to gain a view of it. To witness it for yourself, turn right to follow signs for Wolfe Ranch and the Delicate Arch Viewpoint, about 3 miles north of Balanced Rock. For a decent-size hike, park at the Wolfe Ranch itself and

prepare yourself for a 1.5-mile hike across desert soil and slick-rock to the very base of the arch. Though much of the trail passes along bare sandstone slabs, you'll be able to find your way by following cairns. Despite its 3-mile, round-trip length, this trail is enormously popular and must be shared by many other hikers during the park's busy season. Nevertheless, the trail itself and the views afforded by it render the crowds tolerable.

*If you like this . . . view, but cannot (or do not like to) hike so much to reach it, consider taking one of the two, much shorter trails from the **Delicate Arch Viewpoint Parking Area** to catch a glimpse of the arch. The shortest trail requires a mere 50 yards of nearly flat walk-*

ing on a broad and flat path; at its end stands a viewing area. From the same parking area, another more moderate trail heads to a separate viewpoint; though short (0.5 mile), this path is rather steep and slightly strenuous. Taking this trail will reduce crowding by a good margin and will get your blood moving a little. Delicate Arch sits roughly 0.5 mile to the north of both viewpoints, perched high on a sloping sandstone dome and on the other side of a dramatic and gaping gorge.

Learn a Little

Before heading back to the main road, stop at the Wolfe Ranch to learn a bit about early pioneer life in the region. Built by John Wesley Wolfe, a veteran of the Civil War, this homestead consists of a small, weathered log cabin situated in a part of Arches called Salt Wash. Hoping for prosperity, Wolfe and

Plant life throughout southern Utah is delicate and beautiful.

his family lived at this site for approximately 10 years before yielding to reality and retreating back to civilization in Ohio.

Take a Drive

Those wishing to see the remainder of the park before leaving should extract themselves from the Wolfe Ranch portion of the park and return to the main road. Driving north from here, you'll pass overlooks for the Salt Valley, Fiery Furnace, Skyline, and Sand Dune arches on the road's roughly 5.6-mile journey northward to the parking area and trailhead for the Devil's Garden. For more information on these hikes, see the "Extend Your Stay" portion of this chapter, below.

Lunch before You Go

If you're heading back into Moab to continue your journey, you will have numerous options to investigate (see "Local Flavors," chapter 7). If you're heading north to Salt Lake City, your choices will be greatly reduced; however, if you drive through Green River, you still have one great option. In a sea of truck stops and generic food chains, Ray's Tavern (25 Broadway; 435-564-3511) fires up its grill and opens its taps every day of the week. Ray's is notorious for serving the best burgers in the area. If you're looking for a romantic or quiet lunch spot, don't bother stopping in. But if you'd like a beer and a burger and can tolerate a respectable Western bar, this will be a great lunch spot for you.

Extend Your Stay
If you have more time, try to
see these things . . .

RECREATION

Scenic Driving

Arches National Park has a fairly simple layout: Its one main road, Arches Entrance Road, stretches from the visitors center in the south, up through the center of the park, and to the Devil's Garden trailhead at its far northern point, before bending quickly to the south and terminating in the Devil's Garden Campground. The entire one-way distance on this road alone is approximately 19 miles. However, the park also has two relatively short side roads that depart approximately from the midsection of Arches Entrance Road and head east—one toward the Windows Section of the park, and the other past Wolfe Ranch and toward the Delicate Arch lookouts. Both side roads stretch about 2.5 miles one way, so visitors driving the entirety of the main road, as well as each paved spur road, will travel approximately 46 miles. As the park enforces speed limits often as low as 25 miles per hour (or sometimes even slower), you should expect this drive to take at least two hours. Increase that estimate to three or four with stops. Allow for a full day if adding one or more significant hikes.

Those comfortable leaving the pavement should first check the weather forecast to be sure no rain is predicted, and then locate the Salt Valley Road on a map. If you have a two-wheel-drive car and/or low clearance, you might consider speaking with a ranger about road conditions before opting to take this drive. Though the paved roads in Arches see quiet a lot of traffic, the dirt roads are an entirely different story. However, if you feel like your self-preservation skills and vehicle are up to par, turn onto this road about 1 mile south of the Devil's Garden Trailhead (and 5 miles north of the Wolfe Ranch Road junction). This often decently maintained dirt road heads southwest for a few miles before bending back to the northwest, roughly paralleling the main road, as it tours the Salt Valley Wash. Driving through this utterly desolate valley, rimmed with gently sloping hills, slickrock, and sometimes colorful buttes, you'll forget entirely that you're in a national park.

After 7.5 miles, the road splits in three, with the Salt Valley Road continuing along the same trajectory. It eventually leads out of the park, connecting with US 191, about 10 miles after this split. (See a gazetteer if attempting this drive; a few junctions complicate this journey.) The unnamed fork branching just west of this consists of a passable, well-maintained dirt road. It heads west toward a pit toilet, just 1.3 miles down the road. The southwestern-most branch should be considered a jeep road. It is recommended for high-clearance four-wheel-drive vehicles, hikers, and mountain bikers only.

If you do have the requisite vehicle to explore this bumpy road, you can follow it west for 1.7 miles before yet another junction. Heading north (right), you'll travel another 1.4 miles to the Klondike Bluffs and a collection of twisted spires called the Marching Men. But turning south, you'll now be on the 9-mile Unnamed Four-Wheel-Drive Road, which runs southeast and eventually meets back up with Arches Entrance Road near Balanced Rock. This road, though often composed of alluringly smooth dirt, does sometimes feature deep sand on its steeper sections, so it is recommended for north–south (that is downhill!) travel only—even for those with four-wheel drive. Those with a rugged vehicle and some spare time should think about taking this drive, as it rewards its visitors with numerous arches; great views of surrounding mountains, bluffs, and other rock formations; and occasional slickrock driving.

Hiking

If you've completed the requisite Double Arch, North and South windows, and Delicate Arch hikes (as listed in the 48-hour itinerary of this chapter, above) and find yourself with a few remaining hours or days to spend in the park, think about checking out some more trails.

Many don't have time to drive all the way to the northernmost portion of the park, Devil's Garden. But if you do, it's definitely worth parking the car at the Devil's Garden trailhead and heading north on foot along the Devil's Garden Trail. Take a look at a map before you head out, as this trail system consists of an out-and-back path with one major D-shaped side loop and a handful of smaller side paths branching off of it. If you explore this trail in its entirety, you'll end up walking slightly more than 7 miles and will pass by several arches, distributed satisfyingly along the way.

Less than a mile of hiking on the Devil's Garden Trail leads to Landscape Arch—a worthy destination if you only have time for a truncated version of this hike. This massive arch, with a span of 290 feet and a height of nearly 78 feet, is categorized by the Natural Arch and Bridge Society as the largest arch in the North America, just ahead of Kolob Arch of Zion National Park. Worldwide, only two others in China exceed it in size: the Fairy Bridge at 400 feet and the Jiangzhou Bridge at approximately 300 feet. (To see more about the Natural Arch and Bridge Society's in-depth measuring of these arches, check out their Web site: www.natural arches.org.) If at all possible, make a trip to see this arch; this extremely thin and fragile filament of rock will not stand forever! If you hiked this trail before the night of August 4, 2008, you would have seen Wall Arch. This 71-by-33.5-foot arch collapsed in the middle of that night, causing the Devil's Garden Trail to temporarily close. It is only a matter of time before Landscape Arch does the same.

Landscape Arch   Gordon McArthur

If you find yourself still in the northern end of the park, cruise south to the Devil's Garden Campground and take a hike to Broken Arch along the trail that departs from campsite #40. Though not actually broken, this arch is composed of two large cobra-head-looking lobes converging at a very narrow meeting point; it does not require much effort to imagine this arch crumbling some day soon. Quite a short trail, this crosses through meadows, past fins, and over slickrock as it heads to the arch, loops around it, and returns to the road in just 1.2 miles of walking. Extend this walk by a few minutes by taking the spur from the southernmost end of the Broken Arch Loop to Sand Dune Arch. Though the arch itself isn't particularly reminiscent of dunes, it is utterly surrounded by fine golden-pink sand. Tucked into a cozy rock cove, this arch and its environs have a sandbox-like feel that kids quite like. If you don't have the time or desire to do this entire hike, you can alternatively reach Sand Dune Arch via a much shorter trail departing from Arches Entrance Road, approximately 1.5 miles south of the Devil's Garden Trailhead.

Also in the northern portion of the park, but accessed by the Salt Valley Road, is the Tower Arch/Klondike Bluffs Trail. This pathway departs from the end of that dirt road and stretches 1.7 miles westward toward Tower Arch. Along the way, it passes over steep rock slabs, alongside and among spires and fins, and through sand dunes and meadows to reach this pale arch that somewhat resembles a fireplace and chimney. To get to the parking area for this hike, follow the Salt Valley Road to the pit toilet, approximately 9 miles from Arches Entrance Road (as described in the "Scenic Driving" portion of "Extend Your Stay," above in this chapter).

Given its fragility, you'll need a special permit to hike in the Fiery Furnace. Furthermore, the park requires all persons entering the area to watch an educational video on minimizing impact. But if you stop by the visitors center, sign up, pay your fees, and see the film, you'll be allowed to check out this particularly unique section of the park. From afar, this densely packed series of parallel fins resembles flames; within the feature itself, these fins transform into a maze of cooler corridors that not only provide a bit of respite from the heat to visitors, but also supply habitat to plants and animals that otherwise could not live in the region. If you prefer, you may enter the Fiery Furnace on a ranger-guided walk, on which you'll learn more than you might alone. However, this walk has a prescribed distance and takes about two or three hours to complete. Once on the walk, you must stay with the group, so think ahead about your fitness and commitment level before signing up for one of these tours. The tours are offered twice daily and run April through October. Reservations are accepted and encouraged; tours can fill up days ahead of time. You can make these in person at the visitors center or online (www.recreation.gov) as much as a week in advance of the trip.

Though many of the hikes in the park appropriately tour rock formations, one trail that differs slightly from this theme is the Courthouse Wash Rock Art Panel. This hike, though in the park, is not located along Arches Entrance Road; rather, the parking area sits 0.5 miles north of the Colorado River on US 191 (and about 2 miles south of the turnoff to the park's main entrance). At just 0.5-miles in one-way distance, and with its parking area situated en route to Moab, this short hike can easily be added to your trip as a last-minute outing. The rock art panel reached by this trek spans an impressive 52 feet in width and 19 feet in height and is an excellent representative of the Barrier Canyon rock art style. The figures painted on the wall here have powerful size and clarity. Forms include humans, ghosts, bighorn sheep, scorpions, shields, birds, and more.

Park Tours and Other Educational Offerings

The simplest and most accessible ranger-led activities outside the visitors center are the numerous guided tours of the park's shorter and more popular trails. These typically are offered during the peak season—that is, between April and October—and take place several times every day. If you are interested in joining one of these tours, stop at the visitors center on the morning of your visit and inquire. Though you don't need a guide to follow any of these trails, the leading rangers will point out many features of the environment that you would likely otherwise miss, possibly enriching the experience for you. Rangers also usher hiking groups through the Fiery Furnace; see "Hiking," above.

Those looking for something to do after dark might drive to the Devil's Garden Campground Amphitheater for an evening program. These take place most nights between April and early October and cover a variety of topics. If this sounds tempting to you, ask a ranger at the visitors center what time and topic you can expect that evening; offerings change seasonally.

Rock Climbing

Any climber knows that Entrada sandstone, which largely composes Arches National Park, is quite soft. This presents a number of hindrances to the sport, including difficult and unreliable gear placements, disintegrating anchor setups, potential rock fall, and potential climber-caused damage to the rock itself. Nonetheless, climbers have been tooling around in Arches for decades. Because this often smooth and rounded rock does not lend itself to climbing in the same way that Zion's sheer and hard stone does, the routes in Arches National park are quite thinly spread.

If you do plan to climb, you should make yourself aware of the park's rules. First and foremost, climbing on the arches themselves (as well as on Balanced Rock) is absolutely forbidden. Certain seasonal restrictions apply to other features as well; check online *and* with a ranger to ensure the legality of your climbs. Chalk must be red or orange so as to blend with the rock, and the use of drills is prohibited. Whether free climbing or aid climbing, think "clean" and avoid leaving any gear behind. Approach all climbs via established trails or sandy washes; avoiding stepping on cryptobiotic soil at all costs. For more information, invest in a copy of Eric Bjornstad's *Desert Rock* or Stewart Green's *Rock Climbing Utah,* almost always available for sale in Moab's Pagan Mountaineering (59 South Main Street; 435-259-1117).

Before 2006, there had been no official ban of climbing on the arches; up to that point, tradition dictated that climbers should not ascend named features. However, in May of that year, a famous American climber controversially free-soloed Delicate Arch. Though that act itself left no damage on the arch, scars were visible from previous top-roping exploits. The end result of this fiasco was the official written ban of any climbing on named features.

Biking

As is the standard practice in national parks across the country, all cycling in Arches must be practiced entirely on existing roads. Though no biking on trails is allowed, it is permitted on dirt roads. Because the main dirt roads in the park (Salt Valley, Willow Springs, and the unnamed four-wheel-drive road connecting these two) can be impossible or difficult for two-wheel-drive vehicles to pass, mountain biking is therefore an excellent means for exploring these portions of the park. Be aware that Salt Valley Road can usually be driven by any vehicle; if you find yourself biking this road, watch out for vehicular traffic. Additionally, the four-wheel-drive road connecting Salt Valley and Willow Springs roads contains sections of deep sand that can render biking tedious.

Road bikers also occasionally enter the park. A paved bike path heading north out of Moab and along US 191 conveniently passes by the entrance to Arches, where Arches Entrance Road's challenging climb into the park awaits cyclists. Road bikers do not commonly bike in the park; whenever the weather is pleasant enough for cycling, it's also nice enough to warrant heavy traffic on the entrance road. The park's road itself has no bike lanes, so if you dislike exhaust and road crowding, consider riding in the early morning hours, before the bulk of the visitors arrives.

The same bike path that originates in Moab continues on a path parallel to US 191, all the way up to UT 313—the access highway for the Island in the Sky portion of Canyonlands National Park (see chapter 6) and Dead Horse State Park (see chapter 6 and "Overview of Southern Utah: Its History, Parks, and Monuments"). You may consider riding this route as an alternative to the actual in-park ride if you're a late sleeper and will be in the area during the busy months. Additionally, the Intrepid Trail System in Dead Horse State Park was built especially for mountain bikers and provides excellent views of the Colorado River and surrounding canyons.

CAMPING

Within Arches National Park, only one camping option exists: the Devil's Garden Campground. Located at the far northern terminus of Arches Entrance Road, this 50-site campground accommodates both tents and RVs. Though the campground offers no showers and very little infrastructure, it does provide drinking water, toilets, picnic tables, fire pits, and grills. If you would like to have a fire or use the grills, bring your own wood and charcoal. Each site costs $20 and can be reserved online (www.recreation.gov) for an extra fee; the park itself does not handle reservations for camping.

Plenty of other wild and developed camping options exist within the Moab area, including a campground within the town itself. For information on these varied options, see chapter 7.

6

Canyonlands National Park

PARK OVERVIEW

Canyonlands National Park occupies a nearly 530-square-mile area just west of Moab and south of I-70. Centered around the confluence of Utah's two mightiest rivers, the Green and Colorado, this national park showcases the region's rich geologic history sliced rawly into view by the impressive powers of erosion. Here the Colorado River arrives from the northeast and is joined by the Green River arriving from the northwest; once merged, the mighty river plunges south through the steep and narrow Cataract Canyon. Divided by this Y of rivers, Canyonlands contains three main sections, distinct from one another in flavor and separated by this natural barrier. A fourth and detached area of the park stands off to the northwest of this major land area.

The northern major slice of Canyonlands, Island in the Sky, sits nearest to Moab and is the most easily accessible and therefore most visited region of Canyonlands. The "island" itself, fittingly named, consists of a massive and flat mesa that soars high and alone above the surrounding landscape. To its east, west, and south, the rivers carve deep canyons into the earth, flowing roughly 2,200 feet below the mesa's rim. This section of the park is the location of the famous White Rim and its White Rim Trail. Tracing a meandering path along a midlevel plateau beneath the Island, but above the rivers, this 103-mile loop is a multiday adventure for both jeeps and mountain bikers.

In the southern district of the park, the Needles lies about 1.5 hours southwest of Moab. This portion of the park has a much more untamed feel

LEFT: In the Needles District, the Six Shooter towers of Indian Creek Canyon are visible in the mirror.

than Island in the Sky. The journey to the Needles via US 191 and UT 211 is a trip out of and away from society, as the roads wind out of Moab, up onto high desert plateau, and then plunge down into the ever-broadening Indian Creek Canyon. This canyon, with its jutting Wingate sandstone buttes perched atop steep talus piles, might as well be a national park itself. Once in the Needles, a road, both dirt and paved, explores this appropriately named district of the park. The Needles' roads and many hiking trails feature close-up views of dramatic fins and spires, as well as far-off glimpses of Island in the Sky mesa and the La Sal Mountains, beautified by their complementary desert foreground.

The third main section of Canyonlands, and also its largest, sits to the west of the Green and Colorado rivers. The Maze, as it's called, bears a forebodingly accurate name. The least developed portion of the park by far, the Maze and its ranger station stand 46 dirt road miles away from any pavement. From there, high-clearance jeep roads and wilderness hiking lead into the heart of this district. Also called the Canyons of the Maze, this wild expanse rewards its visitors with a near total absence of other people in this extremely remote, colorful, and complicated geological wonderland. Those entering the Maze should arm themselves with a high degree of self-sufficiency and desert wilderness know-how and likewise bring along generous amounts of water, food, clothing, and maps.

A fourth and much smaller part of Canyonlands, Horseshoe Canyon, is actually an island of parkland sitting off the northwestern side of the Maze. Accessed by two-wheel-drive dirt roads, this section is isolated from highways and towns and stands near the far northern sliver of the Glen Canyon National Recreation Area. Those making the effort to reach this oft-overlooked section of Canyonlands will witness some of the most considerable rock art in North America. Added to the park in 1971, Horseshoe Canyon has been home to humans as far back as 9000 B.C.—when the locals literally hunted mammoths and mastodons. These ancients left behind numerous images on protected cliff bands that are still quite clear today. Like that seen at the Courthouse Wash in Arches National Park, these are classified as part of the Barrier Canyon–style group. The panels in Horseshoe Canyon contain large, detailed, and clear interpretations of ancient life and culture, the most famous of which is called the Great Gallery.

All told, the park receives about half a million visits each year—approximately one-sixth from Zion and one-half from its neighbor, Arches National Park. So even if you happen to visit its most popular section, Island in the Sky, you'll find yourself contending with far fewer cars and RVs for parking spots. If you head to the Island, be sure to check out Dead Horse State Park along the way (see "Overview of Southern Utah: Its History, Parks, and Monuments"). Regardless of where you decide to visit, bring your camera, plenty of water and sunblock, and hiking shoes.

Pick Your Spot
Where to stay and what you'll find nearby . . .

Generally speaking, most people coming to Canyonlands will head to Island in the Sky and will therefore base themselves out of Moab. For all information on lodging and dining within that town, see chapter 7, as well as the suggested 48-hour itinerary for Arches National Park (in chapter 5). Those heading to the Maze likely will not station themselves in any town, as the extreme time and distance required to reach this remote portion eliminates daily commuters. Finally, those heading to the Needles will find themselves putting up in the small towns along US 191, Monticello and Blanding.

MONTICELLO

The Inn at the Canyons (533 North Main Street; 435-587-2458) offers 43 of the best, newly renovated rooms in the area, outfitting its dwellings in Southwestern-themed, non-standard-motel garb. This two-story structure also houses a large, indoor swimming pool and hot tub area. Though the skeleton of this building clearly suggests a regular, roadside hotel, the recent improvements have done a lot to dress it up and place it a notch above its competition.

Also situated right in town, the Monticello Inn (164 East Central Street/US 491; 435-587-2274; www.themonticelloinn.com) provides another option in improved—though still basic—motel-style lodging. This motel provides free wireless Internet throughout the building, and its televisions carry HBO. The rooms are reliably cleaned and moderately priced. Those staying here won't partake of the dirt-cheap pricing typical of rural Utah, but will pay a few extra dollars for a pleasant night of sleep.

BLANDING

Slightly larger than Monticello, Blanding sits a bit farther south on US 191 and will likely be your locale if your trip also includes visits to Monument Valley or the Glen Canyon National Recreation Area. The Four Corners Inn (131 East Center; 435-678-3257; www.four cornersinn.com) may appear like most other hotels from the outside. But on the inside, it's surprisingly superior in terms of décor, updated furniture, and cleanliness. These improvements come at a slightly elevated price, but compared with city lodging, it's not too bad, and is roughly in the range of Moab prices.

The Blue Mountain Inn (711 South Main Street; www.blue mountaininnblanding.com), formerly a Comfort Inn & Suites, still bears many similarities to its precursor, though it now enjoys local ownership. A slightly dressed-up

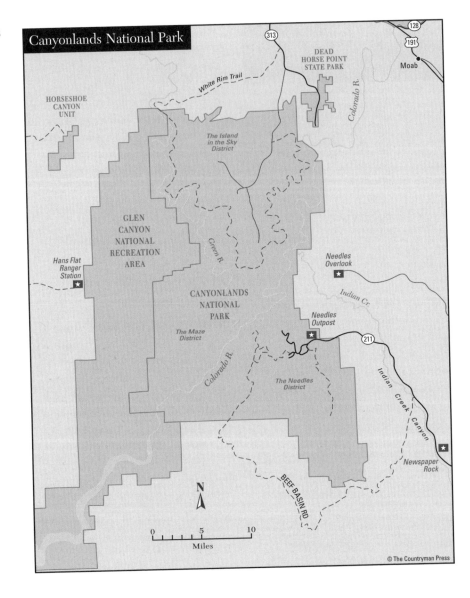

Canyonlands National Park

HORSESHOE
CANYON
UNIT

White Rim Trail

313

DEAD
HORSE POINT
STATE PARK

Moab

128

191

Colorado R.

The Island
in the Sky
District

GLEN
CANYON
NATIONAL
RECREATION
AREA

Hans Flat
Ranger
Station

Green R.

Needles
Overlook

CANYONLANDS
NATIONAL
PARK

Indian Cr.

Needles
Outpost

The Maze
District

211

The Needles
District

Colorado R.

Indian Creek Canyon

Newspaper
Rock

N

BEEF BASIN RD.

0   5   10

Miles

© The Countryman Press

version of its old self, the inn offers slightly more color and pizzazz than a run-of-the-mill, national brand hotel. Like the Four Corners Inn, this establishment charges a bit extra for its improved accommodations.

Blanding Super 8 (755 South Main Street; 435-678-3880; www .super8.com) offers hotel-style rooms of reliable quality in the center of town. Like its sisters across the nation, this AAA-approved hotel offers basic room décor and consistent cleanliness. Wireless Internet reaches all of the rooms within this two-story structure. Rates here are comparable to, but slightly more than, those at the Blue Mountain and Four Corners inns. Pets are also allowed here for a charge of $10 and up.

Local Flavors
Taste of the town—local cafés, restaurants, bars, bistros, etc.

MONTICELLO

The restaurants in Monticello certainly cater to a rural Utah crowd. The vast majority offer a very basic American cuisine and are closed on Sundays. However, a few eateries in Monticello offer some higher quality, fresh-made cuisine.

Come hungry if you're going to eat at the K & A Chuckwagon (496 North Main Street; 435-587-3468). This Monticello restaurant embodies down-home cooking and serves home-style meals beginning with salad and freshly baked bread delivered to the table with honey butter. Grilled chicken, salmon, baby back ribs, and steaks come next with heaping sides of baked beans and country potatoes. If you have room, take a slice of their homemade pies, made fresh every day.

Wagon Wheel Pizza (164 South Main Street; 435-587-2766) presents another specialized option for eating fresh-made, delicious meals. Offering a wide variety of pizza sizes and toppings, this restaurant has an excellent reputation among locals and visitors alike and, though it has a simple atmosphere, serves first-rate food.

Choose from one of their house specialties, design your own, or even split one pie with different toppings on each half.

BLANDING

If all this hiking and fresh air has rendered your tank too close to empty, stop by Fattboyz Grillin' (164 North Grayson Parkway; 435-678-3777) to bring your system back into balance. Perhaps the most popular of all Blanding's restaurants, this specializes in burgers, steaks, sandwiches, and barbecue. Fattboyz typically runs a lunch special every day between 11 AM and 4 PM, offering quite a lot of food for around $5. Think ribs, barbecue sauce, pulled pork, thick burgers, potato salad, macaroni and cheese, beans, and homemade coleslaw.

You'll really know you've reached the heart of rural Utah when you step into the Old Tymer Restaurant (733 South Main Street; 435-678-2122; www.old tymerrestaurant.com), a down-home restaurant offering a full menu, salad bar, and buffet in the presence of utterly shameless pioneer West décor. The cuisine served is somewhat of an amalgamation between Southwestern and Mexican food and includes special choices for vegetarians and children. Don't be surprised that the menu is devoid of alcohol; Blanding is a dry town and offers no liquor, beer, or wine in its restaurants. The Old Tymer serves three meals a day, except on Sunday, when the Mormon ownership observes Sabbath.

The Homestead Steakhouse (121 East Center Street; 435-678-3456) offers huge portions of meat for bargain prices, considering the restaurant's distance from any major town. And while the name would fittingly have you expecting T-bones and top sirloin, you can also order a variety of seafood. Vegetarians dining here will also find themselves able to select among a few substantial entrées. Expect a soup and salad bar as well.

48 Hours

Most coming to Canyonlands with limited time will visit the Island in the Sky portion of the park; it offers the most attractions for the least amount of driving. Additionally, this portion of the park stands within about 30 minutes of Moab, allowing visitors to enjoy the lodging and dining of that famous outdoorsy town. This itinerary will guide you through two days' worth of exploration there; for more options in the park's other districts, read the "Extend Your Stay" section, below.

GETTING THERE

On your first evening, steer your way toward Moab and check into your hotel. (For lodging suggestions in Moab, refer to chapter 7.) If you have arrived with an empty stomach, stop by a real area classic, Eddie McStiff's (57 South Main Street; 435-259-2337; www.eddie

mcstiffs.com). This restaurant-slash-tavern provides both a family eatery (with children's menu) and a place to unwind with a beer or mixed drink. Specializing in pizza, the restaurant also serves sandwiches and burgers, entrées like grilled steaks and various seafood, Mexican cuisine, salads, and dessert. After dinner, you can watch sports any night of the week on the tavern side, or even catch live music. If interested, check online or call for the live music schedule. Eddie McStiff's is open seven days a week, so you can count on being fed and watered.

DAY 1

Breakfast before You Go

Now that you know where Eddie McStiff's is, you can easily return to that same parking lot to get breakfast the following morning at the neighboring Wake & Bake Cafe (57 South Main Street; 435-259-

Eddie McStiff's is one of the most popular restaurants in town.

2420; www.wakeandbakecafe.com). Opening its doors at 7 AM, Wake & Bake serves the full spectrum of espresso drinks and locally roasted drip coffees, as well as quick bites like bagels, croissants, muffins, granola, and cookies. If you crave a more filling breakfast, but without the time requirement and tip duties of a full-service restaurant, you can fill your belly here by simply ordering a breakfast burrito, stack of waffles, or a sweet (or savory) crepe. Other beverages served here include smoothies, fresh juices, and various teas. Unfortunately, the café offers almost no outdoor seating.

Enter the State Park

Head north from Moab on Main Street. Follow this road as heads out of town and becomes US 191 for about 11 miles, keeping an eye out for the clearly marked left-hand turnoff for Canyonlands National Park and UT 313. This road heads west and gradually dips toward the south. After about 14.5 miles, it splits; unless you are extremely tight on time, head south toward Dead Horse Point State Park. A detour to this spectacular state park requires only about 6.5 miles of driving in each direction, rendering it well within reach.

A well-developed and unusually scenic state park, Dead Horse Point features a narrow finger of land, surrounded by sheer cliffs and soaring more than 2,000 feet above the winding Colorado River. A mere 30 feet wide at its neck, this peninsula offers incredible views in all directions but is just one of the attractions of this park. Also situated here is a campground—a good alternative to camping in Canyonlands—a visitors center, as well as a system of trails known as the Intrepid Trail System, which was built

Pack a Lunch

Before you head to the park, make sure to stop and pick up a lunch to go. Many of Moab's restaurants offer sack lunches, including the **Moab Diner** (189 South Main Street; 435-259-4006; www.moabdiner .com) and **Moab Sandwiches** (inside the Chevron gas station, 817 South Main Street; 435-259-2212; www.moabsandwiches.com). If you prefer to build your own sack lunch, head to the **City Market** (425 South Main Street; 435-259-8971), Moab's largest grocery store. Here you can choose from any of their premade deli sandwiches and to-go dishes, as well as from-scratch fixings of any kind. Plus, you don't need to call ahead to order from a grocery store!

especially with mountain bikers in mind. Hikers may choose to tour the 1.1-mile Intrepid Loop; mountain bikers or long-distance trekkers have the option of taking the 4.2-mile Great Pyramid Loop or the 9-mile Big Chief Loop. Built in 2009, these new trails provide a variety of terrain, including shrubby plateau and slickrock. The three different loops are designed to accommodate riders of all levels, with the shortest being the easiest, and the longest the most challenging. Though the parts of the trail flirt with the extremely cliffy edge of this plateau, it stays far enough away from the actual edge to be safe. Well developed and signed, this trail is easy to follow on your own. However, if you want recommendations, maps, or even further reading, talk with rangers at the visitors center who can recommend rides or hikes based on your time frame and skill level; or stop in at the bookstore to purchase riding-specific information.

Stop for Lunch

If you didn't already eat your lunch at the picnic area in Dead Horse Point State Park (about 0.5 mile north of the park road's southern terminus and the Dead Horse Point Overlook), head into Canyonlands National Park before pulling over to ingest your midday calories before embarking on a number of very short and easy, classic hikes in the afternoon.

Enter the National Park

From the turnoff to Dead Horse Point, you have less than 5 miles of driving to reach the boundaries for Canyonlands National Park, and about 6 before you encounter the visitors center. Inside this small, nondescript building, you can meet and talk with rangers, pick up permits if you plan to sleep out in the backcountry, or inquire about the availability of developed campsites. If you don't already have one with you, it is a good idea to pick up a free map and trail guide. The first afternoon in this fantastically exposed section of Canyonlands lends itself to peering over the edge at various overlooks around the plateau rim. Plan to drive around a fair amount and hop out of the car for many short and rewarding hikes to classic vistas.

Take Two Hikes

Leaving the visitors center, the main road heads south for another 6 miles before splitting into two branches. Immediately before this junction, keep your eye out to your left (west) to look for the parking for a trail leading to the classic view at Mesa Arch. From here, a 0.5-mile loop trail heads across the flat, high plateau to this namesake feature. Though itself not overly impressive in size or in shape, this broad and flat, squinting arch sits exactly at the edge of Island in the Sky mesa, framing the view of the incredible drop-off immediately behind it. Through the arch, you see the handiwork of the Colorado River: richly colored spires and buttes, as well as the obvious White Rim outlining the dominant plateau below.

After that short loop, you're probably just starting to feel warmed up in terms of blood flow to the legs and ready for more views of mesa-edge drop-offs. Back in the car, head south and take the southern spur toward the Grand View Point Overlook. Doing this will lead you toward the most famous vista in the park, the parking for which lies just 6 miles

Mesa Arch, located in Island in the Sky, requires just a short hike to reach. Gordon McArthur

Looking down from Island in the Sky at just a portion of the White Rim   Gordon McArthur

beyond this junction. From the trailhead, a 1-mile trail extends to the south, reaching Grand View Point. Almost entirely flat, this well-maintained, extremely popular trail loses only 50 feet along the way, making it an accessible hike for almost any fitness level. The trail terminates at the southern edge of Island in the Sky mesa, where interpretive signs point out the major features visible from the viewing area. These include the massive Henry Mountains, which top out at 11,506 feet and are the home of a free-ranging buffalo herd; the massive Boulder Mountain Plateau, which sits sandwiched between the Capitol Reef National Park and the Grand Staircase–Escalante National Monument and whose top elevation is 11,313 feet; the deep rust and purple spires and fins of the nearby Needles District to the south; and the Green River, responsible for the fantastic erosion below and whose waters have traveled all the way from the Wind River Range in northwestern Wyoming to reach this point. A set of stone steps leads yet farther from the first viewing area toward the edge of this high plateau; those willing to literally stand on the cliff edge will see White Rim Plateau more than 1,000 feet below. With any luck, you'll be either at the Grand View Point Overlook or at the White Rim Overlook ("If you like this . . ." below) as the sun starts to set; this late day, low-angle light wildly enriches the already stunning views.

If you like this . . . and feel like adding (or substituting) another nearby hike of similar length, return to your car and backtrack north a little bit more than 1 mile to the parking area for the **White Rim Overlook Trail.** *Just 0.9 mile in length and similarly flat, this out-and-back hike quite resembles the Grand View Overlook Trail; however, its viewpoint looks out toward the southeast and is situated at the far end of a thin filament of Island in the Sky mesa, providing a panoramic view of Gooseberry Canyon to the north and Monument Basin to the South, as well as views of White Rim Road as it winds for miles between these two features. Even though the trail is much less famous than its Grand View sister, it certainly is not inferior in any way, plus it typically has a touch less crowding than the Grand View area.*

Dinner

Unless you're camping and are outfitted with a camp stove and fixings, you'll need to head back into Moab for a bite. Hungry and thirsty, you'd be well served to stop in at Zax (96 South Main Street; 435-259-6555; www.zaxmoab.com), a very casual restaurant serving a variety of food to please any taste. Dinner possibilities include wood-fired specialty and classic pizzas; roughly 15 sandwiches and burgers; steaks, ribs, and poultry from the grill; and salads, pasta dishes, and soups. Whether you feel like splitting a

pizza among the family or ordering a full-blown entrée each, you can feel confident that you'll be able to find a meal to match your appetite, preferences, and budget at this eatery.

Evening Out

After dinner, slide over to Zax Watering Hole (on location at Zax Restaurant), which offers plenty of bar stools, high-top tables, and booths for resting your legs while sampling Utah's local brews and wines. With a full bar, Zax also offers mixed drinks. Or if you'd like to enjoy the weather outside, head to Frankie D's (44 West 200 South; 435-259-2654; www.moabfrankieds .com). A bar friendly to both locals and tourists, it offers pool tables, a late-night menu, horseshoes, and frequent live music with a dance floor. If you're interested in seeing one of their shows, check out the "Entertainment" portion on their Web site for up-to-date offerings.

DAY 2

Breakfast before You Go

For a satisfying cup of organic coffee and a full, hot breakfast, head to the Eklecticafe (352 North Main Street; 435-259-6896). This liberal outfit serves some of the most interesting and nutritious breakfasts you've never heard of, including steamed seaweed with a choice of scrambled eggs or tofu (vegan), banana nut whole wheat pancakes, salmon cakes with eggs and tarragon tartar sauce, and scrambled tofu burritos. For those with more conservative tastes, plenty of more traditional options exist like egg, pinto bean, rice, and cheese breakfast burritos, bagel breakfast sandwiches, quiche du jour, buttermilk pancakes, and oven-roasted taters with eggs, cheese, and salsa. Whether you're vegan or meat-eatin,' you'll have plenty of filling and delicious items to choose from. Additionally, the café makes boxed lunches, which include a choice of sandwiches with chips, a cookie, fruit, and water. If ordering for four or more persons, you must call 48 hours in advance of your pickup time.

*If you like this . . . but prefer a lighter breakfast, head to **Moab Coffee Roasters** (90 North Main Street; 435-259-2725; www.moab coffeeroasters.com). Opening at 6:30 AM during the summer (and 8 AM during fall, winter, and spring), seven days a week, this staple Moab institution gives you plenty of time to stop here before beginning a long day. Enjoy a cup of organic, fair-trade coffee or an espresso drink. Grab a quick bite of pastries, muffins, or smoothies.*

Take a Hike

To finish your exploration of the park on this in-and-out tour, head back north to the Island in the Sky

The entrance to the Needles District   David Sjöquist

Upheaval Dome

Located at the end of the road, this peculiar features sits just 5 miles away from the junction by Mesa Arch and serves as the starting point for multiple trails. A completely unique landform in the park, this round, craterlike area stretches 3 miles across and contains radically tilted and otherwise deformed rock layers along its edges, as well as a rising dome in its center. As nobody was around to witness the formation of this curious feature, no one can say with certainty what created it.

Two primary theories have been formulated by scientists to explain the formation of Upheaval Dome. One group believes the dome is an impact crater formed when a meteorite collided with the earth. If true, this particular meteorite must have had a diameter of approximately 0.3 mile and impacted the earth roughly 60 million years ago. A dome in the center of the depression formed after the impact, as the meteorite left a massive hole in the earth where it hit; the rocks beneath, now rid of the weight of formerly overlying crust, rose.

The second theory postulates that Upheaval Dome is a massive salt dome. Much as happened in Arches National Park, the feature originated from massive salt beds that formed as a sea evaporated. Atop these salt areas other sediments collected and eventually formed rock layers. With enough rock above it, the salt beds became more fluid under the enormous amounts of pressure. This salt bed then formed a massive blister under which yet more layers of rock were deposited. The theory holds that the salt bubble then eventually burst, collapsing under the crust above, and rendering a massive hole in the earth's crust. The debris from that collapse were eroded away over time, leaving a circular void.

District. For time-saving purposes, a return to this district of the park is the most efficient; it requires only about half the driving time from Moab than the Needles District. However, if you would like to see something new and don't mind about 45 minutes extra driving in each direction, check out "The Needles" in the "Extend Your Stay"

section below for suggestions.

Once in the park, wave hello, pass the visitors center, and head south to the junction just beyond Mesa Arch. Instead of heading south toward the Grand View Overlook, this time bear right to head northwest and toward the parking and picnic area situated at the gateway to Upheaval Dome (see

"Upheaval Dome," below). To tour this massive, circular landform, you have two main options: the Syncline Loop Trail, which circles the dome, and the Overlook Trail (below), which makes a much shorter journey to a viewing point. If you do just one hike today and have come prepared for a fairly substantial outing, you should take the 8.3-mile Syncline Loop Trail. Not only serious in terms of length, this trail also requires a good bit of climbing power, as it has more than 1,300 vertical feet of elevation change. Hiking down into the canyons of this formation, you'll pass through a beautiful desert landscape and twisted and tiled cliff bands. Though the hike does offer some shade, you should plan to wear plenty of sunscreen and bring more water and food than you'd expect. Allow six hours for the hike, or less if you're quick on your feet.

If you like this . . . but really don't care to hike 8.3 miles, or your allotted time won't allow doing so, take instead the Upheaval Dome Overlook Trail, which departs directly from the same parking area and heads toward the bull's-eye of the dome. Along the hike, you'll pass by one overlook at 0.4 mile and another at the end of the trail, 0.5 mile later. Not only is this hike less serious than the Syncline Loop Trail in terms of distance, it also cuts the elevation change down to only about 10 percent of that trip.

Lunch before You Go

Once you've completed this hike, you can take your time to explore some of the park's many scenic overlooks (in "Scenic Driving" under "Extend Your Stay," below), head directly back to Moab (chapter 7) for lunch, or hit the road and be on your way.

Extend Your Stay
If you have more time, try to see these things . . .

Because Canyonlands' three major sections and its smaller and separate district, Horseshoe Canyon, all must be accessed via completely different routes, this chapter's "Extend Your Stay" section consists of four sections, one for each portion of the park. Choose which portion of the park you'd most like to visit, and read below to learn about the various recreation options you have there.

ISLAND IN THE SKY

Though this chapter's 48-hour suggested itinerary took place in this portion of Canyonlands, there remains much to be explored there. Centered around a lofty mesa with abrupt edges, this region of the park lends itself readily to short hikes along the mesa rim. Once at the rim, however, almost all the

Rounded domes in Island in the Sky   Gordon McArthur

hikes quickly become a lot more serious, descending more than 1,000 feet
to reach the next major mesa below, the White Rim Plateau—with a few of
the trails even dropping more than 2,000 feet in total to reach the shores of
the Colorado River. Most paths leading down to the White Rim Plateau also
meet up with the White Rim Road, a famous 103-mile loop popular among
jeepers and mountain bikers with the requisite permits and reservations to
camp during the multiday journey this trail presents.

Recreation

Scenic Driving

Island in the Sky mesa, with its cliffy edges, allows only for a finite number
of road miles—20 along the paved scenic drive, to be exact. Just 2 miles
after crossing into the park's borders, the Schafer Trail Road splits off this
main road to the east and begins snaking down the plateau. The first mile or
so can be passed by almost any regular vehicle; but quickly after that, the
road becomes quite steep and is best taken by vehicles with four-wheel
drive only. Though the road surface itself is generally passable by any vehicle, the severe pitch of the road and the very steep drop-offs immediately to
its side render it much more dangerous to those with insufficient traction
and power. Imagine a road in the high Alps, only with narrower shoulders
and a dirt surface. The road reaches the White Rim Trail 5.3 miles after
leaving the scenic drive. Beyond that, this road continues on its own path

and connects with Potash Road (see the "Scenic Driving" portion of chapter 7) just on the northern bank of the Colorado River.

A mile south of the Scafer Trail turnoff is the visitors center with its maps and rangers aplenty. Another mile farther south comes the parking area for the Neck Spring Trail (see "Hiking," below). Two miles beyond this you'll find the Lathrop Trailhead, another backcountry footpath that leads down to the White Rim Trail in 6.8 miles. After these trailheads, it's pretty smooth sailing and uninterrupted viewing until you reach the parking for Mesa Arch (see "Take Two Hikes" in Day 1 of this chapter's 48-hour itinerary), which sits immediately north of a Y junction in the scenic drive.

Heading south, you'll pass by the trailhead for Murphy Point in just a few minutes, and the Buck Canyon Overlook in just 1 more mile. Don't bypass this viewing area. Reached by a 2-mile trail, this overlook affords expansive views of the massive White Rim Plateau, below, and the massive namesake canyon that eats into it. Next up comes the White Rim Overlook, just a couple of miles south and also on the west side of the road. A couple of footpaths lead east from this overlook, the Gooseberry Trail and White Rim Overlook trails (see Day 1 of this chapter's 48-hour itinerary). The final stop on this road is its most famous, the Grand View Point Overlook. From here, you'll have to do an about-face and retrace to the Y junction.

Once there, take a left here to head northwest. Quickly after making this turn, you'll want to take another left toward the Willow Flat Campground and the Green River Overlook, from which you'll see yet another fantastic and yet different view of the plateaus and river canyons below. Across the main road from this turnoff sits the parking for Aztec Butte Trail (see "Hiking," below). Between this and the end of the road, just a few more trailheads exist, one for the 6.1-mile Wilhite Trail, another for the 0.5-mile

Some of the expansive views afforded by Island in the Sky.   Gordon McArthur

Whale Rock Trail, and another for the 5.6-mile Alcove Spring Trail. Both of these longer hikes depart from the road and descend more than 1,300 feet to reach the White Rim Trail. Of these, Alcove Spring reaches the north-easternmost part of the White Rim Trail within the park boundaries. Finally, at the end of the road sits the parking for all the trails situated around Upheaval Dome (see Day 2 of this chapter's 48-hour itinerary, above).

Once you've reached Upheaval Dome, you've literally passed by all the pavement in the park; from here, turn back south to eventually find the exit for the park. However, just because you've completed all of the drives within Island in the Sky, the park still offers other scenic driving possibilities (in their sections of this chapter, below). And if you have interest, you wouldn't be wasting your time to check out the many other scenic driving opportunities in the Moab area (chapter 7) and in Arches National Park (chapter 5).

Hiking

Neck Spring Trail, located 1 mile south of the visitors center, stretches for 5.8 miles, on the western side of the park's scenic drive. This interpretive loop trail is adorned with numerous signs depicting the various natural features and creatures and human ranching history along the way. This ranching past is also illustrated by remnants of equipment scattered by the trailside. Because it has very little elevation change, this hike is quite easy to complete, despite its fairly significant length.

Just south of this, the Lathrop Trail heads downhill for 6.8 miles to the southeast, connecting eventually with the White Rim Trail. Beyond that, it extends for another 4 miles, eventually descending all the way to the Colorado River. The trail begins as a flat path, cutting across the flat and grassy top of Island in the Sky mesa. This easy section lasts for 2.5 miles until the trail reaches the plateau's edge, and then begins to drop 1,600 vertical feet to the White Rim, providing great views of the La Sal Mountains, seen above Moab, to the east. The next 4 miles only loses another 400 vertical feet to reach the shores of the Colorado River.

If you like this . . . but want to head west and toward the White Rim Trail above the Green River instead, take the **Wilhite Trail,** *a 6.1-mile path that drops quickly off Island in the Sky and down 1,600 vertical feet to the White Rim Plateau. Because of its westward trajectory, this path offers views of the Henry Mountains to the southwest. The trailhead for this sits just about 2.5 miles southeast of Upheaval Dome. Or consider taking the* **Alcove Spring Trail,** *another trail of similar length that instead trends to the north. This 5.6-mile trail departs from the main road about 1.5 miles south of Upheaval Dome, passing through a large alcove with a sizable amphitheater eroded into its walls. This hike loses "only" 1,300 feet to reach the White Rim Trail's in-park northeastern terminus.*

White Rim Trail

Probably the most famous trail in the entirety of Canyonlands National Park—and among the most well known in the entire state of Utah— the White Rim Trail stretches for 103 miles along the distinct rim of the incredible White Rim Plateau, more than 1,200 feet beneath Island in the Sky. Providing plateau-edge views of the Green and Colorado rivers beneath it and ever-changing views of the Island in the Sky cliffs above it, this road would be passable by any low-clearance, two-wheel-drive car, if it weren't for a few sections. But because of these rough patches of road, anyone planning a trip here should a have high-clearance vehicle or a mountain bike. Due to the popularity of this road, the park service limits the number of users on it at any given time. Nineteen campsites exist along the way, and camping outside these is prohibited. If you hope to do this trail, be sure to call the **Reservation Office** (435-259-4351) well in advance of your trip—even more than a year in advance—as permits are required to sleep in any of these sites, and the demand for them is quite high.

The Murphy Point Trailhead, located on the way to Grand View Point, about 2.5 miles south of the Scenic Road's Y junction, offers a number of branching trails. The shortest of these heads to Murphy Point after just 1.8 miles of flat, plateau-top walking. The Murphy Loop departs from this trail just 0.5 miles after its origin and heads to the edge of the mesa before dropping 1,700 vertical feet to reach the White Rim Trail. It joins this famous path for just 1.3 miles before turning back toward the plateau and reascending its slopes.

If you crave a physical challenge and want to pack it into a midlength power hike, think about taking the Gooseberry Trail. Not to be confused with Gooseberry Mesa (outside Zion National Park), this steep path shares its trailhead with the White Rim Overlook Trail (Day 1 of this chapter's 48-hour itinerary, above). However, instead of hiking across flats to an overlook, this path plunges 1,400 feet in just over 2.7 miles to connect with the White Rim Trail below.

Sitting just a jiggle northwest of the scenic drive's major Y junction is the parking for the Aztec Butte Trail. Another plateau-top hike, this short journey actually is not as flat as you've grown to expect. Rather, it climbs sandstone slabs to reach an ancient granary. Left behind by the namesake tribe, this stone structure sits under a scenic overhang with natural rock pillars and a fantastic view of the canyons beyond and below. The total hike is just 2 miles in length.

Just before reaching the end of the road at Upheaval Dome and all of the trail options there (see Day 2 of this chapter's 48-hour itinerary, above), you'll see the parking for Whale Rock. This short trail climbs just 0.5 mile and about 100 vertical feet to reach the top of a naked, slickrock dome. From atop this mound, hikers have a slightly elevated view of the surroundings below.

Park Tours and Other Educational Offerings

Between the months of March and October, the park service offers three ranger-led programs each day. Rangers give two talks at Grand View Point in the morning, covering the park's geology, and one at the visitors center in the afternoon on various subject matters. Stop at the visitors center to confirm exact times and topics during your visit.

Rock Climbing

Though rock climbing in Canyonlands National Park has been practiced for several decades, the only established climbing routes in Island in the Sky are found on its towers like those in Monument Basin (in the southeastern area of the Island) and on the Monster Tower (accessed by Shafer Trail and the White Rim Road). For exact route locations and descriptions, head to Moab's climbing shop, Pagan Mountaineering (59 South Main Street; 435-259-1117; www.climbmoab.com) to pick up copies of Eric Bjornstad's Desert Rock or Stewart Green's Rock Climbing Utah.

Biking

No single-track mountain bike riding exists within the park, and riding on hiking trails is prohibited. Therefore, all riding must be kept to paved and dirt roads. The most popular biking route in Canyonlands is the White Rim Trail (see "White Rim Trail," above). Outside that, biking can be done along dirt roads like Shafer Trail and the connecting Potash Road. However, if you crave some great mountain biking in this beautiful country, you must only head as far away as Dead Horse Point State Park (see "Enter the State Park," Day 1 of this chapter's 48-hour itinerary, above) to ride on the biker-friendly Intrepid Trail, a nested system of three loops.

Camping

Willow Flat Campground, immediately west of the scenic drive's Y junction, offers the only established camping in Island in the Sky. Only 12 sites are available and are assigned on a first-come, first-served basis only. RVs up to 28 feet will fit into the spaces.

All other camping within the park requires a hike (or a drive on the White Rim Trail) and a permit to occupy. Because of the popularity of the sites along the White Rim Trail, reservations are typically required for them and can be made by calling the Reservation Office (435-259-4351).

If none of these options satisfy your camping requirements, consider going up to Dead Horse Point State Park (Day 1 of this chapter's 48-hour itinerary), checking out some of the Moab area camping (chapter 7), or even heading to Arches National Park (chapter 5).

The visitors center in the Needles District

THE NEEDLES

More remote and much less visited than the Island in the Sky District of Canyonlands, the Needles nevertheless offers its own visitors center, an extensive and complex system of hiking trails, and a branching paved scenic drive with viewpoints. For backcountry hikers, this district of the park might well be the best and most accessible region of all; much tamer than the Maze, it offers miles and miles of hiking trails without the extreme isolation of that western section of Canyonlands. If you find yourself in the Needles during evening, consider checking out one of the park service's stargazing programs.

Recreation

Scenic Driving

The drive itself from Moab to this region of the park is an incredibly and increasingly aesthetic stretch of well-maintained, two-lane road, with a total length of 70 miles from town to the park's border. Before leaving Moab, be sure your car has plenty of gas; aside from a seasonally open (and therefore seasonally closed) Needles Outpost (at the eastern border of the Needles), Moab is your last chance to refill. And even though you'll be on paved roads for the entirety of your journey, cell phones essentially stop working entirely once you've left US 191.

The route begins by following US 191 south and out of Moab. As the homes and businesses fall away, the speed limit increases. You'll see the La Sal Mountains passing to your east. This proud range, which contrasts beautifully with the desert-scape below, rises to an elevation of 12,721 feet at Mt. Peale—and all of its other 11 significant peaks stand at least 12,001 feet. Just as with the Henry Mountains (southeast of Capitol Reef National Park and north of Lake Powell), the La Sal range is characterized by laccoliths, and was formed by igneous intrusion. (For an intimate view of this range, check out the "Scenic Driving" section of the "Extend Your Stay," in chapter 7.)

US 191 continues along its southbound path, passing the clearly signed Hole N" The Rock (435-686-2250; www.theholeintherock.com) about 13 miles south of Moab. This completely unabashed and bizarre tourist spot sits at the bottom of a hill and showcases, among other things, a 5,000-square-foot home that was literally dug into the rock over a 12-year period by one man during the 1940s and 1950s. For $5, you can get a tour of this home, see a few zebras, buffalo, and other animals, witness historic tools and artifacts, and purchase some art and touristy stuff.

About 25 miles south of Moab, you'll pass by Wilson Arch. Ninety-one feet in width and 46 feet tall, this thick rock window sits immediately east of US 191 and can either be seen on the fly or by pulling into the large scenic pullouts on either side of the road. Forty miles south of Moab, look for the obvious turnout for UT 211 toward Canyonlands National Park. (Don't be lured prematurely by a Needles Overlook turnoff earlier on US 191, unless you have extra time to drive to this preview.) If you need confirmation, this junction is marked with a rock formation on the east side of US 191 that, from some angles, strikingly resembles the Yellow Submarine.

Wilson Arch sits about 25 miles south of Moab on US 191.

The Hole N" The Rock must rank high in the nation for poorly spelled names.

This smaller highway winds generally westward across a high desert plateau before suddenly plunging into the top of Indian Creek Canyon. Observe the suggested speeds at curves in the road, as a few of them are incredibly tight and sit immediately above steep and long drop-offs. Once the road reaches the bottom of this distinct descent, keep your eye out for Newspaper Rock on the right side of the road (see sidebar).

Continuing along, the road winds past cottonwood trees and the base of ever-growing Wingate sandstone mesas and their skirting talus piles. The canyon steadily opens up and deepens, exposing much wider views of many more buttresses. Watch the deep red cliffs carefully; those darkly varnished walls host some of the world's most famous and popular crack-style rock climbs. Especially toward the top of the canyon, where the cliffs sit nearest the road, you should be able to see climbers during any pleasant day.

Eight miles past Newspaper Rock (and 20 miles from US 191), you'll notice the turnoff to Beef Basin Road, marked by a kiosk and pit toilet. Numerous campsites exist along the branches of this road (see "Camping," below), most of which lie just beneath the obvious and jagged mesa. Called the Bridger Jack Mesa, this toothy fin of rock also holds quite a few multip-itch rock-climbing routes. Farther along the UT 211, keep your eyes out to the left to see a set of twin towers perched high above their own pedestals. Called the North and South Six Shooters, these were so named because of their approximate resemblance to revolvers.

A total of 70 miles from Moab, you'll reach the park's border, marked

Newspaper Rock Petroglyphs

Driving through Indian Creek Canyon en route to the Needles provides more than just spectacular natural scenery. As UT 211 heads west from US 191, it squirrels suddenly down into the cottonwood-lined top of Indian Creek Canyon. Once the road has finished its major descent,

Newspaper Rock sits near the top end of Indian Creek Canyon.

keep an eye out to your right-hand side for the signed News-paper Rock (12.3 miles west of US 191) and a large parking area complete with pit toilets. This small historical site features just one rock art panel, but that panel alone contains hundreds of etched figures on its 200-square-foot, rust-colored Wingate sandstone surface. The incredibly dense collection of figures includes representations of humans, animals, and various other items created by the Fremont, Puebloan, and Basketmaker cultures. Thought to date back approximately 2,000 years, these images are protected by a natural rock overhang, making the slab provide a perfect and lasting canvas on which these figures will continue to remain. If you're passing this site, you have no excuse not to stop; the distance from the parking area to the viewing area is just a handful of feet.

by a sign. The turnoff for the Canyonlands Needles Outpost (435-979-4007; www.canyonlandsneedlesoutpost.com) will appear 2.5 miles later. Only open seasonally, the outpost provides your last opportunity to get gas if you forgot to do so in Moab. The small shop offers a limited amount of groceries and camping supplies, as well as a grill serving breakfast and lunch and a campground. (See the Needles "Camping," below.) The Needles Outpost is open during late spring through early fall only.

Once inside Canyonlands and past the visitors center, you're officially

The Six Shooter towers west of the Needles can be seen for miles around.

The Needles Outpost, just inside the park boundary, provides camping and some wares during the peak season.

on the scenic drive. Just west of the visitors center, the road passes the Roadside Ruin. Though not exactly on the roadside, the ruin can be visited by hiking a 0.3-mile loop trail. This small prehistoric granary was built by Ancestral Puebloans. Staying right at the next fork in the road will keep you on track to see the Wooden Shoe Arch Overlook. (Heading left will take you to the Cave Spring Trail, mentioned later in "Hiking," below.) A surprisingly far distance afield, this accurately named piece of rock can be seen by looking for light coming through the narrow opening along its sole. Continuing along, you'll notice the turnoff to the Squaw Flat Campground (see "Camping," below). Beyond the campground, the road turns to

Monticello: A Backup Fueling Spot

The best advice for those heading to the Needles is to leave Moab with a full tank of gas. That tip is especially important for those visiting the Needles during the off-season (late fall through early spring), when the Needles Outpost closes. If you happen to find yourself dangerously low on fuel, your next best bet is to return to US 191 and head south toward Monticello. This town, just 13 miles south of the UT 211 junction, sits nearly 27 miles (and about 1 gallon of gasoline!) closer to the Needles than Moab. If you happen to run out of gas, you'll have to wait for another passing vehicle to pull over and assist you; virtually no cell phone service exists along UT 211. You'll have to return to US 191 to pick up even a faint signal.

graded dirt and leads to the Elephant Hill Trailhead and Picnic Area. Those with four-wheel-drive vehicles or mountain bikes can continue as this dirt road dramatically worsens and enters a network of backcountry jeep trails that also connect with numerous hiking trails and campsites.

Staying on the main scenic drive (and bypassing Squaw Flat), your trajectory will bend to the north, affording views once again of the now distant La Sal Mountains. Next up, is the Pothole Point Trailhead, from which a short loop trail departs; after this, the road passes by a picnic area from which Slickrock Trail departs (see "Hiking," below). Finally, the road terminates in the Big Spring Canyon Overlook. From here you can see quite well Island in the Sky to your north, soaring above the complex canyons carved out by the Green and Colorado rivers.

The Roadside Ruin in the Needles requires only a few minutes of hiking to reach.
David Sjöquist

Hiking

A wealth of opportunities exist within the Needles for both day hikes and overnight trips. If you look at any map, you'll see that the central portion of the Needles is

covered with a interwoven web of
trails, which is mainly anchored to
the roads at Squaw Flat, Elephant
Hill, and the Big Spring Canyon
Overlook. From these points,
numerous interconnected trails
head west and south, forming
dozens of possible loops through
Lost, Squaw, Big Spring, Elephant,
Devil's Lane, and Cyclone canyons.

In the Needles District, Wooden Shoe
Arch can easily be missed.

As this network rather resembles a spiderweb of paths, it is best to take a
park-issued map and trail guide.

The Needles does contain a handful of quite short hiking trails that are
distinct from this larger trail network. As these stand alone, they can easily
be followed. Cave Spring Trail is one of these and is reached by taking the
spur road of that name (just south of Roadside Ruin). It requires just 0.3
miles of hiking and passes through brush and over rocks to reach pictographs and an old cowboy camp. This camp sits sheltered under a sandstone overhang and contains an old table, shelves, a hitching post, a stove,
and other items for cooking. The pictographs also sit in the shelter of a fairly deep overhang and are accompanied by an interpretive sign. Along the
way, hikers must climb two wooden ladders. This hike is a great way to
check out a little bit of the park's human history.

*If you like this . . . hike for its brevity and want to see a bit more
human history, park your car just south of the visitors center and take the
0.15-mile stroll to **Roadside Ruin**. This short loop takes just a matter of
minutes to walk and leads to an ancient Puebloan granary that sits safely
in the shelter of a much larger sandstone roof.*

For a hike with a focus on geology and expansive views of the surrounding region, take the 0.6-mile Pothole Point Trail. Forming a loop
over bare slickrock just a few miles south of the Big Spring Canyon Overlook, this leads to collections of potholes or naturally occurring basins
carved into the sandstone by swirling winds. Given the vegetation-free
nature of the rock slabs along the way, this hike offers much more open
views than the Cave Springs Trail, affording views of mesas, the Needles'
signature spires, and distant mountains.

*If you like this . . . but would like to exercise your legs a bit more,
head north on the scenic drive a few miles from the Pothole Point pullout
and stop at the **Slickrock Trail**. Covering a distance of 2.4 miles, this
trail makes a much broader loop away from the road, across sandstone
expanses, and toward grand views of distant red mesas and nearby, colorfully striated needles.*

Given the park's location in the Colorado Plateau, a high, dry, and utterly unsettled region of the world, it has excellent stargazing opportunities. With no urban light pollution, very infrequent clouding, and almost no relative humidity, the thin, dry air above the Needles renders it a perfect place to observe the night sky—both with the naked eye, as well as with with telescopes. Check at the visitors center to learn whether any stargazing events will take place during your visit.

Alternatively or additionally, you can mosey on over to the Squaw Flat Campground for ranger-led talks. During the warmer months of the year, these occur most days of the week. Topics vary, and events last about an hour.

Rock Climbing

Almost anyone traveling to the vicinity of the Needles to rock climb will head directly to Indian Creek, immediately to the east of the Needles. This famous Wingate sandstone climbing area draws in crack climbers from around the world, luring them there with dozens of buttresses stacked with pure crack lines. Usually one pitch in length no more than a few seconds' walk from the next route, these climbs satiate any climber's appetite, with each cliff offering vastly more climbing than one body could do in a day. The canyon also offers a number of multipitch routes on the Bridger Jack Mesa and on towers like the Six Shooters. If you want to experience this legendary area for yourself, bring every cam you own and purchase a copy of David Bloom's *Indian Creek: A Climbing Guide.* This book depicts hundreds upon hundreds of routes, and also includes gear suggestions and many brilliant photographs. Pick this up at Pagan Mountaineering in Moab (59 South Main Street; 435-259-1117).

If you want to climb in the park itself, Canyonlands does offer some limited and regulated climbing. Much of the routes here are on towers in the general vicinity of the Needles and Indian Creek. The most famous of these, Moses, has a handful of free-climbing classics like Primrose Dihedrals and the Dunn Route. Be prepared for a full outing, as these towers typically require hours of off-trail hiking to reach, and then require several pitches of climbing to summit. Information on these climbs can be obtained by purchasing Eric Bjornstad's *Desert Rock* or Stewart Green's *Rock Climbing Utah,* also for sale in Pagan Mountaineering.

Camping

The Needle's only developed camping area is the Squaw Flat Campground, located at the end of the road of the same name. The 26 sites in the campground come with a picnic table, fire ring, tent pads, and drinking water available all year. RVs fit in the campground if they're 28 feet or shorter. All sites are assigned on a first-come, first-served basis.

An alternative developed campground, sitting almost exactly on the park's eastern border, is the Canyonlands Needles Outpost (435-979-4007; www.canyonlandsneedlesoutpost.com). This privately run facility has firewood for sale and offers sites with running water, fire pits, and tables. Showers can be had here for a cost of $3 (or $7 for noncampers). The Outpost accepts reservations for sites, a few of which enjoy some shade cover.

Indian Creek Canyon itself holds numerous, cost-free camping opportunities. Though most of them are somewhat tricky to find, a very obvious and well-established (though undeveloped) collection of campsites sits right under Bridger Jack Mesa. To get there, head almost 14 miles west from the turnoff to Needles Outpost, and take a right onto Beef Basin Road; here you'll see a pit toilet and climber bulletin board. Driving farther along this road, you'll cross quickly over a river (generally totally passable in normal vehicles), and soon after, take the first right-hand turn. About 10 minutes of very rugged road leads to a few dozen numbered sites. Aside from their labels, these sites are otherwise unimproved; please treat them respectfully and camp only in preexisting sites. This road can be passed by vehicles with low clearance, but only with a high level of driving skill and patience. Driving all-wheel-drive and high-clearance vehicles helps greatly to access these sites.

THE MAZE

The most rugged portion of Canyonlands, the Maze requires at least two hours of dirt road driving just to reach its entrance and the Hans Flat Ranger Station. And that's only the beginning; from the ranger station on in, the Maze grows ever more rugged and remote, with roads becoming only passable to those with high-clearance, four-wheel-drive vehicles or mountain bikes. Abutting the Orange Cliffs portion of the Glen Canyon National Recreation Area to the west, these two regions share the same wild landscape and national-park-style regulations.

To get to the Hans Flat Ranger Station, head south from I-70 on UT 24, passing the turn for Goblin Valley State Park, and turning left at the Canyonlands National Park sign after a total of 24 miles. Continue for 46 additional miles of graded dirt driving, which leads directly to the ranger station, a tiny building rather looking like a mobile home. Depending on current road conditions and when the roads were last graded, interior routes may be passable with a normal vehicle. However, the more common circumstance is that roads much beyond the ranger station will only be navigable by four-wheel drive. If a two-wheel-drive car is all you have, it

Jet Boat Access

If you would like to access the Maze, but don't have an all-wheel-drive vehicle or care much for long drives on backcountry dirt toads or you simply want to experience a completely different means of transportation, look in to hiring a jet boat from Moab to the Maze. Traveling down the Colorado River and through its beautiful canyons, you'll pass beneath Island in the Sky, the Needles, and by the Green River confluence before stopping at Spanish Bottom in the Maze. This pullout is mandatory for jet boats, as it sits just upstream of Cataract Canyon— one of the most popular and serious whitewater stretches of its kind, within which are a few of the biggest river drops in North America. As you pass by the confluence of the Green and Colorado rivers, note the green waters of the Green swirling together with the brown of the Colorado. Regardless of which service you hire, the boats will let you out at a trailhead to the Doll House, a collection of colorful, knobby spires, 1,000 vertical feet high. Call **Tag-A-Long Expeditions** (435-529-8946; www.tagalong.com) or **Tex's Riverways** (435-259-5101) to talk about availability and pricing.

may be worth calling the ranger station (435-259-2652) before your trip to inquire about road conditions. If you've come to backpack and don't have a jeep, you can leave your passenger car at a parking area located 2.5 miles south of the ranger station (at North Point Road).

Recreation

Hiking
Depending on your comfort level, navigational skill, and degree of self-sufficiency in desert wilderness, the Maze either has nothing to offer you, or nearly unlimited exploration. Unlike most national parks, hiking within the Maze consists of largely undeveloped routes rather than established and improved footpaths. Be sure to stop at the ranger station to discuss potential outings, as off-road hiking inherently can present varying levels of technical difficultly, with some passages in the Maze even requiring hikers to carry short lengths of rope to safely pass over cliffy sections. Because of the length of time required to reach the Maze and the difficulty of reaching any of the hikes within it, a large percentage of people actually come to backpack; as such, a long approach trip (and the lack of any developed scenic drive within the Maze) hardly seems warranted if you're only going to hike for an hour or two. Just as within any other part of Canyonlands, any people

heading out on an overnight journey must possess a backcountry permit. Regardless of the length of your trip, it would be worth your time to discuss your plans with a ranger so at least someone knows your whereabouts in case you run into difficulties.

Camping

All camping within the Maze is considered backcountry camping and must therefore be done only with a permit. To acquire a permit and discuss camping opportunities and regulations, stop in at the Hans Flat Ranger Station at the park's entrance.

The Green River flows into the Colorado River in the center of Canyonlands National Park.

HORSESHOE CANYON

Added to the park in 1971, this island of Canyonlands sits just off the northwestern edge of the Maze. Horseshoe Canyon features a remarkable collection of ancient rock art, the most famous panel of which is called the Great Gallery (see "Hiking," below). As with the Maze, the canyon is reached by driving quite a while on graded dirt roads: Head south on I-70 for 24 miles and turn left as for the Maze, but drive 30 dirt road miles to reach Horseshoe Canyon (instead of the 46 required to get to the Hans Flat Ranger Station). Despite the canyon's close proximity to the Maze, no through roads connect these two sections of Canyonlands. Please keep in mind that pets are not allowed beneath the rim of Horseshoe Canyon.

Recreation

Hiking

The main attraction within Horseshoe Canyon, the Great Gallery, requires a decently challenging hike to see. The trail heading to this fantastic rock art panel stretches 3.5 miles in each direction along an old jeep road and loses 750 feet of elevation along the way. The panel itself contains 7-foot-tall figures of impressive detail and clarity, thought to be painted between 2,500 and 4,500 years ago. Classified as part of the Barrier Canyon rock art style, this bears many similarities to that of Arches National Park's Courthouse Wash Rock Art Panel (see the "Hiking" portion of "Extend Your Stay" in chapter 6). Both engraved art (called petroglyphs) and painted images (pictographs) of humans, spirits, and even possible pets can be seen on this and other panels in the canyon. Located in a broad alcove and situated on slightly overhanging rock, these figures have been protected from erasure from rock overhead. Parking for this West Rim Trailhead is located at the BLM campground just outside the park boundaries. Follow the path southeast, into Canyonlands National Park, and down into Horseshoe Canyon, turning to the southwest at the canyon bottom to reach the Great Gallery.

Park Tours and Other Educational Offerings

Even if you consider yourself to be a self-sufficient explorer and hiker, you may want to look into taking a guided walk through Horseshoe Canyon. You'd be surprised how much more information you can glean from a ranger-led hike than by a solo trek. Between mid-September and mid-October of each year, guided walks depart from the West Rim Trailhead (and BLM campsite) at 9 AM on Saturdays and Sundays. All hikers are responsible for bringing their own water and food and are expected to be physically fit enough to cover these moderately strenuous 7 round-trip miles. Other trips may be scheduled, depending on demand and staff availability; call Hans Flat Ranger Station (435-259-2652) to discuss this possibility if the weekend trips don't fit your trip, or to verify the exact time and day of scheduled hikes (as the times may change).

Horseback Riding

Horseback riding is permitted within Horseshoe Canyon. In order to preserve the balance of indigenous plant life within the area, all animals must consume pellet food only for the 48 hours preceding the trip. Permits are required for all horse trips and can be obtained in person at the Hans Flat Ranger Station or by telephone (435-259-2652).

Camping

Because of the fragility of Horseshoe Canyon and its archaeological richness, no camping is allowed within the canyon itself. However, BLM provides a campground immediately outside this island of Canyonlands and shares a location with the West Rim Trailhead. Though the campground does have an outhouse, it offers no water; come prepared with all of your own food and water needs, and pack out all trash.

7

Moab

TOWN OVERVIEW

Of Utah's cities, Moab stands second only behind Salt Lake City in world-wide fame and is one of the state's biggest tourist attractions—both for in-state residents and international travelers alike. Today a renowned hub for mountain biking, river running, jeepin,' hiking, national park exploring, rock climbing, and all other modern outdoor pursuits, Moab certainly was not born that way.

Originally home to members of the Ute and Navajo tribes, the Spanish Valley experienced its first European settlement with the establishment of the Elk Mountain Mission by 41 Mormon men in the summer of 1855. The group constructed a fort and lived in uneasy peace among these two indige-nous tribes for just a few months. In September, tensions broke, and a con-fusing battle took place, rendering two missionaries dead. At this point, the group considered residency in the Spanish Valley too risky and abandoned the mission. It wouldn't be until the 1880s that ranchers and cowboys would reestablish any significant form of European residency in the area. This time the effort was successful, and the town of Moab was platted in 1884 and incorporated in late 1902.

Over the next decades, vanadium, uranium, potash, manganese, oil, and natural gas were taken from the area around Moab, shaping its industry and population. Signs of former mining activity today are visually obvious throughout the entire area. During the 1950s and early '60s, an enormous boom in the uranium industry brought a flourish of economy to Moab.

LEFT: Climbers approach the route Fine Jade, in Castle Valley. Zac Robinson

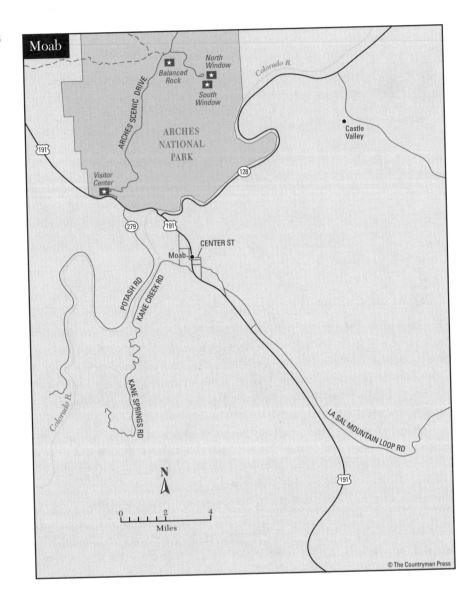

However, when this business died, the town shriveled to a skeletal existence.

With the unofficial completion of I-70 in the 1970s, Moab's nearness to Arches and Canyonlands National Parks, the Spanish Valley's beautiful natural surroundings, and the emergence of the outdoor industry, the town seized the opportunity to save itself with modern tourism. Over the next few decades, Moab enjoyed a steady growth in its annual visitor count. Today the city of Moab, with around just 5,000 residents, estimates that it receives about 1 million visitors each year.

The Labyrinth and Stillwater canyons of the Green River are quite near Moab.

Today, people literally travel from around the world to test Moab's famous slickrock mountain bike trails, raft the Colorado River's Cataract Canyon and the Green River's Labyrinth and Stillwater canyons, hike the many regional trails, explore ancient rock art panels, visit Arches and Canyonlands, and rock climb. When you drive through town on Main Street, you'll see at least one shop, guide service, and rental outfit for each activity, as well as an even greater number of restaurants and hotels.

Pick Your Spot
Where to stay and what you'll find nearby . . .

Looking at any map, you'll understand that Canyonlands and Arches national parks sit extremely near to Moab. That said, people visiting those parks typically dine and slumber in the town of Moab; if this chapter's suggested eateries and accommodations do not exactly satisfy your requirements, peruse the "Pick Your Spot" and suggested 48-hour itineraries of chapters 5 and 6.

One of Moab's best in-town

bargains, the locally owned Kokopelli Lodge & Suites (72 South 100 East; 1-888-530-3134; www.kokopellilodge.com) stands just one block away from Main Street. While avoiding the bustle of the main drag, it still provides perfect in-town walking access to all amenities. The rooms of this tiny motel have been dressed up colorfully and charmingly, making the sleeping quarters much more fun than other hotels in the area. Kokopelli charges quite a bit less than some of its competitors, with rates starting well within the double digits for a single room during peak

Jeep Safari Weekend

If you happen to find yourself anywhere near Moab—or along any of the roads leading to Moab—during April, you will inevitably experience Jeep Safari Weekend, whether you intend to or not. Though the exact date changes each year, this infamous off-road festival usually falls around Easter and includes the same elements year after year, that is: four-wheel-drive slickrock jeeping, rock crawling, and trail driving. Hosted by the Red Rock 4-Wheelers of Moab (www.rr4w.com), this typically contains nine official trails each day, with a culmination event on Big Saturday, on which roughly 30 groups convene in the center of Moab and then simultaneously depart for the trails. The entire event is quite a spectacle and utterly saturates the town's restaurants and hotel rooms. Whether or not you plan to partake in the festival, if you intend to visit Moab anywhere near this weekend, you should reserve a hotel room as far in advance as possible.

season and dropping to half during the winter months.

Also immediately in the center of town is the much larger Gonzo Inn (100 West 200 South; 435-259-2515; www.gonzoinn.com). Like Kokopelli, this enjoys a one-block insulation from the traffic of US 191/Main Street. When compared with those of other hotels in town, the rooms in the Gonzo are certainly a bit fancied up but still quite durable with the front desk offering a bike concierge service. Rates run a bit steeper for the increased luxury here—usually at least double those at the Kokopelli Lodge. Several size options exist for accommodations.

If you want to remove yourself a bit from Moab, perhaps sleep next to the Colorado River, and—better yet—share your backyard with a winery, look into staying at the Red Cliffs Lodge (Mile Marker 14, UT 128; 435-259-2002; www.redcliffslodge.com). This Western-style lodge occupies an historic ranch and sits directly adjacent to the Colorado River, with all guest rooms overlooking the water. The structure itself has wood-paneled walls and 20-foot ceilings, with expansive windows to match. If you prefer a little more privacy, look into renting a cabin on the property. Beyond just beds, the lodge also specializes in making activities available to guests; you can opt to horseback ride, mountain bike, river raft, rent an ATV, take a scenic flight, or chose from many more options. Don't forget to stop in at the Castle Creek Winery next door and the Moab Museum of Film and Western Heritage, right on-site.

Local Flavors

Taste of the town—local cafés, restaurants, bars, bistros, etc.

For an isolated town in rural Utah with just 5,000 people, Moab certainly has a generous selection of dining options. As with the lodging establishments, many of this book's Moab-area restaurants have been listed in the "Local Flavors" sections and 48-hour itineraries for Arches and Canyonlands National Parks and can be found in chapters 5 and 6. See the 48-hour suggested itinerary in chapter 5 for information on the Moab Brewery, Moab Diner, Castle Creek Winery and Red Cliffs Lodge (also see Red Cliffs Lodge, above), Jailhouse Cafe, and City Market grocery store. Look in the same section of chapter 6 to find Eddie McStiff's and neighbor Wake & Bake Cafe, Moab Sandwiches, Zax, Frankie D's, Eklecticafe, and Moab Roasters coffee shop.

For a romantic evening with a spouse or a special treat to yourself, call for a reservation at the Desert Bistro (1266 North US 191; 435-259-0756). One of Moab's only true upscale dining establishments, this restaurant operates out of a historic ranch home and has two dining rooms. The menu changes constantly to adapt to the season but always features local cuisine with continental European, new American, and Southwestern influences. Service hours vary significantly with

the time of year, but dinner is served from the beginning of March through October; details are posted online. Reservations are highly recommended but not required.

If fancy or spendy isn't your scene on a Desert Southwest trip, and you want something quick and utterly casual, try Milt's Stop and Eat (356 Mill Creek Drive; 435-259-7424; www.miltsstopandeat .com)—a popular restaurant on the complete opposite end of the formality spectrum. One of Moab's top favorites among locals and tourists alike, this classic retro diner serves an enormous list of burgers including some deluxe specialty items, home-cut fries (if you don't believe it, they cut them right in front of you), a whole bunch of savory sides, shakes and malts, and desserts. For those who have been active all day and might want to take it easy on the heavy foods, no worries: Milt's offers a good selection of grilled dinner sandwiches, salads, garden burgers, as well as fish and chicken options. Extremely limited seating exists inside; if you want to dine at Milt's, you'll find yourself sitting on high stools at the counter.

For a full sit-down dining experience without sacrificing your hearty meat portions, call Jeffrey's Steakhouse (218 North 100 West; 435-259-3588; www.jeffreyssteak house.com). This restaurant buys all of its Wagyu-style beef from the Snake River Farm in Idaho, which raises hormone-free, American

Kobe cattle. Entrées feature various cuts of steak, as well as numerous poultry, lamb, pork, and seafood selections. You needn't worry if you don't feel like consuming a huge chunk of meat; smaller portions of each dish are also offered on the menu. Side orders such as rice pilaf, mashed potatoes, green beans, creamed spinach, and seasonal vegetables come to the table family style. Located in an historic brownstone home, this restaurant includes multiple intimate dining spaces, both up- and downstairs, as well as outside. Prices run rather high—but after all, this is a high-end restaurant in southern Utah serving specialty cuisine.

48 Hours

Unfortunately, two days is hardly enough time to become acquainted with the town of Moab itself, let alone its vast and varied natural surroundings. However 48 hours still gives you enough time to get a lasting impression of the area—and hopefully one that brings you back again soon.

GETTING THERE

Moab lies a little more than four hours from Salt Lake City and six from Denver. Regardless of your point of origin, you will leave I-70 at exit 182 and head south on US 191 for just 31 miles to reach Moab. Once in town, check into your hotel and park your car there; almost everything in town can be reached easily on foot. Whether you need a light or serious dinner or just a beer, stretch your legs for about 15 minutes and walk toward the southern end of town toward the Moab Brewery (see the 48-hour itinerary of chapter 5). This Moab classic offers locally brewed beers and a generous and varied menu.

DAY
1

Breakfast before You Go

Wake up early enough to enjoy a cup of gourmet coffee or an espresso drink with some freshly baked goods at the Love Muffin Cafe (186 North Main Street; 435-259-6833; www.lovemuffincafe .com). In addition to its pâtisserie items, it serves a healthy selection of breakfast burritos, waffles, paninis, eggs, sausage dishes, potato plates, and the like. The Love Muffin favors organic, local, wholesome, and natural items and offers vegetarian or vegan options on most dishes. Unlike some of Moab's eateries, this stays open year-round, excepting a handful of short holiday and restorative closures. The restaurant offers indoor and outdoor seating, so you can enjoy fresh air on pleasant days. Don't forget to pick up lunch here, as you'll likely be exploring the great outdoors all day. Ask your server about their creative, nutritious, and savory sandwiches that can be ordered to-go.

Leave Town, Take a Drive, and Learn a Little

An excellent way to get a sampling of this area's complex terrain and diverse scenery is to tank up the car and head out on a 2.5-hour, 62.3-mile drive along the Colorado River, through Castleton Valley, and on the La Sal Mountain Loop. Departing from the center of town, you'll head north on Main Street/US 191 for about 2.5 miles. Take a quick right onto UT 128 just before the Colorado River. Follow this highway as it heads east through a narrow passageway of sheer cliffs, paralleling the winding Colorado River and the southern border of Arches National Park. Along the way you'll pass by the Castle Creek Winery (see chapter 5's 48-hour itinerary) and the Red Cliffs Lodge (see "Where to Stay," at the beginning of this chapter). Stop here to check out the Moab Museum of Film and Western Heritage. Located in the lodge, this free museum documents the area's place in film and Old West history.

Go 15.5 miles east of US 191 (and just 1.5 miles beyond the Red Cliffs Lodge), and take a right onto Castleton Road as it leads south

into the picturesque Castle Valley. Keep your eyes peeled, especially to the west, to catch views of fantastic Wingate sandstone mesas and spires, sitting atop glorious talus piles. These features rise more than 1,000 feet above the valley floor. Called the Nuns, Priest, Rectory, Castleton, and Sister Superior, these distinctive towers have been the subject of uncounted photographs and films. These excellently solid pieces of rock also hold numerous multipitch rock climbs (see "Rock Climbing" under "Extend Your Stay," below); if you drive slowly enough, you will likely spot climbers ascending them on pleasant days.

If you aren't a climber but want to get an up-close look at these Castle Valley towers and an elevated view of the entire valley, you should consider hiking to their base. Keep an eye out for any number of unmarked dirt roads heading east toward the main tower formations, about 4 miles south of UT 128. Drive these roads until you can't drive them anymore, then continue on foot trails; though none of the trails are marked, the area's lack of vegetation and the popularity of these features among climbers make them easy to access. Follow your instincts! The trail to the saddle beneath Castleton Tower takes only about an hour to hike each way.

As it nears the southern end of Castle Valley, the road's name changes to Mountain Loop Road. As it begins its initial ascent into

Fisher Towers Detour

If you're are as far east as Castle Valley and aren't on a tight schedule, you would find it worth your time to extend this day's trip a little by checking out the Fisher Towers. These extremely peculiar and unique sandstone towers stand as tall as 900 feet, with their tallest being the Titan Tower. Resembling mud corkscrews, they make any onlooker wonder how they could possibly exist. The pedestals of the towers are composed of a sandstone belonging to the Cutler Formation called Organ Rock Tongue, which is capped by Moenkopi sandstone. Unbelievably, the towers are a world-famous and popular rock-climbing destination. (See "Rock Climbing" under "Extend Your Stay," below in this chapter.) Titan Tower, the first climbed of all of these, saw its initial ascent in 1962. Today, the towers are climbed more for their extreme novelty than their rock quality.

A 2.2-mile trail leads up to the base of these towers and slightly beyond them, ending just short of a stream called Onion Creek. If you think the towers look familiar, you may have seen them before; often photographed and sometimes filmed, they appeared in *Against a Crooked Sky*, *The Comancheros*, *Wagon Master*, and *Rio Conchos*.

To get there, ignore the turnoff for Castle Valley and stay straight on UT 128 for an extra 5.4 miles; turn right onto Fisher Tower Road, just east of Mile Marker 21. Two dirt road miles later, you'll arrive at the picnic area and trailhead. This detour extends the day's trip by about 15 miles, turning the entire outing into an approximately 77.5-mile route.

the La Sal Mountains, you'll have to take a sharp right turn to stay on this Mountain Loop Road (and later follow signs to remain on this road at subsequent junctions). This scenic byway loops higher and higher onto the shoulders of this massive range, climbing through ever-changing ecosystems. From the desert valley floor, it ascends first through evergreen stands and then into aspen groves. Drive carefully; the road picturesquely meanders quite near the edge of steep slopes, providing excellent views, but also perilous drops. To properly see the area and take photographs, pull over onto any widened shoulders or side roads.

The Mountain Loop Road winds down from the mountain exactly as it ascended, steeply reentering the desert climate. You'll have to use your head or a map to pick your way through various junctions and back to US 191. Once at US 191, simply turn right to head back north and into town.

*If you like this . . . and happen to be a cyclist, consider renting a road bike at **Poison Spider Bicycles** (497 North Main Street; 435-259-7882; www.poisonspider bicycles.com) and embarking on this journey under your own power. However beautiful, this is no ordinary 60-mile loop; along the way, it features roughly 5,500 vertical feet of climbing and reaches elevations of roughly 8,300 feet. Because of the high altitude, this ride usually first becomes accessible in late spring or early summer.*

Take a Hike

An obvious natural inclination for hikers visiting Moab would be to head into Arches National Park, just five minutes north of town. If that tickles your fancy, see chapter 5. However, if you want to check out some of the area's out-of-bounds trails, think about hiking in Negro Bill Canyon. Located 3 miles east of US 191 along UT 128, this actually sits just across the Colorado River from the southern edge of Arches. From the parking area, a trail heads south through this pleasant and oft-wet, narrow canyon, staying along its floor for 1.5 miles. After this, turn to hike 0.5 miles up a side canyon and gain views of the 243-foot-long Morning Glory Natural Bridge. A massive span, this bridge is the sixth largest in the country. Beware the poison ivy that grows here; this plant loves the relatively wet environment of the canyon. If you've packed a lunch, you can combine this with the drive of the La Sal Mountain Loop (above). To enjoy your picnic lunch, drive about 4.5 miles east of

The towers of Castle Valley can be reached by anyone willing to hike an hour.

this trailhead to sit in a sweeping kink of the Colorado River called Big Bend, which has ample space for parking and sitting away from the road.

Dinner

After a full day of sightseeing and physical activity, Mexican food and a cold brew can be the perfect thing before bed. If this idea tickles your appetite, drive to Miguel's Baja Grill (51 North Main Street; 435-259-6546; www.miguelsbaja grill.com). Serving cuisine of the Baja tradition, this brightly colored restaurant furnishes a much dressed-up version of Mexican cuisine, incorporating fresh ingredients, many seafood items, herbs, and vegetables. If you're hankering for a margarita, theirs are made from scratch; but if you're not a tequila person, they also offer a wine and beer list, as well as a full bar.

DAY 2

Breakfast before You Go

Roll out of bed and get ready for a morning cup of coffee and breakfast. Like yesterday, you'll also want to pick up a lunch to carry with you. Head to the Red Rock Bakery & Net Cafe (74 South Main Street; 435-259-5941), where you can accomplish all three tasks at once. Serving baked goods, breakfast, espresso drinks, and notoriously good sandwiches (that can be taken

away) crafted with your choice of bread, this allows you to meet your dietary needs and be on your way.

Take a Hike

For a stroll with more views than yesterday's hike of the confined Negro Bill Canyon, head to the intersection of US 191 and Kane Creek Boulevard. Drive 2.6 miles northwest on this road as it nears the Colorado River. Just a few hundred yards after the first cattle guard, look for a parking area. The Moab Rim Trail heads south and uphill from here, following at first a jeep trail, climbing higher and higher onto sandstone domes. The trail reaches an overlook of the Moab after just about 1.5 miles, and then continues through a wash, farther uphill, to another view of the Spanish Valley and of sandstone fins. This trail has many branches but stretches roughly 3 miles from the parking area to a place called Hidden Valley. If hiking around the time of Jeep Safari Weekend, avoid this trail, as this is a very popular route among off-roaders.

Learn a Little

If you're curious about how all of the pieces of Moab's history fit together, you can stop by the Museum of Moab (118 East Center Street; 435-259-7985; www .moabmuesum.org) for some answers. On display, you'll see numerous installments covering the region's natural and cultural story. Topics include mining, paleontology, archeology, geology, and pioneer history. The museum hosts numerous events and traveling exhibitions, so check online to see what's happening during your visit. First opened in 1957, the museum has been a staple of the cultured community since Moab's uranium mining boom days.

Lunch before You Go

For a quick, satisfying bite before leaving town, heading into Arches (chapter 5), or driving to Canyonlands (chapter 6), stop by Paradox Pizza (702 South Main Street; 435-259-9999; www.paradoxpizza.com). Offering Italian cuisine that can satisfy almost any palate, this restaurant creates all of its soups, salads, crusts, sauces, and ingredients from scratch. Choose from their numerous specialty and classic pizza options, or build your own. Dine in the restaurant, or take it on the road.

Extend Your Stay

If you have more time, try to see these things . . .

RECREATION

Scenic Driving

Anywhere near Moab, nearly all of the driving will be, by default, utterly scenic—a fact that you surely will have noticed on your drive there. US 6, a major highway and popular "shortcut" between I-15 and I-80, sweeps over high plateaus and past the San Rafael Swell on its roughly 120-mile stretch between the two interstates. I-70, as it heads east from I-15 and toward Moab, cuts through the gut of the San Rafael Swell, rolling through fantastic topography and diverse geology.

The drive from Moab to the Needles of Canyonlands (as described in "Needles" under "Extend Your Stay" in chapter 6), rambles through increasingly empty and beautiful, high desert south of Moab before plunging down through Indian Creek Canyon and into Canyonlands National Park. Needless to say, the nearby roads in Arches and Island in the Sky of Canyonlands provide spectacular vistas. And don't forget the La Sal Mountain/Castle Valley Loop, as listed in Day 1 of this chapter's 48-hour itinerary.

Potash Road stands as one of the only roads near Moab not discussed in this book up to this point. Departing west from US 191, just 1.5 miles north of the Colorado River crossing, this road pinches in toward that river and runs parallel to it, as both snake into a deep bend before heading southwest, beneath Dead Horse Point State Park (see "Enter the State Park," chapter 6), and eventually connecting with the White Rim Trail, Shafer Trail, and finally the scenic drive of Canyonlands National Park. Any vehicle attempting the Shafer Trail portion of this route should be prepared to climb steep, dramatically exposed dirt roads. (For more information on these roads, see "Scenic Driving" in chapter 6's "Extend Your Stay" for Island in the Sky). This route stretches about 23 miles from Moab to the park's border, requiring about an hour of driving each way. Be sure to pause about 4.5 miles west of US 191 to observe dinosaur tracks that are visible from the road. You can use the existing spotting scope to get a better view of them or walk directly up to the site. Study a map when attempting this drive; many other possibilities exist along the way that offer both scenic alternatives and potentially confusing intersections.

Hiking to rock climb on a tower in Kane Springs Canyon, west of Moab

Exactly on the other side of the river, Kane Springs Road quite resembles Potash Road at first, tracing closely parallel to the Colorado River for about 3 miles before bending due south and simultaneously away from the river to enter Kane Springs Canyon. From here, the road turns to dirt and follows a totally separate path than the Colorado River and Potash Road, passing by famous rock formations called The Tombstones. These massive and sheer pieces of sandstone are popular among climbers (see "Rock Climbing," below). South of this, this road takes a few steep switchbacks into an ever-deepening canyon with multiple stream crossings. Eventually, the route bends back to the north, running again parallel with the Colorado River (about 17.5 miles from town). To reach this road, look for Kane Springs Boulevard (just north of the McDonald's), heading west from Main Street.

Hiking

As with much of the scenic driving in the Moab vicinity, so too will a good portion of the area's hiking be found within the boundaries of Arches and Canyonlands National Parks (chapters 5 and 6). However, the area contains many hiking trails outside these parks that warrant exploration. Each trail has its own flavor, and many afford views of the area or of peculiar geological formations. Of these, the hike to Fisher Towers, is one of the most classic. For more information on this route, see the "Fisher Towers Detour," Day 1 of this chapter's 48-hour itinerary.

For a very short, self-guided tour of a natural dinosaur footprint and fossil area, head north of town to the Mill Canyon/Copper Ridge Dinosaur Site. This completely cost-free, self-guided, and signed area contains numerous, partially excavated dinosaur remains and a short hiking trail. This unregulated sight is an experiment run by the Bureau of Land Management see whether visitors can successfully preserve such areas without supervision. To get there, head about 13 miles north of Moab, turning west onto a dirt road near Mile Marker 141. Park at the clearly signed trailhead. If you have any questions about the site, call the Moab Field Office (435-259-2100).

If you like this . . . and don't mind driving 10 miles farther north of town, extend your dinosaur discovery day and check out the Sauropod Dinosaur Tracksite. These fossilized footprints can be seen on the Salt Wash Member of the Morrison Formation. As with the Copper Ridge area, these theropod tracks are not protected with guards or fences so visitors must take care. If you'd like to visit one more instance of dinosaur remnants, remember that Potash Road (in "Scenic Driving," above) has visible dinosaur tracks along it, just 4.5 miles west of town.

For a slightly longer hike, aim for the trailhead for Corona Arch, 10 miles west of US 191 on UT 279/Potash Road. This 1.5-mile trail leads uphill and to the north, through a gap in the canyon rim, up a wash, over a pass, and then across slickrock slabs. When the existing terrain becomes too rough, man-made improvements like chipped steps and hand cables assist with your safe passage. To the end of the hike, a flat, open slickrock approach leads directly to the base of this massive arch, whose opening is 140 feet wide and 105 feet tall. With just more than 400 vertical feet of climbing, this trail offers a perfectly moderate outing.

Just across the way, on Kane Springs Road is the trailhead for Hunter Canyon. This 2-mile trail departs to the south from a parking area about 7.5 miles west of town and follows along a narrow canyon occupied by a flowing stream and associated vegetation. After hiking about 0.5 mile, keep your eyes open to the right to see an arch on the side of the canyon.

Rock Climbing

Though not as much on the public radar as the local mountain biking, the greater Moab area contains some of the greatest and most iconic sandstone crack climbing in the world. To begin any rock-climbing trip here, you may want to stop by Pagan Mountaineering (59 South Main Street; 435-259-1117; www.climbmoab.com) to acquire some guidebooks like David Bloom's *Indian Creek: A Climbing Guide*, Eric Bjornstad's *Desert Rock*, or Stewart Green's *Rock Climbing Utah*.

The Six Shooter towers are visible from the trail leading to the Roadside Ruin.

Nearest to town, a crag called Wall Street literally offers roadside climbing. Though certainly not the best climbing in the area, this crag offers warm, sunny, single-pitch cragging during cooler months. Scores of side-by-side routes give the office workers of Moab an opportunity to squeeze in a few evening pitches after a day at work. Located along Potash Road, this crag is reached by turning west off of US 191 onto Potash Road/UT 279 (about 4 miles north of Moab). Wall Street can be recognized as the very obvious, long, chalked-up wall on the right side of the road. Farther along Potash Road, you'll find dozens of other scattered routes; talk with the people at Pagan Mountaineering for tips, and peruse the guidebooks for Utah's desert climbing.

On the opposite side of the river, you'll find Kane Creek Road/Boulevard and another collection of climbs scattered around it. Some of its most famous and best lines are found on The Tombstones, obvious and appropriately named features. (These vertical sandstone Goliaths sit directly above the left side of the road after the road comes into Kane Springs Canyon.) However, these five or so pitch lines are not the only routes along this road; check the guidebooks to learn about other routes of varying length, difficulty, and style. The simplest way to access this road is to turn off Main Street/US 191 onto Kane Creek Boulevard right in town and north of the Moab Brewery; stay on the road as it nears the river.

East of Moab stand some of the most famous and iconic towers in all of Utah's legendary desert. The Fisher Towers are the most unique and peculiar of all. Composed of Cutler sandstone covered with a thick layer of mud, they are dirty and difficult to climb. However, the tallest of these, The Titan, has been climbed since 1962. Though the rock on these towers most certainly does not compare to the bullet-hard Wingate of Indian Creek, the uniqueness of these formations has put them on the top of the all-time classics list. And believe it or not, some of the most popular routes on the towers like Ancient Art have cleaned up quite a lot. (For driving directions, see Day 1's "Fisher Towers Detour" of the 48-hour itinerary, above.)

The turnoff to Castle Valley stands just 5.4 miles west of the Fisher Towers turnoff (see Day 1's "Leave Town, Take a Drive, and Learn a Little," in the 48-hour itinerary, above). This massive valley is home to some of the world's most classic tower climbs—both in terms of rock quality and aesthetics. Composed of the coveted Wingate variety of sandstone, these towers hold a whole host of roughly four-pitch routes. The towers bear the names Castleton, Sister Superior, the Nuns, the Priest, and the Rectory. Reached by extremely pleasant trails, the approach hikes afford not only an hour of warming up but also views of the entire valley (including the distant Fisher Towers to the northeast). All told, these routes provide an all-day experience that can't be beat. Just be sure to check the weather forecast to avoid a storm sneaking up behind you while ascending these natural lightning rods.

Between Castle Valley and Moab, there is even more climbing to be found along UT 128 and the Colorado River. Though sheer cliffs line the entire length of the canyon, only a few of these are actually featured and fractured enough to hold lines. Some of these roped climbs, as well as a collection of easily accessible boulder problems, can be found around the obvious Big Bend area, about 7.5 miles east of US 191.

Mill Creek Canyon is commonly associated with Moab-area climbing, but is actually a solid hour southwest of town. To check out this thoroughly top-notch, world-class area, under "Rock Climbing" in the "Extend Your Trip" section of chapter 6.

The Monuments on Kane Springs Road, just west of Moab, hold numerous rock-climbing routes.

Biking in Moab requires encyclope-
dias to cover properly. Though it has
earned most of its fame for its peer-
less slickrock riding, Moab's riding
also includes a number of unsung
single-track cross-country and downhill rides and even fantastic road biking. To get yourself oriented on any
of the trails, you'll need to consult
detailed maps and directions. Head
to either Moab Cyclery (391 South
Main Street; 435-259-7423; www
.moabcyclery.com) or Rim Cyclery
(94 West 100 North; 435-259-5333;
www.rimcyclery.com) to rent a bike,
pick up some guidebooks and sweat-
proof maps, or to sign up for a guided tour.

The most famous trail of all, the
Slickrock Trail, stands just 1 mile
east of Moab and takes a 10.6-mile
loop across spectacular Navajo sand-

Bouldering area at the Big Bend on the
Colorado River, just 7.5 miles east of US
191 on UT 128   David Sjöquist

stone slabs and knolls. For skilled riders, the natural features of this domed
rock form a playground; for less apt riders, this can prove overwhelming.
However, don't let that discourage you; you can always jump off the saddle
and push the bike through excessively technical sections. If you are a truly
inexperienced rider, you can get your own kicks on the much less aerobically
and technically demanding 2-mile Practice Loop. To get to both of these
trails, take Sand Flats Road (400 South Street) as it climbs east out of town.
There is an entry gate to the Sand Flats Recreation Area and a small fee ($5
for cars; $2 for bikes) to be paid; from there, it's 0.5 miles to the parking
area.

Not as famous as the Slickrock Trail, but just as cool and totally different,
is the Porcupine Rim Trail. This downhill course is the best of its kind in the
area and a must-do for skilled riders. The 15.6-miles are most often taken as
a one-way, descending ride with a shuttle vehicle; a loop version is possible,
but makes this already upper-level ride into a much bigger adventure.
Though the ride is considered primarily a downhill route, the first 20 percent
of it consists of a climb ascending roughly 1,000 vertical feet. Once at the top

of the climb, take a moment to look to the north to catch views of Castle
Valley. Catch your breath, lower your seat, and switch gears, as you're about
to drop about 3,000 feet over the next 10 miles. This descent is quite
demanding of skill, so be prepared—especially for the final 3 miles, which
consist of oft-exposed single track.

If you're interested in riding one of the area's most spectacular road
bike loops, the La Sal Mountain Loop, check out the "If you like this . . ."
section above that discusses riding Day 1's suggested driving loop on a
road bike.

ACCOMMODATIONS AND RESTAURANTS

For an extended selection of accommodations and dining in the Moab area,
flip through this chapter's 48-hour suggested itinerary, as well as those for
chapters 5 (Arches) and 6 (Canyonlands). Many of the hotels and restaurants in Moab have been allotted to those chapters.

CAMPING

Nearly everyone visiting the Moab area comes expressly to re-create in
the outdoors. And for many people, this goes hand in hand with camping.
Those seeking established campgrounds in the area might first look in the
national and state parks. Arches (chapter 5) and Canyonlands (chapter 6)
national parks each have their own established and backcountry sites; Dead
Horse Point State Park (chapter 6 and "Overview of Southern Utah: Its
History, Parks, and Monuments") has its own, too.

For camping directly in the town of Moab, head to the Canyonlands
Campground (555 South Main Street; 435-259-6848; www.canyonlands
rv.com). This privately owned facility offers spots for both tent campers and
RV sleepers, as well as a swimming pool, bathroom facilities, running water,
and recycling. Though it is located in town, the park has been set back sufficiently from the road to prevent noise disturbances. If you don't have the
equipment or desire to camp, ask whether any cabins are available to rent.
Call ahead to book a site or cabin based on your preferences and length of
RV, if applicable.

Kane Springs Campground (on Kane Springs Road, 4 miles west of its
junction with US 191; 435-259-4484) is another privately operated campground right on the banks of the Colorado River. This tent- and RV-friendly
campground offers a slightly more wild sleeping experience but is still located quite close to town.

For the numerous other wild camping opportunities in the area, contact the Bureau of Land Management's Moab Field Office (82 East Dogwood; 435-259-2100; www.blm.gov). This agency oversees much of the vast public land in the vicinity. Other wild camping opportunities exist around the peripheries of the area's national parks; for information on that, take a look at this section of chapters 5 and 6.

Index

LEFT: The Castle Creek Winery and Red Cliffs Lodge sit next to the Colorado River.